THE
SPRINGER SPANIEL

POPULAR DOGS' BREED SERIES

Sh. Ch. Hawkhill Royal Palace

Sh. Ch. Teesview Tarama

THE
SPRINGER SPANIEL

DOROTHY MORLAND HOOPER

Revised by Ian B. Hampton

POPULAR DOGS
London

POPULAR DOGS PUBLISHING CO. LTD
3 Fitzroy Square, London W1

AN IMPRINT OF THE HUTCHINSON GROUP

London Melbourne Sydney Auckland
Wellington Johannesburg Cape Town
and agencies throughout the world

First published (as The Popular Springer Spaniel) *June 1963*
Second edition, revised July 1971
Third edition, revised December 1972

This book has been set in Baskerville type, printed in Great Britain
on antique wove paper by Anchor Press, and
bound by Wm. Brendon, both of Tiptree, Essex

ISBN 0 09 115120 1

*For Ranger of Ranscombe 1915–1927 and his
descendants, past, present and to come.*

CONTENTS

ILLUSTRATIONS

In the text

ACKNOWLEDGEMENTS

I have to acknowledge with many grateful thanks all the help and information given me by Mr E. Holland Buckley and his staff at the Kennel Club, to Mr Henry Cecil for allowing me to quote the paragraph from his book *Alibi for a Judge* at the beginning of Chapter 7, to Mr Wilson Stephens, Editor of *The Field*, for permission to quote from Mr William Arkwright's preface to Mr H. W. Carlton's book *Spaniels, Their Breaking for Work and Field Trials*, published in 1915 by *The Field*, to Mr Maxwell Riddle for quotations from *The Springer Spaniel for Show and Field* published by The Cleveland Press, to Mr Chas. S. Goodall for quotations from *The Complete Springer Spaniel* published by The Howell Book House, Inc., and the Secretaries of Kennel Clubs and Spaniel Societies mentioned in the various sections dealing with Springers in other countries as well as the many friends in all parts of the world who have given me so much helpful information.

I am greatly endebted to Mr John Kent for reading my notes on training a Springer and to Mr J. A. Fleming, M.SC., M.R.C.V.S., for so thoroughly 'vetting' the chapter on Ailments, and I thank them both very much indeed for the time and trouble they gave to helping me.

My sincerest thanks are due to Miss Barbara Bourne and to Mr F. W. Simms for allowing me to use so many pictures appearing under the name Fall and F. W. Simms respectively and to Mr Alan Lambert the photographer and Mr E. K. Sinclair, Editor of *The Age*, Melbourne, Australia, for permission to reproduce the picture of Whittlemoor Flicker and her grandchildren facing page 81. For the first page of illustrations facing page 32 I am indebted to Mr R. R. Kelland, who owns the engraving of Spaniels belonging to Richard Nowell, Esq., and to the Kennel Club, possessors of the Maud Earl painting of the Welsh Springers. Mr J. C. Quirk has been very kind in giving me permission to use photographs of his American Field Trial Champions and I am grateful, too, to the many British owners who have sent me photographs of their dogs. I should have liked to include them all but this was impossible in a book of this size.

AUTHOR'S PREFACE

Dogs were always part of my home life as a child, but it was not until I bought the dog I named Ranger of Ranscombe in 1915 that I owned my first English Springer Spaniel. (I was living in Cheltenham then and those who knew the Promenade in those days will understand why, when I first took him there, I was puzzled when suddenly I found myself the object of interested glances, in fact stares, from the many obviously retired army officers and tea planters passing by. I soon realised, however, that it was not I but the outstandingly beautiful Springer at my heels that was attracting attention!) So many people admired Ranger that I was persuaded to show him at the first championship show after World War I, held by the old Kensington Society at the Holland Park Rink, and I showed him again at Cruft's in the following February. Here he was seen by Mr H. S. Lloyd and Mr David MacDonald, who both admired him greatly.

At this show the English Springer Spaniel Club was formed and I felt honoured to be elected on the committee, a position I have held ever since; indeed I am the only original member still holding office.

All my records up to the beginning of World War I were destroyed in the blitz, so that I am largely dependent on memory for what I say of my dogs during the early period of Ranscombe history.

All my working life I have been engaged in teaching (someone had to earn the dogs' living!), and so, except when a show was held on a Saturday, which was not very frequently in those days, I had to depend on friends or relations to show my dogs for me, though from 1925 until 1932 Miss M. A. Brice lived with me and was able to do a great deal to help in this way.

The first field trial I attended was the first trial held after World War I, under the auspices of the now defunct Horsham and District Field Trial Society, and after this I became, as the Americans say, completely 'sold' on field trials. It was here that I saw Horsford Hetman, who was to become our first Dual Champion.

My own first venture at running a dog at trials was at Idsworth, at the English Springer Club Trials on Lady Howe's wonderful ground. She was judging and I was delighted to be awarded a Certificate of Merit with my home-bred Reuben of Ranscombe.

I purchased a bitch which I named Rival of Ranscombe to mate to Ranger. She was a great-grand-daughter of Ch. Beech-grove Donaldson on her sire's side and a grand-daughter of Tellax (winner of the Horsham Trials in 1912 and 1913) by F.T. Ch. Velox Powder. Ch. Reipple, Ross and Romp were three from this breeding that I retained all their lives and from which my Ranscombe strain derives. Reipple mated to Ch. Little Brand produced Int.Ch. L'ile Buccaneer and Reuben of Rans-combe, a Challenge Certificate and field trial prize-winner. Mated to Nurscombe Prince she was the dam of Reipple and Ranter of Ware, Rae and Roan of Ranscombe and many other workers and winners. Romp was the dam of many good-looking and good-working puppies, including my greatly loved Rompson, John to his friends. He won the Bryngawr Cup for the best field trial dog at Cruft's on at least two occasions. Ross, through his daughter Regalia, is the ancestor of Aust. Dual Ch. Curtsey George, now in England.

Among the puppies in Reipple's last litter, by L'ile Marquis was Ronald, a particularly beautiful dog, but who was never shown; he spent his entire life at work, but, mated to Ch. Mediant of Canfordbourne, sired Rostre of Ranscombe, still the only English Springer bitch to win a Challenge Certificate on the bench and a first prize in an Open Stake at trials. Had the war not come she *might* have been our first English Springer Dual Champion bitch. Alas! she was eleven years old when trials were resumed.

During the war I had to give up my home and kennels and the dogs went first to the care of Mr C. Tyler, the head keeper at Hill Hall, Epping, and afterwards spent the rest of the war years at Dr Rickard's, near Windsor, in the faithful care of Miss Emsden. During this time I bred a litter from Rostre by Rompson in which was the outstandingly beautiful bitch Roxana. Rostre's next litter by Ch. Higham Tom Tit produced Replica of Rans-combe, whose name appears in many of the present-day pedigrees. His son, Reveller, mated to Roxana, and so combining two very good-looking and working lines, produced Rollicker and Reverie, and Reverie, mated to Mr John Kent's F.T.Ch. Silverstar of

Chrishall, was the dam of Runner and Reporter, both field trial prizewinners, and Rilla, whose son Rilson of Ranscombe by F.T.Ch. Pinehawk Sark was third in the American Field Trial Championship Stakes in 1961.

In 1929 I had the great pleasure of having an article by Mr A. Croxton Smith on English Springers in general and the Ranscombes in particular published in *Country Life*, illustrated by a number of very beautiful photographs of my dogs taken by Messrs Fall.

In 1927 I was jointly responsible with Mr Lewis D. Wigan in forming the Eastern Counties Spaniel Society and have been its hon. treasurer since 1929 and its hon. secretary since 1936. After I retired and had more leisure I became the hon. secretary and treasurer of the Eastern Counties Branch of the Utility Gundog Society and in 1951 took over the hon. field trial secretaryship of the English Springer Spaniel Club. I am the delegate for the Spaniel Club to the Field Trial Council.

I judge at championship shows; English Springers, Welsh Springers and the Clumber Spaniel Club have twice honoured me by asking me to judge their club show at Windsor. In 1955 I had the honour and the great pleasure of judging English Springers at Cruft's.

D.M.H.

1963

REVISER'S NOTE
TO SECOND EDITION

Dorothy Morland Hooper died in April 1970; a veteran in the breed. With her passed a vast knowledge and understanding of the spaniel breeds with which she had been associated for much of her life.

It has been both an honour and a pleasure to bring her book up to date at the suggestion of her publishers. I found it almost completely unnecessary to revise her main text so my additions are confined to the ends of appropriate chapters. The appendices have been fully revised and a handful of photographs have been replaced.

I.B.H.

1971

REVISER'S NOTE
TO THIRD EDITION

I was pleased to be asked by the publishers to carry out a further revision of the late Miss Hooper's book. It is good to know that the breed is commanding attention for the English Springer is a grand working dog and a wonderful companion. I have had the honour to be an official of the parent Breed Club since 1953 and have seen registrations grow from 1,398 to 2,683 in 1971. This illustrates the high regard for the breed in the Spaniel world.

This latest revision includes some slight alterations to the main text and some additions at the end of appropriate chapters; the appendices have been fully revised. Only one photograph has been changed to allow for the inclusion of Sh. Ch. Hawkhill Connaught. In a succession of five General Championship Shows so far this year, he has gained 5 Best of Breed, 1 Best in Show and 3 Reserve Best in Shows. A great credit to our breed and an achievement long to be remembered by his owner/breeders.

I.B.H.

1972

Chapter 1

HISTORY OF THE BREED

A LTHOUGH excavations and drawings on cave walls indicate
that dogs were the companions of man perhaps 10,000 or
more years ago none could be described as of Spaniel type: they
were all definitely hounds which could run their quarry down
for their masters.

Mr J. H. Walsh, one-time Editor of *The Field* and a nineteenth-
century authority on the dog, writing under his nom de plume of
Stonehenge on *The Dog* (a classic for all dog lovers), says that
hawking was known and practised by the Ancient Britons;
when the Romans invaded the country they were intrigued by the
sport and, I imagine, with the efficiency which characterised that
race, they proceeded to improve the sport by importing the land
Spaniel, and probably the 'water dog' too, to flush the game out
of the thickets and marshes.

An ancient law of Wales of A.D. 300 mentioned dogs particularly as Spaniels and another law of A.D. 942 also speaks of
Spaniels.

The name Spaniel is certainly thought to be derived from this
type of dog, its having been brought originally from Spain,
probably by Caesar's conquering armies, whence it bore the
French name for Spain, Espagnol, and sometimes the Latin
name for Spain, Hispania.

In following the history of the Spaniel from these early times
one is helped by some very interesting original manuscripts in
the British Museum dating from the reign of Henry IV, trans-
lated from the French by Edward Plantagenet, Henry's nephew.
in which Spaniels are described, and the work for which they are
particularly praised was that of springing the game for the hawks
and for hounds to chase.

Dr Caius, physician to Edward VI, wrote on dogs about 1570
and uses the term Springers for the land Spaniels, and this is
perhaps the first time that the actual name 'Springer' was
used.

After the introduction of gunpowder, Spaniels became even
more useful to sportsmen and the description and the method of

B   17

their 'manner of working in front of the hunter' is delightfully given by Richard Surflet, a sportsman of the seventeenth century:

'The spaniel is gentle, loving and courteous to man more than any other dog, of free untiring laborsome ranging, beating a full course over and over, which he does with a wanton playing taile and a busie laboring noise, neither desisting nor showing less delight in his labors at night than he did in the morning.'

He describes the Spaniel's beauty in his colour: 'of which motleys or pieds are the best, whether they be black and white, red and white or liver and white—or solid colours without any spots. The solid colour is not so comeley in the field although the dog may be of excellent cunning', which infers that though the broken colours are the easier to see in the field 'a good horse cannot be a bad colour'. Present-day sportsmen are in two camps here: some say a whiter dog can be more easily seen by his handler when at work, while others say the nearly self-coloured dog is not so easily seen by the game it is hunting.

The term 'springing Spaniel' was gaining ground as a description, not of a particular variety but of the fact that these dogs sprung their game, and all land Spaniels came under this general heading. The varieties we know now as Clumber, English and Welsh Springers, Field, Cocker, Norfolk and Sussex were all springing Spaniels.

About 1800 the Boughey family of Aqualate in Shropshire developed a distinct strain of Spaniel and bred it very carefully, keeping a stud book from 1813 onwards for their 'Springer Spaniels'. For over a century the strain was kept by successive geneations of the family and in 1903 Sir Thomas Booughey bred F.TCh. Velox Powder, later owned by Mr Eversfield and winner of twenty F.T. stakes, whose pedigree goes right back through the *Aqualate Stud Book* to Mop I, whelped in 1812. I often think how lucky I was that, in my first days as a Springer owner, and ignorant as I was of Springer pedigrees I should have bought a daughter of Cuxton Nellie, a grand-daughter of Velox Powder on her dam's side and a grand-daughter of Ch. Beechgrove Donaldson on the sire's side, as my foundation bitch. Rival as I called her, was a grand-daughter of Tellax, and so combined the Aqualate strain and the Foel Strain. The Boughey family continued its interest in English Springers right into the 1930s and I remember Mrs Boughey, wife of Commander E. V. F. Boughey, telling me that Sir Francis Boughey once used a French Poodle in his breeding to secure extra sagacity. I saw a number of the Aqualate dogs during the 1920s and 1930s and they were really good-looking and active dogs, well able to do a long day's work. I should be very interested to know if there are any of the direct strain left now.

There were a number of quite typical Springers during the latter part of the nineteenth century, described as Norfolk Spaniels, perhaps because such a large number of them were in Norfolk and were spread over the country from Norfolk. My first dog, Ranger, whelped in 1915, was descended from a Spaniel from the Sandringham Kennels, sent by King Edward VII, when Prince of Wales, to the Earl Fortescue of that day after he had been on a visit to him, and this Sandringham dog and his descendants were called Norfolk Spaniels for a number of years, but before 1900 they had become known as Springer Spaniels.

Great interest in the working abilities of Spaniels developed during the 1890s and the first field trial was held by the Sporting Spaniel Club on Mr William Arkwright's estate at Sutton Scarsdale, Derbyshire, on January 3rd, 1899, with Mr William Arkwright and Mr Elias Bishop as judges, but none of the winners was a Springer.

Some years ago, while in Derbyshire, I met on several occasions the late Mr Ned Seedhouse, who as a very young man had been a keeper on Mr Arkwright's estate at Sutton Scarsdale, and he told me many interesting details of how Mr Arkwright worked his dogs and how the shoot and this first historic field trial were run.

The club held a second trial on December 12th, 1899, on the estate of Mr B. J. Warwick near Havant, Hampshire, but again no Springer was in the first three.

The Spaniel Club, though founded in 1885, did not organise a field trial until January 1900. It was held at Welbeck Abbey with Mr James Farrow and Mr C. A. Phillips as judges but still no Springer occupied the first place. It was won by Mr Winton Smith's Beechgrove Bee, a Clumber. However, at the Spaniel Club's second field trial held in the following year a Springer won the Open Stake for the first time. This was a dog called Tring, owned by Mr Gardner.

In 1902 the Kennel Club gave separate classification for Springers, and it was not long before the breed had bench Champions, the first dog being Mr Winton Smith's Beechgrove Will and the first bitch, Major Harry Jones's Fansom. It was a great deal longer (actually 1913) before the first English Springer attained the title of Field Trial Champion. This was a dog called Rivington Sam, sired by Spot of Hagley, ex a Cocker bitch, Rivington Ribbon, and bred and owned by Mr C. A. Phillips, and it is fitting that the honour of owning this first English Springer Field Trial Champion should go to a man who had done so much to establish the breed as a definite type and towards perfecting it as a working dog.

Firmly established during the decade 1902 to 1912 the English Springer went forward in popularity, both as a shooting dog and on the bench.

Famous English Springer prefixes of the beginning of the century onwards were those of the Duke of Hamilton's 'Avenda le', Mr C. A. Phillips's 'Rivington', Mr C. C. Eversfield's 'Denne', Mr John Kent's 'Chrishall', Mr Winton Smith's 'Beechgrove', Mr W. Humphrey's 'Horsford', Mr A. L. Trotter's 'Dalshangan', Mr A. Byrnes's 'Tedwyn', Mr Selwyn C. Jones's 'O'Vara', Lady Portal's 'Laverstoke', Mr D. MacDonald's 'L'ile', Sir Hugo FitzHerbert's 'Tissington', Mr MacNab Chassels's 'Inveresk', Lady Howe's 'Banchory', Mr L. D. Wigan's 'Cairnies', Mr John Forbes's 'Glennewton', Mr E. E. Trimble's 'Matford', Mr R. R. Kelland's 'Nobel', Mr H. S. Lloyd's 'Ware', and many others.

It is sad to think that so many of these great sportsmen, builders of the breed as we know it today, have passed on. They made their prefixes famous wherever their dogs went throughout the world and I hope that the value of what they did for English Springers will be realised by the many who have come into the breed just before and after World War II and that they themselves will do their utmost to maintain the principle that these pioneers held so strongly, that the Springer is essentially a dual-purpose dog and that, to misquote the Scriptures, 'looks without work avail nothing'.

It is good to know, however, that some of these stalwarts of the breed are still with us. Mr Kent was handling his F.T.Ch. Speckle of Chrishall at two recent Kennel Club Spaniel championship trials. Cruft's would not be Cruft's if we did not see

Mr MacNab Chassels and Mr E. E. Trimble at the Springer ringside, while the 'O'Vara' prefix lives on in the ownership of Mr T. J. Greatorex, who trained and handled so many of this famous strain in the past. The recent death of Mr H. S. Lloyd has deprived the gundog world of one of its most outstanding personalities but we are happy to know that the famous 'Ware' Kennel is being continued by his daughter, Miss Jennifer Lloyd. Very fittingly Mrs E. Thomson, daughter-in-law of Mr Thomson, Senr, trainer and handler of F.T.Ch. Rivington Sam and Mr C. A. Phillips's trainer for so many years, now owns the 'Rivington' prefix and has handled two Springers, Rivington Michele and Rivington Rachele, to field trial championship status in recent years. Mr John Forbes tells us that he has retired, but we see him each season at trials with winning dogs.

In 1921 a meeting was held at Cruft's Show and the English Springer Spaniel Club was formed with Mr William Humphrey as secretary and a strong committee of enthusiastic show and field trial owners. This marked another big step forward, and English Springers have never looked back as *the* Spaniels for the shooting field, while they have maintained great popularity as show dogs. During the first few years the secretaryship changed several times, but in 1933 Mr R. R. Kelland took over this position and continued to guide the club's activities very successfully until 1939, when World War II put an end to all but the small wartime shows in which the club had no part. Until 1934 Major Maurice Portal, D.S.O., was the president, and Lady Howe the chairman. In 1935 Captain O. P. Traherne became president, a position he held until his death in 1950. Mr H. S. Lloyd was the chairman from 1935 until 1937, when Lady Howe resumed that position until 1946. In that year, when canine affairs woke to life after the war years, Mr Kelland restarted the work of the club and was able to hand it over in a flourishing condition in 1947 to the new joint honorary secretaries, Major and Mrs W. Travers. For four more years Mr Kelland continued his help to and interest in the club as chairman, and on Captain Traherne's death was elected as president, a position I know he valued highly. During the years he was president Mr H. S. Lloyd resumed the office of chairman and their combined knowledge of canine matters was of the greatest help and benefit to the club. Towards the end of 1955 they both felt that the younger generation should take a hand in the management of the club and in 1956 the Earl of Northesk consented to become the president and Miss C. M. Francis was elected chairman of committee. After five years of hard but very successful work as secretaries Major and Mrs Travers found that other calls on their time made it impossible for them to continue, and, by what must be considered a most fortunate circumstance, two young and very keen Springer owners were found in Mr and Mrs I. B. Hampton, who consented to undertake the work of joint honorary secretaries. In 1957 Mr Hampton became honorary treasurer and assistant secretary, with Mrs Hampton continuing as honorary secretary. Prior to 1951 the field trials had been part of the work of the general secretary but since that date I have been responsible for the field trial section of the club.

The past few years have seen the passing of a number of very experienced and enthusiastic Show and Field Trial personalities.

The English Springer Spaniel Club lost its President with the death of the Earl of Northesk in November 1963. The office of President was then filled by Lady Lambe whose Whaddon Chase prefix was known throughout the spaniel world. After a few years in office, Lady Lambe died in April 1968 following an accident at her home. She was succeeded by the present President, Miss C. M. Francis, who has been associated with the Club since its formation. Her Higham prefix is well known in both Show and Field Trial sectors.

In December 1966, Miss Hooper retired after some 15 years in office as Honorary Field Trial Secretary to the E.S.S.C. Her untiring efforts and great organising ability established the annual Field Trials of the E.S.S.C. as one of the best in the Spaniel world. The E.S.S.C. elected as her successor an experienced Field Trialler and administrator, Lt Colonel Lewin Spittle.

I.B.H.

Chapter II

KENNEL CLUB STANDARD OF POINTS

BEFORE giving thought to the actual selection of a Springer from which to start breeding, and as the foundation of a kennel, a knowledge of the Kennel Club Standard of Points for the breed is necessary. The official standard of points is given below in smaller type followed by explanatory comments.

CHARACTERISTICS.—The English Springer is the oldest of our Sporting Gundogs and the taproot from which all our sporting land spaniels (Clumbers excepted) have been evolved. It was originally used for the purpose of finding and springing game for the net, falcon or greyhound, but at the present time it is used entirely to find, flush and retrieve game for the gun. The breed is of ancient and pure origin, and should be kept as such. The Springer's gait is strictly his own. His forelegs should swing straight forward from the shoulder, throwing the feet well forward in an easy and free manner, not a paddle nor a chopped terrier-like stride. His hocks should drive well under the body, following in a line with his forelegs. At slow movement many Springers have a pacing stride typical of the breed.

The Springer should move with an easy, swinging, effortless action, the back feet following exactly the line of the front ones. In the show ring one sees at times a hackney action, which is quite alien to a Springer movement and in a Springer most unattractive. One wonders how a dog trained to this movement could possibly work on heather, bracken or through briars.

GENERAL APPEARANCE.—The general appearance of the modern Springer is that of a symmetrical, compact, strong, upstanding, merry and active dog, built for endurance and activity. He is the highest on the leg and raciest in build of all British land spaniels.

The Springer must above all be an *active* dog, and too heavy bone, body and head must be avoided; all or any one of these detract from the appearance of a quick-moving, very active dog. On the other hand, a whippety or greyhound type, with too light a body is equally to be avoided. His expression when in repose should be gentle, serene and trustful; at work he should be gay, very happy but intensely purposeful.

1. *Head and Skull.*—The skull should be of medium length and fairly broad and slightly rounded, rising from the foreface, making a brow or stop, divided by a fluting between the eyes gradually dying away along the forehead towards the occiput bone, which should not be peaked.

This means that the skull must never be narrow and never flat; on the other hand, it must never be domed. The stop must

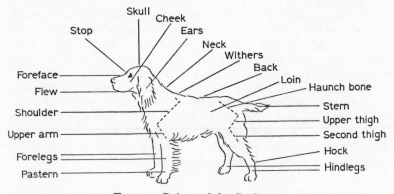

FIG. 1.   Points of the Springer

be clearly marked but rising gradually between the eyes. A sudden upward bone formation gives an apple-headed appearance which is most objectionable. The fluting gives great character and quality; without it the head is extremely plain.

The cheeks should be flat, that is, not rounded or full. The foreface should be of proportionate length to the skull, fairly broad and deep without being coarse, well chiselled below the eyes, fairly deep and square in flew, but not exaggerated to such an extent as would interfere with comfort in retrieving.

The length of head from midway between the eyes to the tip of the nose should be the same length as from midway between the eyes to the occiput. The chiselling below the eyes, together with the fluting, gives great refinement and makes all the difference between a quality and a plain head. A snipey muzzle is certainly undesirable, but is almost preferable to the very deep flew sometimes seen, which is more like that of a St Bernard and destroys all Springer character as well as being a handicap in retrieving.

Nostrils well developed, underjaw strong and level mouth, that is neither over nor undershot.

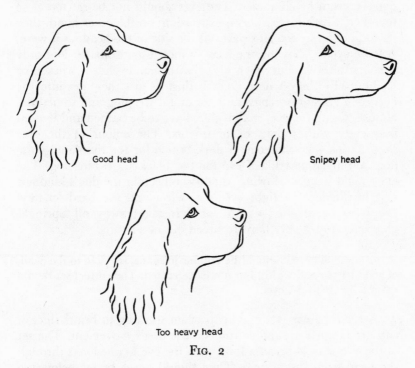

Good head

Snipey head

Too heavy head

FIG. 2

A strong underjaw is needed to take the weight of a heavy retrieve. A partridge or pigeon is an easy matter, but a big pheasant or hare needs a strong, well-developed jaw to take the weight. The nostrils, in a liver-and-white dog, must be liver; in black-and-white dog, black. A 'butterfly' or 'dudley' nose, that is, one partially flesh-coloured, detracts greatly from a pleasing appearance.

2. *Eyes.*—The eyes should be neither too full nor too small but of medium size, not prominent nor sunken, but well set in (not showing haw), of an alert, kind expression. A mouse-like eye without expression

is objectionable, as also is a light eye. The colour should be dark hazel.

The eyes should be well set in the head; a protruding or goggle eye is utterly alien to the breed. The shape of a Springer's eye should be oval, slightly triangular and in no circumstances round. This shape is peculiar to the breed. The round eye detracts from its character. The eyes should not be set too close together, which gives a mean expression; on the other hand, they should not be set too far apart, on the side of the head, as it were. A loose eyelid, showing the haw, is most objectionable. Not only is it unattractive, but when a dog with such eyelids is worked or is about anywhere where there is dust or grit these get into the eye, soon causing soreness and continual weeping and sometimes almost closing the eye, so that they have to be bathed and treated frequently with lotions or ointments. The colour of the eyes should tone with the coat: a dark brown for the liver-and-white dog and an almost black eye for the black-and-white dog. The eye should have a 'glowing' quality, reflecting the dog's kindness and intelligence. A light eye is a defect and the hard 'chalky' eye is to be avoided at all costs. It takes away all Springer character and is very hard to breed out of a strain.

3. *Ears.*—The ears should be lobular in shape, set close to the head, of good length and width, but not exaggerated. The correct set should be in a line with the eye.

A too long ear is a handicap when working in briars since it can get tangled up and so impede the dog's movement. The set of the ears should be on a level with the eye as one looks through the head from the nostrils. They should never be set below the level of the eyes, as this gives a Cockerish character to the head.

4. *Neck.*—The neck should be strong and muscular, of nice length and free from throatiness, well set in the shoulders, nicely arched and tapering towards the head—this giving great acivity and speed. A ewe neck is objectionable.

Here again, not only is the long neck attractive, but it has been developed for a practical purpose. It is essential in work: a dog with a good length of neck can pick up almost in its stride when retrieving. A short-necked dog going at any pace will almost fall over itself as it stoops to pick up. Throatiness, the baggy loose skin in the front of the neck, is not only ugly; I have seen it torn when a dog has been working in thick thorns.

5. *Forequarters.*—The forelegs should be straight and nicely feathered, elbows set well to body and with proportionate substance to carry the body, strong flexible pasterns.

Front: good   Front: too narrow   Front: too wide

FIG. 3

Feet: good pasterns   Feet: weak pasterns

FIG. 4

The forelegs should have flat, round bone and be set well into the body, with a good slope back from the shoulder to the upper arm so that the legs are well under the dog, not at the corners of his body. A straight shoulder gives a very ugly outline and poor movement. Loose shoulders are equally to be avoided.

6. *Body.*—The body should be strong and of proportionate length, neither too long nor too short, the chest deep and well developed with plenty of heart and lung room, well-sprung ribs, loins muscular and strong, with slight arch and well coupled, thighs broad and muscular and well developed.

The general length of the body from the withers to the set-on of the tail should be proportionate to the length of leg, so that in looking at a Springer one sees a square dog. It is important that there should be good width between the forelegs and a deep brisket, for a well-developed chest combined with the deep brisket gives plenty of heart room; a Springer is a hunting dog and is required not merely to retrieve as is a Retriever, but to hunt forward and put up game, often through thick briars and woodland and for long periods. A narrow chest and 'slab sides' both militate against sustained effort, for there must be plenty of room for the lungs and heart, the bellows and the pumping systems! The loin should not be over-long but needs to be strong and very muscular, to give the dog spring and force; the arch should be very slight indeed—a too arched, whippety loin is very undesirable. The upper thighs need to be strong and, with the second thighs, well muscled up to give the drive essential to quick movement, ability to jump well and to go out fast and make long untiring retrieves.

7. *Hindquarters.*—The hind legs should be well let down from hips to hocks. Stifles and hocks moderately bent, inclining neither inwards nor outwards. Coarseness of hocks is objectionable.

A straight stifle, often seen with a weak second thigh, detracts both from appearance and the drive needed for work. Too great length from the hock to the foot is not good, while cow hocks or bow hocks are serious faults, as well as being extremely ugly.

Hindquarters: good bend of stifle   Hindquarters: too straight stifle

FIG. 5

Backlegs : good   Backlegs : cow hocked   Backlegs : bow hocked

Fɪɢ. 6

8. *Feet.*—Feet tight, compact, and well rounded, with strong full pads.

Feet are most important. A loose open foot usually has soft spread pads, and both pads and the flesh between quickly become sore.

9. *Tail.*—The stern should be low and never carried above the level of the back, well feathered and with a lively action.

A gay tail, one that is carried at an angle above the body or, worse still, straight up like that of a terrier is most objectionable, and a tail that is carried stiffly with no rapid motion gives no indication of a Springer's pleasure and interest. The tail should be left a really good length, for when at work its happy rapid motion tells the handler so much, warning him as it moves faster and faster as to when game may be expected to rise from the ground that is being hunted, or be pushed out of covert. All too often at shows one sees tails cut far too short and frequently clipped of feather, in some cases trimmed to a point at the end, so looking thoroughly unnatural and very ugly, completely destroying all Springer character.

10. *Coat.*—The coat should be close, straight and weather resisting without being coarse.

This is, of course, the ideal coat from the show point of view, and if there is a dense undercoat it is excellent for work. For show it is easy to prepare and, with a lovely bloom, it is most attractive, but I am heretic enough to be quite happy to own dogs with a wavy coat when it is a question of work, for it usually means that there is a dense undercoat. The pre-1934 standard allowed a wavy coat. I am not claiming that it is right according to the present standard, but such a coat will turn the briars and resist any amount of rain and water, and, too, dogs with this type of coat usually excel at swimming. No one, I am sure, will deny the late Countess Howe's knowledge and experience of the Springer as a working dog, and she always wrote and spoke most emphatically of the value of this wavy coat in a Springer. When I take Dr Wilson's Dally (Aust. Dual Ch. Curtsey George) as my companion to the Spaniel Championship the first comment made on him by the field trial enthusiasts who gather there is, 'Oh, what a wonderful coat for work!'

11. *Colour.*—Any recognised land spaniel colour is acceptable, but liver and white, black and white, or either of these colours with tan markings preferred.

The only colour that is not desirable is the red of the Welsh Springer. Liver and white is perhaps most generally seen, and with tan markings it is a beautiful combination; black and white is equally acceptable, and the tricolour—black and white with tan markings—is most attractive. There is no rule as to the proportion of dark colour to white; lightly or heavily marked dogs can be equally pleasing.

12. *Weight and Size.*—The approximate weight should be fifty pounds. The approximate height should be twenty inches.

Let the dog be well covered, but do let it be muscle, not fat. A too heavy Springer cannot even move well in the ring and it certainly cannot be the active dog needed for a spaniel's work in the field.

There is a tendency for the show Springer to exceed this height, often because it is so long in the leg. On the other hand, the working Springers are often below it. While one does not want Springers to be just the size of big Cockers, it is worse if they get nearly to the size of Retrievers; they are needed for working through undergrowth, not for going over the top of it.

Chapter III

ONE'S FIRST SPRINGER

MY EXCUSE for accepting the invitation to write this book on English Springers is that the breed has been my great love and interest for nearly fifty years. I have in that time bred very many puppies, all in direct line from my original dog and bitch, and have retained a number from each generation to grow up to be shown and as working dogs. I know that it is the Springer's sweet nature, absolute devotion, great intelligence, ability and usefulness at work that keep one devoted to it for life.

There is, I know, a certain type of person who drifts in and out of all breeds. I have seen them in Springers. They have started to keep and show Springers because they have seen them winning at shows. They have bought a dog or bitch, had a certain measure of success at shows and perhaps bred a winner or two, but coming to a period when their dogs have failed to win under one judge after another, with harsh words about the shortcomings of all judges, they have drifted out of the breed, and very often out of the dog world. Sometimes they have 'taken up' other breeds which may be numerically small and found satisfaction in the awards more easily gathered. But these are the people who go into the breed in the hope of gain and are, happily, soon forgotten by those to whom the companionship and love, given unstintedly by the Springer, is such that it is impossible to think of life without it.

It is on the show side that this casual ownership of a Springer more often occurs. There is, I admit, a great thrill in winning a Challenge Certificate or other award, especially with a dog of one's own breeding, but once one has trained and worked Springers I think there are very few people who give them up. It is in the working side of the breed that such very special interest lies and in which it is so fascinating to watch a puppy's progress from its first 'Kindergarten' lessons to the time when it becomes a well-trained gundog, or perhaps takes its 'degree' by obtaining an award at a field trial.

At this point the established owners of English Springers

should cease to read this chapter, which is entirely for the help and guidance of the real novice.

First and most emphatically I would say to anyone considering the acquisition of a Springer: if you live in a house or flat in a great town where there is no easy access to commons, woods or fields or other open spaces, don't have one. It is not that a Springer is not a most accommodating dog, it will settle down and adjust itself to practically any environment, provided it has the affection and care of its owner, but you will be denying it so much of the instinctive pleasure of its life, its natural inheritance, that it would be better if you chose a breed more suitable to town conditions. If, however, you can give your dog exercise over open spaces, not just fenced town parks and recreation grounds surrounded by bricks and mortar, then a Springer is the dog to own, for it will mean many years of mutual affection and pleasure and interest for you both.

It is a matter of individual choice whether, if it is to be the one dog in the home, a puppy or a grown dog is selected, or whether you decide on a dog or a bitch. I have often heard it said that a bitch is more affectionate and makes the better companion in the house, but with this I cannot agree. I have had many dogs and many bitches as personal companions, and have never found that one sex has given me greater devotion or more happiness than the other.

If a puppy is decided on, it must be remembered that much more time and patience must be given to it than if a start is made with a grown dog, who one expects will be house-trained, used to going well on a leash, and generally behaving in a manner that makes it easy to take it about. In these days, too, one expects that it will travel well in a car.

Assuming that a puppy is chosen, do not buy one too young. At six weeks puppies should be finishing with their mother as 'milk bar' and general provider, and should have been having a certain amount of food—meat, meal and milk—during the two previous weeks. They are still too young, however, to leave the companionship of their brothers and sisters and the conditions to which they have been used in their little lives. In another two weeks, during which they will become used to food provided entirely by human agency, and not by their mother, they will be old enough for a new life.

The utmost care should be taken to see that a puppy's diet

Spaniels belonging to Richard Nowell, Esq., of Stanstead, Suffolk. From an original engraving published July 25th, 1803

(*F. W. Simms*)

The Welsh Springer Spaniels, Ch. Longmynd Calon Fach and Ch. Longmynd Megan. Painting by Maud Earl, 1906

Sh.Ch. Hawkhill Connaught

Dark Ranger
of Crosslane

and times for meals are, so far as is possible, the same as those to which it has been used and when buying a puppy it is wise to ask for a diet sheet for guidance in this respect. Above all, it is important that it should be kept happy and contented. Taken suddenly from its family and put to sleep in a box or basket or, worse still, a strange outside kennel, it will feel utterly forlorn. I always suggest that a stone hot-water bottle, well covered in an old, thick, woollen stocking which it cannot remove, be put in the bed with it. To this it will cuddle up, and the warmth gives the puppy the illusion that one of its brothers or sisters is still with it.

When choosing a puppy, watch the litter at play for a time and pick a bold, confident, active pup. Always avoid one that runs back into its kennel at your approach. Look for a sturdy, compactly built one, with promise of a good muzzle, stop and length of head, straight legs and well-set tail. If possible see the dam, and if the sire is in the same ownership look carefully at him too, and then hope that you will pick a puppy with the merits of both and, with luck, the faults of neither.

If it is decided to buy a grown dog, look for a gay, confident one, with a good head, well-set dark eyes, straight front, well-laid-back shoulders, good bend of stifle and a well-set and well-carried tail—a gay tail is anathema.

If the puppy you buy has not been inoculated against distemper, hard-pad, nephritis and the other diseases for which veterinary science has found a preventive, have it done as soon as the veterinary surgeon advises it. If a grown dog is bought it may have been inoculated; if not, have it done at once.

And now, a very important piece of advice. A young puppy cannot travel far or fast, so it is easy to keep it within bounds, but an older dog can do so and it can jump too. Do not let a newly purchased dog—and here I include a young dog whose age may still be counted in months—out for a walk without a leash until it has become thoroughly accustomed to its new owners and new surroundings. Further, if it is let loose in kennel run or garden, see that there is absolutely no possibility of its getting out, either by jumping over or breaking through a hedge or fence. I have heard of so many cases of dogs of many breeds who, let loose before they have really settled in their new homes, have escaped and run distractedly about the countryside for a fortnight or more, sometimes never being found. One case that I

C

can never forget was that of a Springer bitch that I sold as a five-months-old puppy. She became a field trial prize winner and qualified to run at the Spaniel Championship. Her owner became ill and could no longer continue shooting, so sold her. The new owner was warned that she was an exceptional jumper, and so put her in a run with high, but, alas, not high enough, wire. She jumped out, endeavoured to find her way to her old home and was found dead on the railway line. So please, do be careful.

I suppose it happens in most breeds that owning one dog leads the owner to wish to breed a litter, and Springer puppies are such fascinating little creatures that after one litter it is hard to resist starting a kennel, which, of course, one has dreams of making famous, either on the show or working side, or, perhaps, on both.

Chapter IV

BREEDING FOR SHOW

GENERAL COMMENTS

HERE there must come a division in what I write about breeding Springers. There are two very distinct camps: the owners who find all their pleasure in breeding for perfection of form, and the owners who breed for the perfection their dogs can attain as workers and field trial winners.

In the 1920s there were several strains that could win both on the bench and at trials, notably the Horsfords, which produced Horsford Hetman, the first of the only three Dual Champions in the breed, and Colonel F. H. B. Carrell's Hartings, from which the second Dual Champion in Thoughtful of Harting came. The Duke of Hamilton had a brilliant line of field trial winners, but I remember Flint of Avendale only as a show dog; he became the third Dual Champion in the breed. Lady Portal had a strain of very good-looking Springers, mostly black and white with the prefix Laverstoke, and they were well to the top in awards on the bench and at trials. Mr Oswald Ellis also had a very good-looking dual-purpose strain; one in particular, Nurscombe Prince, was a most attractive liver-white-and-tan dog which won in both spheres, and mating Ranger's daughter, Ch. Reipple of Ranscombe to him, I bred a number of bench and trial winners, including Reipple and Ranter of Ware. For many years Miss C. M. Francis with her Highams, I with my Ranscombes, and, since the war, Mr D. C. Hannah with his Stokeleys and Mr W. Manin with his Northdowns, have endeavoured to show that a good-looking dog is not necessarily one that cannot at least gain some awards at trials and certainly not disgrace the breed as workers.

I do not wish to infer that there are many Springers today that are not both good-looking and able to do an honest day's work, for I know some of the show winners are shot over, but their owners are diffident about running them at trials. I know too that there are many hundreds of Springers who will never enter a show ring nor compete at a field trial because their owners have no desire for them to be anything but companions at home and in the field.

However, in this book the breeding of Springers as show dogs will be dealt with first, written primarily for the novice breeder, not for people who over a number of years have established successful show kennels. The latter know what they want, have decided on the methods by which they will attain it and now have a number of winners to their credit.

Many novices have bought their first Springer—with luck a good one, sometimes a mediocre one or even a very poor one— and brought it to me for my opinion and advice. If the ambition has been to win on the bench, and the animal is a good one, I have encouraged them; if only a second- or third-rate one, particularly if it has a pedigree likely to reproduce faults in the next generations, I have tried to be kind, but explained that the dog in question will almost certainly bring them nothing but disappointment and had much better be retained as a family friend and a fresh start made with a Springer chosen carefully with a reasonable hope of success. I know, because I was a novice myself and made the mistakes most novices make—perhaps more than many!

THE BROOD BITCH

My first advice to anyone who is starting a kennel of English Springers is that it is much wiser to begin with a bitch. I admit that I did not do this myself, but then I was most extraordinarily lucky in finding such an outstandingly beautiful dog as Ranger and, of course, at that time I had no idea of either showing or breeding.

The strength of a kennel lies in its bitches, and if one owns a good bitch one can always obtain the service of the pick of the dogs of the whole country, whereas it would be a very lucky novice who could find and purchase a winning dog who would suit all the bitches he might acquire.

Look for a bitch of really good temperament, friendly and neither shy nor nervous, with a soft, kind eye and pleasant out-look. I put these points first because it is easy to breed a nervous disposition into a strain, but very hard to breed it out. In the 1920s and early 1930s I knew one strain that, although good-looking, was so shy that every member of it literally shuddered when a judge attempted to handle it, while another strain was so sour that every dog bred from it snapped at every other dog in the ring, at every handler but its own and at the judge. And these unpleasant traits persisted in generation after generation.

There is one axiom which should never be forgotten in breeding: Never breed from the second generation of a fault. In choosing a bitch it is most desirable to know both the sire and the dam and, too, the grand-parents. A fault, like a good quality, can miss a generation and reappear in the grand-children, and a physical fault, such as a bad front, a light eye or a gay tail, can recur in the first, second and third generation, or even farther on, just as easily as bad temperament.

It is not always easy to find the exact bitch that one hopes will breed the puppies one wants, and perhaps do some winning herself, and I do advise novices not to rush into buying a bitch too hurriedly. Study the pedigree and see that the forbears in it are of the type and character you desire. If you do not know these dogs, and as a novice this is very likely, ask the advice of an experienced breeder and exhibitor, who will be able to tell you of the make, shape and temperament of these ancestors.

Do not be tempted to buy a bitch simply because there are numerous Champions among the sires in the pedigree. Some people, because certain dogs have done a lot of winning and have become well known, use first one sire Champion and then, with the offspring of that, mate another Champion, totally unrelated, with no regard to line breeding. No real type can be fixed in this way. 'Twice in and once out' is a good motto, but in going out it is wise to see that the 'out' has some of the same blood lines. Don't be led away by the idea that, because a *very* high price is being asked for a young maiden bitch, she must necessarily be *very* good; she may be, and therefore be worth what is being asked for her, but in that case it is unusual for the owner to want to sell her, unless there is a very good and convincing reason for it. Find out by judicious enquiries what price a reasonably good bitch should cost, and unless you have unlimited funds do not spend too much money at once. Keep a reserve in case of any untoward happening which may necessitate a fresh start. Look for a bitch who conforms to the standard for the breed and, above all, has quality and, that most essential attribute, a good temperament. Do not absolutely refuse to consider one because she is a little long in body. A bitch with just that little longer body carries her puppies well and is usually a good whelper.

Some special points to remember: As Springer bitches with few exceptions come in season first at about ten months and then at six-month intervals, the choice of time for having a litter can be fairly certainly decided on. Unless there is any special reason against it, I like to wait until the second season at least before breeding from a bitch. If the first season is delayed until fourteen months or more it may be desirable to mate a bitch then, especially as it may help to improve a light or shelly bitch, but I do like Springers to have their childhood just like other young things and enjoy their youth and, too, have time for their education.

Never breed from a bitch twice running, unless it is one who comes in season only at yearly or even longer intervals. To breed every six months, or even at two out of every three seasons, is putting a strain on her, mentally and physically. Dogs are not machines and should not be expected to grind out products like a factory. It is, putting it mildly, unkind to the bitch and it leads to a deterioration in the puppies. I can think back to the occasions when one or another breed has become very popular, and bitches have been bred from at every heat and the puppies kept and bred from as soon as possible. I remember how physique, temperament and mental ability fell; it does not take long for a breed to be inundated with weaklings, who, in addition to being poor in shape and size, are shy, nervous and stupid. Fortunately for such breeds there have been sturdy supporters who have kept their dogs for love of the breed, and as popularity waned and the craze died out the good standards they maintained all the time have triumphed, and the breed has returned to sound, typical specimens.

So, to all beginners in English Springers, I say breed with judgement and restraint, produce what authorities in the breed can tell you are good specimens and likely to maintain the standard, and do not overbreed.

Two final points. It is wise to ascertain beforehand that there is no stricture in the bitch's vagina which would prevent a mating. It is no use waiting until the actual time and then discover that it is impossible for the dog to mate her. If one has the slightest suspicion of such a thing it is best to take the bitch to a veterinary surgeon, who will, in many cases, be able to break the stricture down; if this cannot be done it is useless to think of her as a brood bitch.

The Kennel Club made a rule that no dog which is either monorchid or cryptorchid could be shown but this rule has been rescinded. It is desirable, however, to make sure that the dog chosen as a sire has in its ancestry no history of the lack of one or both testes in the scrotum and the same applies to the bitch's pedigree. It has been shown that breeding from a line in which this condition has occurred anywhere brings a risk of its happening with one or more of a litter in future generations. It must be remembered that it may be a considerable time before the condition can be definitely known and one does not want to hold on to a puppy, however promising otherwise, with the risk that there may be disappointment in the end.

Once you have decided on the dog you would like to use get in touch with his owner and book a service, well before the bitch is due in season. For if a dog has become known as a successful sire his owner will want to arrange that his services shall be available at a given time. If he has accepted a reasonable number of bookings he cannot be expected to fit in extra bitches 'out of the blue'. One generally knows within a little when a bitch should be in season and the approximate date should be given to the owner of the stud dog. Directly the bitch comes in season he should be informed and an appointment made for the eleventh to the thirteenth day afterwards. Should circumstances seem to make it necessary for you to ask for an earlier (or possibly later) date, telephone at once.

If it is at all possible take your bitch to be mated. For one thing she is much happier if her owner is about, and for another she does not have to chance the vagaries of the British railway system. If she must travel by train, and the journey is a straightforward one with no changes at all, it should be reasonable to expect that the bitch should arrive at the proper time and be put out of the train at the station to which she is booked, but I have known cases where the travelling-box has been carried on a considerable distance, then put out on a platform and returned to the station marked on the label, or even to the station from which it started. And this in spite of the most careful labelling!

If I could not take a bitch I always telephoned or wired, saying that she had been despatched by a certain train giving the time of arrival at her destination. I also telephoned the

stationmaster at this station, asking him to be sure that the train
was met and the box taken out.

But when it means a cross-country railway journey there is
no knowing when the bitch may arrive, in spite of her owner
having spent endless time in working out connections. It does
help to write *and* telephone to the stationmaster at each station
at which the travelling-box has to be transferred. If the journey
means that London has to be crossed and you cannot go up and
see the bitch into the train on another region, use the very
efficient service run by Miss Kay Stafford and others, who undertake for a most reasonable fee to meet the train at the arrival
station, transport the box across to the station of despatch, see it
into the train and wire or telephone the time of arrival to the
person named on the label. If the journey is a long one, say to
Scotland, it is a good idea to send the bitch by a night train; she
will quite possibly follow her home routine and sleep.

The bitch's kennel name should be shown on the address
label and a large notice should be attached prominently to the
box, stating that it must not be opened by a railway official but
only by the person to whom it is addressed. I heard only recently
of a bitch whose box was opened by porters at a station 'to see if a
dog *was* inside'. She escaped in a panic, got on the railway line
and was killed!

The travelling-box must be big enough for the bitch to stand
upright and to travel in comfort. It should be of light but strong
construction, and ventilated in such a way that in no circumstances can it be blocked by luggage being piled upon it in the
guard's van. For this reason an ark-shaped top is best, as luggage
and mailbags cannot be piled on it easily, also, more obviously,
it contains a live animal.

THE STUD DOG

The choice of a stud dog is a matter for the greatest thought and
care. A very sound axiom is 'mate the pedigree as well as the dog'.
It is no use thinking that just because one has taken a liking to a
particular dog and mates it to one's bitch the results *must* be those
for which one hopes. It is essential that, so far as possible, line
breeding should be followed when selecting a sire. This means
that the same ancestors should appear, following definite lines in

both pedigrees to a certain extent. A half-brother and -sister mating can, depending on the common grand-parents, produce excellent results, but on no account mate full brother and sister; physically it may not appear too disastrous, but mental weakness and nervousness are almost certain. If one or two grand-parents appearing in both the dog's and the bitch's pedigrees are known for their good characteristics, there is reason to hope that the puppies may inherit them. This repetition of the best of the breeding can go back several generations, with good results.

The stud dog itself must be considered very carefully, for however suitable the pedigree appears it is not wise to use a dog that is bitchy in appearance and expression, even if it has won well at shows. This dog might suit a heavy, doggy type of bitch, but I am assuming that a typical bitch has been chosen and is to be mated, a strong, masculine type of dog then being essential. It is equally important to choose a dog with no outstanding fault. The perfect dog is not yet born; if he had been, dog shows would be very dull affairs for all but his owner! In English Springers certain faults have been very apparent in recent years, and not only should one avoid them in selecting a stud dog but one should endeavour to remember, if one has seen them, what sire and dam and grand-parents are like. If one does not know these forbears ask, tactfully, what experienced breeders can tell you of them. The worst faults one sees in the ring at the present time are oversize, straight shoulders, straight stifles—the last two causing bad movement—gay tails, too heavy muzzles and throatiness, and round hard eyes. Any one of these faults can so easily be reproduced that it is wise to avoid using a dog in whom any one of them is strongly noticeable.

Look at as many of the bitches that have been mated to the dog you have in mind, and then at as many of the progeny, as you can. Do not forget that the bitch has as much influence on the puppies as the sire and also that a dog who has made a certain reputation as a winner will have had a number of the best bitches in the country sent to him, so that it is reasonable to expect that the outcome of such matings should be typical, and themselves good winners. Very often the dog is given all the credit; the fact that the bitch was exceptionally good is not mentioned. Had the dog been mated to a series of mediocre bitches only, his reputation might be very different.

It sometimes happens that the father of a successful Show

Champion proves a better sire than the son, and may have a number of very good winners to his credit. Such a dog should be very carefully considered when selecting a mate for one's bitch.

At this point it may be suitable to consider the duties and responsibilities of the owner of a stud dog; for having mated your bitch you may look forward to breeding a puppy who in time may be a successful show dog and sire himself. If you should be fortunate enough to breed such a dog I would suggest mating him at about ten to twelve months to prove him as a sire and only once or twice afterwards until he is at least eighteen months old. Then, if he has made up well and breeders are interested in him, he can be placed at stud, but at first only to a limited number of bitches.

On the arrival of a bitch be sure her box is opened in a place from which she cannot escape. Remember that she is a stranger to you and possibly upset by being confined in a box and by the journey. Advise her owner of her safe arrival, for which I am sure he will be grateful unless he is just a 'dog factory' owner, which I do not believe can be the case with anyone owning and being privileged to be 'owned' by Springers. Exercise the bitch and feed her and put her in your special visiting-bitch's kennel for a quiet night's rest, mating her the following morning and returning her the next day.

The owner of a maiden bitch may ask for her to be mated a second time, and to this it is reasonable to agree, though I have found that most maiden bitches breed after one mating. It is a good thing to let the dog and bitch run round and play together for a time, when they may mate naturally, but some young bitches, and some older ones too, are inclined to snap and to refuse to accept the dog; then it is better to hold her and prevent her hurting the dog or putting him off, if he is young and inexperienced. It may be necessary to muzzle a really difficult bitch who is inclined to snap, and for that purpose I was shown a most effective appliance specially made by a saddler for the owner of a bitch they knew to be troublesome and really bad-tempered with other dogs. It consisted of a flat pad of leather with four slits in it, through which a leather strap was threaded, so that it could be loosened to make a cross-band over the nose, with the leather pad underneath the jaw (Fig. 7). The strap-ends came down below the pad and could be drawn as tight as was necessary, and then taken round the neck and buckled like a collar. It cannot hurt the bitch, and is better than a tape which can sometimes be dragged off with the paws. This device worked excellently and the owners of this bitch had a second one made for me, in case anyone brought another bitch with a temper like that of their bitch! There have been times when I have been glad to use it.

Once a tie has been effected, the service may last from about ten to forty minutes. Puppies have been known to result without a tie, but it is not very usual.

After the bitch has been mated, feed her and leave her quietly in her kennel. Return her the next day, and be as particular in

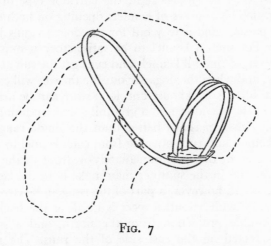

FIG. 7

advising her despatch to railway officials and her owner as when sending one of your own bitches by train.

Stud fees should be paid at the time the bitch is sent, and if she has to come and return by train a cheque for fee and the return fare should be sent to arrive shortly before the bitch. If any arrangement for a puppy or puppies, instead of a fee, is made it should be in writing and in duplicate, signed by both parties. So many misunderstandings can arise over a 'gentleman's agreement'.

Should a bitch fail to prove in whelp a return service is usually given free, though this cannot be demanded as a right. It is, of course, conditional on the dog's being alive and in the same ownership. Should either of these contingencies arise the owner of the dog might offer the services of another dog, should he possess more than the one concerned, but this again is a favour, not a right.

Chapter V

KENNEL MANAGEMENT

KENNELLING

N O DOG can do well unless it is given a kennel that is airy, light and comfortable and, above all, free from draughts.

If many dogs are to be kept, the corridor type of kennel is ideal, Fig. 8. This consists of kennels opening on both sides from a central passage and a way out for the dogs to runs behind on each side. For such a kennel to be satisfactory it must be sited east and west, so that all kennels and runs get the sun at least part of the day, and when the dogs are outside the sun will come down from both sides. A cookhouse and food store can be arranged on the north of the corridor, and a grooming and trimming room on the south. This is perhaps better than the single range, with a corridor behind and runs opening from each kennel to the south, as, unless part of the run immediately in front of the kennel is covered, the sun in the summer may make both the kennels and runs very hot. If, however, a part of the run can be covered, then a single range with a south aspect is ideal, as the back corridor provides double protection from the north, and a screen can easily be erected on the east side of the runs. The north-east winds so prevalent in this country can do a good deal of harm to a dog who is perhaps off colour but who will, for some reason known only to himself, decide to sit out in a run instead of lying in a comfortable bed. A partly covered run, too, allows a dog to be out in the air even on a wet day, and Springers are outdoor dogs and do enjoy a fresh-air existence.

It is, however, not always possible or even necessary to have a big range of kennels. For the novice with only a few dogs, and the strong-minded person who, having decided to keep a very limited number of dogs, sticks to that decision, the smaller separate kennels (Fig 9), say 6 ft. long by 4 ft. deep, 5 ft. high in front sloping to 3 ft. 6 in. at the back, can be made very comfortable for a couple of dogs. A sleeping bench, 2 ft. wide, placed to the left of a central door, and a similar sized strong wooden cover placed on the battening below the window and on the battening at the side and back of the kennel at the same height, makes a draughtproof, sheltered sleeping place, and the window above can be kept open to provide plenty of fresh air.

A kennel for a bitch in whelp, and where she has had her puppies, must be one apart from the main kennels, and it must be high enough for the owner to be able to stand upright in it with comfort (Fig 10).

I have found that the most satisfactory kennel for this purpose is one that is 6 ft. square and 6 ft. high in front, with a slope of 6 in. to the back, and with a large window at the front. It is best

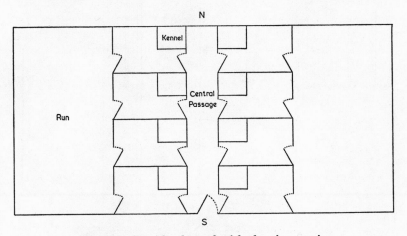

FIG. 8. Corridor kennel with sleeping section

if the door is made in two halves, like a stable door, the top half and inside the upper half an inner barred half-section that can be fastened back when both sections of the door are shut, or brought into use when the top section is opened and fastened back outside (Fig 9). There can also be a 'dog-hole' similar to the hen-door fitted in many chicken-houses. The shutter for this 'hole' is fitted on the outside of the kennel and can be fastened up to a hook. It allows the bitch and, when old enough, the puppies to go in and out to their run without the main door being open, so preventing cold winds chilling the inside atmosphere at ground level. The slots in which this dog door runs must be fixed with a good margin over the actual hole, so that when shut no draught comes through. There should be a ramp fixed from the kennel to the ground outside.

Beds. First the arrangement for the bitch's kennel. A strong upright post should be fixed 2 ft. 6 in. from the back and exactly equidistant from the two sides of the kennel. At the height of the battening that goes round the kennel, and exactly opposite the centre post, nail two battens down the wall to the floor, an inch apart. Fix similar battens on the inside of the centre post exactly

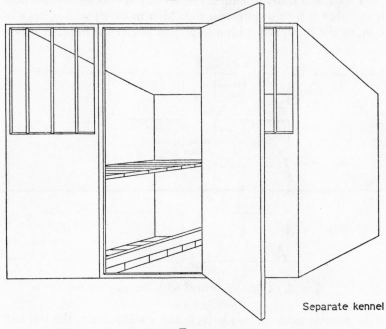

Separate kennel

FIG. 9

opposite the ones on the back wall. Boards the length between the back of the kennel and the centre post can then be dropped down to build up a complete division between the two sides of the kennel, and the sleeping bench can be placed equally well on either side. Battens are nailed to the left- and right-hand side of the centre post and to the sides of the kennel, so that boards can be dropped down in front of the sleeping bench. These can be added to or removed as required for keeping the puppies in the nest or letting them out as they grow up. I had two sleeping benches, and as only one could be in use at a time, the other was ready in the other section to change the bitch and her family over each day, thus enabling the first bench to be thoroughly washed and dried. I found this a most efficient method of keeping the sleeping compartments scrupulously clean and hygienic when the puppies were tiny, and until it was possible for them to have the run of the kennel at night. To begin with, only one or two boards

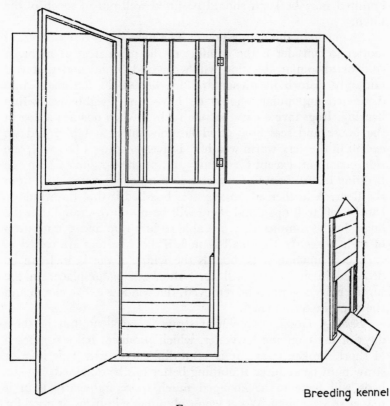

Breeding kennel

FIG. 10

need be inserted, but as the puppies grow older extra boards can be added, so that they do not climb out and perhaps get 'mislaid' by Mother in the night. All the boards used must be tongued and grooved, so that they slot into one another without leaving gaps.

A cover made of three-ply, and with firm battening, should be laid over the sleeping bench, resting on the battening of the kennel at the back and side and on the middle dividing section. This prevents all down-draughts and can be transferred from side to side as required. In very cold weather, if an infra-red lamp is not in use, a sack dropped down over two-thirds or three-quarters of the front ensures that the nest is kept really warm, but the bitch can get in or out as she wishes.

In these puppy kennels a shelf, on which any articles frequently required may be kept, should be fitted well out of reach of the bitch.

So much for the puppy house. The next and a very important matter to consider is the comfort of the other dogs at night. A cold or uncomfortable dog will wake and 'wail', and that will not only disturb its owner and his household but make him distinctly unpopular, should he have any neighbours within hearing. Dogs love a cave, as one realises when one has a dog in the house and sees how often he goes under a table; and so, except in the very warm weather, I give each dog a box with one side taken out, except for about 5 in. at the bottom to keep the bedding in. All boxes should stand on a bench, raised 3 in. from the floor. A further advantage of a box-bed is that the windows can be left well open and there will be no down-draught on the dogs. In the summer they are able to jump up and sleep on top of their boxes. In the small kennel, if short battens are nailed at each end, making slots, boards the width of the kennel can be dropped in and these will keep the bedding in place. In the summer the cover can be removed, the window above closed and the opposite one opened.

Bedding. Good, long wheat straw is excellent, but in these days of the combine harvester, which produces bales composed of short, broken straw, it is very difficult to get. This inferior straw must be endured if nothing better can be obtained, but the beds will have to be changed much more frequently than if reaper straw is used. Wood wool, obtainable in bales, is good for grown dogs, but it is not advisable to use it for puppies because they can get tangled up in it. Avoid the use of barley straw.

The flooring in all the kennels I have described has been of wood, and wooden floors must be kept scrupulously clean. For daily cleaning nothing is better than a pail and mop, for very much hotter water can be used, as well as more soda than one could bear on one's hands if washing it with a scrubbing-brush and floor-cloth, though, of course, all floors and other parts of the kennels need thorough scrubbing at regular intervals to get

(*C. M. Cooke*)

Sh.Ch. Woodbay Prima Donna

(*Fall*)

Reveller of Ranscombe

(F. W. Simms)

Reeve of Ranscombe

(Fall)

Rollicker, Reverie and Remembrance of Ranscombe
at three months old

dust and dirt out of grooves and corners. In the winter, when the weather is wet day after day and the whole atmosphere damp, it is most difficult to get floors dry, especially in the puppy kennel, where it is particularly important. The best and quickest way is to sprinkle the floor with sawdust and brush it vigorously backwards and forwards with a hard broom, using two or three lots of sawdust if necessary. Before the dogs or puppies go back into the kennels the floors should be thickly covered with sawdust, easily obtainable from any sawmill or woodyard.

Kennel Runs. All kennels should stand on solid concrete platforms, and concrete runs should surround the kennels. The concrete in these runs should not be a mixture of ordinary cement and gravel because this is very cold. Cement and clinker should be used. This is warm, and dogs lying out on it do not get chilled as on gravel cement. I used this mixture for many years and found it most satisfactory.

From my concrete runs I always had a gate opening into a big grass run, and although I know space has sometimes to be considered it is most desirable to have a grass run where the dogs can play if the weather is suitable. If a grass run cannot be managed a run covered with clinker, well rolled in, is excellent. Needless to say, all gates should open inwards. It is much easier to push a dog back and slip in oneself than if the gate opens outwards.

The kennel for the bitch in season should be as far as possible from the other kennels and should be wired in very securely, with 7 ft. high, strong, penfold wire, well set into the ground and with a cement fillet all round. The whole of the top of the run should be covered in with strong wire netting: it is astonishing how high a determined dog can jump and how high a bitch can jump if she has made up her mind to get out. The gate, which must open inwards, should be very strong, ideally on an iron framing, so that there is no chance of its 'whipping' if the bitch drags at it at the bottom. A board, the width of the gate, should be let well down into the ground and cemented. The best arrangement is to have two gates, as in a bird aviary, so that the first gate is shut before the second one is opened.

D

VITAMINS

It is now recognised that all animals as well as humans require vitamins, which means that in feeding dogs one must consider the foods that will give the particular vitamins required naturally. In some cases special treatment with a pure vitamin product may be required.

Vitamin A. This is the one, particularly, that protects against infection and is necessary for maintaining health and producing growth in the young animal. Cod-liver oil is the stand-by here. Halibut oil in which Vitamin A is very concentrated, so that only a very few drops are needed, can be used if the larger quantity needed of cod-liver oil is found not to suit a particular dog, but I have never had any difficulty in this respect with Springers. Cod-liver oil for cattle is much less refined, which means that much less of the valuable vitamin has been extracted, and I have used it on my veterinary surgeon's recommendation with excellent results.

Milk, egg yolk and ox liver can also be used for their high vitamin A content.

Vitamin B. This is a very extensive group.

The lack of vitamin B1 can retard development, be the cause of wasting of the muscles, even paralysis, nervous trouble, uncertain appetite, gastric upsets and hysteria.

White bread is one of the worst causes of many of these troubles, certainly of hysteria, and should never be fed to dogs in any circumstances. Real wholemeal bread contains vitamin B1 and can be used as a bulk food. Egg yolk is good, and dried brewers' yeast, crumbled on the food, or wheat-germ oil are two of the most practical concentrated forms. There are a number of nerve tablets for dogs obtainable from veterinary surgeons and/or chemists, which I understand show good results if used over a long period, but as I have been fortunate enough not to have had any nervous dogs requiring treatment of this sort I cannot recommend one or another specially, from my own experience.

Vetzyme tablets, a yeast product made by Phillips' Yeast Products Ltd, are a most useful method of supplying yeast, and with few exceptions dogs love them. A regular daily ration, according to the breed and size of the dog, should be given either in the food or handed out to each dog after its meal, as a treat. A full-grown Springer should have six tablets daily.

There are many forms of vitamin B2. Foods containing this vitamin are wheat-germ oil, dried yeast, yeast extract (Marmite), meat-juice and meat essence. The two latter, obtainable as Brand's Essence, are very valuable in illness when little or no food can be taken.

Vitamin C. This, the vitamin for keeping a skin healthy and for preventing gastric trouble, is contained in lemon- and orange-juice: the former is too sharp for dogs to take it willingly, but if orange-juice is used from the time puppies are weaned they grow up to enjoy the flavour, and I always include it in the diet. In the good old days before the war, when one could buy excellent oranges at seven for sixpence, the dogs used to have the oranges, peeled and quartered, added to their feed, and never left a fragment.

Vitamin D. This is the anti-rachitic vitamin. In the 1920s Professor and Mrs Mellanby did a great deal of research work on this vitamin, particularly in reference to dogs, and we should be thankful to these scientists for the long and patient work they put into their experiments. It is largely their work which gave us the knowledge which, used intelligently, will ensure that rickets cannot occur in our puppies.

Puppies grow at a tremendous rate. A Springer puppy a few days old can lie comfortably on one's hand and weighs only a few ounces. At three months old it weighs several pounds, at six months 25 lb. or more and at twelve months 40 lb. Calcium and phosphorus are essential, in combination with vitamin D, for the formation of good bone and teeth, development of muscles and nerves, and all three must be present and work together for satisfactory results. Calcium is controlled in the bloodstream by the parathyroid gland and is supplied by milk and cheese. Phosphorus is also in these foods but is also supplied by eggs, white fish and ox liver. Vitamin D comes from cod-liver oil and halibut oil, and above all from real sunshine which has not been filtered through having to pass glass. Vita glass and infra-red lamps can do a certain amount, but nothing can equal unrestricted sunshine.

Puppies must have a good supply of nutriment for bone formation. What starts as cartilage must quickly calcify and grow into straight, strong bone, and this means not only vitamin D, calcium and phosphorus after they are born, but the bitch, during pregnancy, must be so fed that she passes these essentials on to the unborn pups. From the time she is mated the bitch should have cod-liver oil or halibut oil regularly; eggs, milk, fish and liver; and, in addition, five drops of Radiostoleum daily. This product of British Drug Houses Ltd is particularly rich in vitamin D, and the dose should be increased gradually during the time the bitch is carrying the puppies. Radiostoleum can be used in cases where cod-liver oil in any quantity upsets a dog. I have used it for very many years and feel sure that given to the bitch during pregnancy and while nursing her litter, and to the puppies directly weaning begins, it is impossible to have anything but straight, strong-limbed pups. Even when puppies have shown bad signs of rickets, bent forelegs, weak hind quarters, etc., a wonderful improvement has been seen when I have persuaded the owner to use this most valuable product. There are a number of other products containing vitamin D, but of this one I speak with experience and most strongly recommend its use.

Vitamin E. This is the anti-sterility vitamin. Wheat-germ oil is undoubtedly the best form in which to ensure a supply of this vitamin. It is most useful for toning up stud dogs and is given to bitches which have been uncertain breeders. It almost always produces good results if given regularly for a period before the bitch comes in season. This vitamin is not a wasting value, that is, the effect of it does not pass off but remains stored in the body.

PROTEINS

The dog in its natural state was a meat-eating animal; it hunted *and caught its prey, devoured it, flesh, entrails and skin and often bones,* and throve on what formed for it a complete diet. The dog now, however, is the product of our modern civilisation and its food requires as much thought and balanced selection as that of its human owners.

Meat is still the most valuable food for dogs, but since the war it has not always been easy to get a reliable and thoroughly wholesome supply.

Butcher's meat is all very well if there are only one or two dogs to feed, but at 2s. 6d. a lb. (and a Springer needs his 'pound of flesh' daily), kennel costs would be very high if many dogs were kept.

If a bullock's head can be obtained regularly from a butcher it provides pounds of good meat which can be cut off and fed raw. The head can then be chopped up and simmered—for preference in a slow-combustion oven or in a pressure cooker—and the broth used for soaking meal.

Horse-meat is lean and good, and provides all the meat values, but it is stronger in protein content than beef or mutton and, therefore, a somewhat reduced weight should be given. Meat from the knacker's should be used with great care. It is essential to know that your supplier will tell you from where he has obtained the animal from which he is cutting your meat. If he is one to whom you go regularly you will soon discover whether you can rely on him; if not, do not use knacker's meat at all. A healthy animal which has been killed for a good reason, such as a broken leg or other injury, is one thing; an animal that has died or been killed when nothing more could be done to keep it alive is quite another.

Heart, liver, kidney are extremely valuable as part of the meat ration; cooked they provide a good stock in which meal can be soaked; bullock's and/or sheep's paunches (tripes) should be included in the bill of fare. They are very nourishing, easily digested and the fat is of great value, particularly for dogs which are poor doers and difficult to get into good condition. Dogs all seem to love paunch and will select it from all other foods offered them: an excellent method of feeding it, either cooked or raw, is to give each dog a portion to take out into the grass run, where it will sit and gnaw it to the last scrap. This is good for the teeth and induces a flow of saliva, and the dog has a much longer period of enjoyment of his food than when he swallows his portion of cut-up meat or paunch in a few seconds. It is wonderful how quickly a dog can clear up a dish of cut-up meat. In feeding paunch, however, it is most important to see that no nails or pieces of wire are imbedded in it. Cows, apparently, can swallow such things with impunity, but dogs could come to grievous harm, either by biting on them and hurting the mouth or, worse still, by swallowing them.

It is a good plan too, for the same reasons, to give dogs their ration of meat in a lump, each one retiring to its favourite corner of the grass run and eating steadily. But a word of warning: Never let the dogs eat their hunk of meat on a clinker or gravel run—on a concrete one, yes—because they may drag the meat or paunch about on the clinker or gravel, neither of which is a desirable addition to the diet, and could be a real danger if rough lumps of either were swallowed.

Rabbits, before that foul disease myxomatosis spread across the country, were a great help in feeding dogs. The flesh has not so great a food value as meat but is easily digested, and, as it is tasty too, it is excellent as a change for puppies and will often tempt sick dogs or dainty feeders. In the halcyon days before the last war, when I had a number of Springers, I used to visit a big shoot regularly and bring back five or six rabbits for the stew-pot, a weekly change from the ordinary rations. These were cooked all night in a covered pot in a slow-combustion oven—pressure cookers were not so much used then. Now, of course, I should be very chary of feeding rabbit: after seeing 'myxy' rabbits I no more fancy using rabbits for my dogs than I fancy eating them myself. But if an absolutely disease-free supply can be guaranteed, rabbit might be considered to give variety to the diet.

Another great help in supplying meat and varying the diet, especially in times of difficulty in obtaining raw meat, is the granulated meat supplied by F. C. Lowe & Son, Ltd, of Sitting-bourne, Kent. This lean dried butcher's meat, of which 1 lb. is equal to $2\frac{1}{2}$ lb. of fresh meat, is soaked in boiling water or broth. The broth is poured off later on to meal into which the meat can be mixed and makes a very sustaining and appetising dish which the dogs enjoy. I have used this granulated meat and found it very satisfactory, as have a number of my friends, particularly those who use their dogs for shooting and who run them at trials. If one lives in the country, and the nearest town for a regular meat supply is ten or more miles away, this product is an excellent stand-by.

Fish, particularly herring and mackerel, is extremely good as part of the protein diet, and as fish contains iodine and phosphorus, both important essentials to a dog's well-being, it is a valuable food and should appear regularly in the menu.

Eggs—especially the yolks—and milk are also valuable protein foods and are particularly good for sick dogs and puppies.

Tinned meats are useful in emergencies and when one is away for a few days, but not long enough to make arrangements for a supply of fresh meat where one is staying. A certain amount of raw or lightly cooked meat can be taken for a day or two, but this is not practicable for longer, especially in the summer, and then the 'iron rations' are a help. I would recommend that the tins chosen should be of meat only, not the meat-and-cereal varieties. There are many good brands on the market. Buy a tin and 'try it on the dog' beforehand—some dogs have very decided preferences and dislikes. The meat may look much the same to us but dogs have their own ideas, unless, of course, they are the dogs that will eat anything placed before them—much the easiest to feed.

Never feed 'lights' (lungs) to any animal. They have no nutritive value whatever. This is often not realised by the owners of the one pet dog, who buy it regularly, thinking they are giving their dogs meat. When I am at the butcher's and hear them ordering it I sometimes have great difficulty in retraining myself from begging them not to buy this useless and repulsive-looking stuff!

CARBOHYDRATES

Under this heading come all the biscuits, biscuit-meal, whole-meal bread, flaked maize, oatmeal, etc. They are not muscle-building foods like meat, but they provide bulk and are useful in that they contain starch, sugars and glycogen—fuel- and energy-producing elements.

Hard wholemeal biscuits are good for keeping the teeth clean and free of tartar, and I much prefer them to bones for this purpose. Wholemeal biscuit meal is excellent, fed dry occasionally or regularly soaked in good meat or fish gravy, but when this is done care must be taken to see that the food is not sloppy. It must be just crumbly; continuous use of sloppy, wet meal will cause stomach upsets and skin trouble. When soaked the meal should be soft all through. In no circumstances should it be soaked hurriedly, a short time before it is to be used, because the centre remains hard. The boiling stock should be poured over it some hours before it is required and the container covered so that the meal is steamed, which results in its being crumbly all through. Meal with cold stock poured over it in each bowl, just as it is being served to the dogs, makes a tasty dinner for a change. The meal remains hard, and the gravy adds flavour but is not on it long enough to 'half soften' it.

There are many excellent meals made by the well-known dog-food manufacturers. Some are made from wholemeal only, others have malt and milk added, and a further selection can be made from wholemeal with meat added, or wholemeal and meat meal. For Springers, the size described as 'Terrier size' is most suitable.

I have never been fond of oatmeal as a food for dogs because it is heating, and dogs given too much of it become fat and soft, and, in extreme cases, rickety. Flaked maize will put weight on a dog rapidly, but again it is no favourite of mine for it is no use as a body-builder or sustaining food.

Professor and Mrs Mellanby, in carrying out their experiments in feeding values, fed rusked brown bread to puppies and other animals, and their findings certainly justified the use of such bread. The bread should be cut in slices and baked for a long time in a very slow oven and then fed to the dogs instead of biscuits. Broken, it can be mixed with their cut-up meat ration and then they 'champ' the mixture up together, which is much better than just swallowing the meat, in fact 'vacuuming' it.

It must be remembered that the bread to be rusked must be *real* wholemeal bread, not any of the fancy breads sold under special trade names. Stone-ground brown bread is quite the best and is much easier to obtain in the country, where the baker in a village or small town makes and bakes his own bread, often from flour milled locally. In and near large towns the bakers' shops are just distributing centres for the electric- or steam-baking 'bread factories', and the so-called brown bread is rarely wholemeal.

Fats are converted in the body to give heat and are the most valuable source of energy. They digest more slowly than lean meat and meals and so form a stand-by against greater expenditure of energy. Fish, fat meat, the fat of bullocks or sheep's paunches are very useful in supplying this need in the dog's body. Beef suet is excellent in conditioning a dog, as I found when I had a very beautiful young Springer during the war. Nothing would put any flesh on him until he was given my ration and the rations of several of my self-sacrificing friends, then he put on weight and glowed with condition.

Healthy, adult Springers need only one good meal a day, the quantity varying with the dog. Some will fatten on a much smaller amount than others, and it is only by watching each dog carefully that one learns how much to give it to keep it in perfect condition. An average diet is 1 lb. of meat for the main meal on days on which meat is served—say four days a week if fish is given once and paunch twice—together with some soaked meal or rusked brown bread, a small teaspoonful of cod-liver oil, a small pinch of Epsom Salts and an equally small pinch of flowers of sulphur. We used to call the last two the dog's 'salt and pepper', and they certainly helped to keep them in good bloom.

Never feed the dogs from a common dish. Each one must have its own bowl and you can then be sure that it is getting its proper ration and, too, that it is eating all its food. Directly a dog fusses over its dinner, leaving it, yet returning when it sees another dog approach, but not finally clearing up its platter, take special note of it and, if it seems in any other way off colour, take its temperature.

For an average Springer a feeding bowl, of the type that cannot be upset, about $7\frac{1}{2}$ in. across filled level with its meat and meal should be sufficient; for bigger or smaller dogs allow more or less in proportion. This principal meal should be given at any time in the afternoon or early evening that is most convenient to the owner and found suitable for the dogs. It is desirable to give this meal so that the dogs can have a quiet time in their kennels or runs before being taken out for exercise. Dogs should never be worked or allowed to take violent exercise immediately after a heavy meal.

It is important to keep to a regular hour for feeding, bringing the time forward gradually as winter approaches, for feeding in the dark is to be avoided unless under very exceptional circumstances.

After the Springers have finished their dinners it is a good idea to give them a piece of hard biscuit or some Crunkles or similar dainty; it gives them pleasure and cleans up the teeth.

In the morning I like each dog to have one or more biscuits, according to the size of the biscuit, or some pieces of rusked bread. They enjoy this snack after their night's rest and again it is good for their teeth.

Every Springer should be trained from puppyhood to sit down and wait until its bowl of food is placed on the ground and its name called. This trains them to orderly habits of eating and keeps the greedy ones from snatching at the first bowl of food put down.

BONES

Except for the big shin-bone which can be bought whole from the butcher I do not like bones. Small chop-bones, mutton leg- and shoulder-bones and beef bones splinter easily, lumps gnawed off are swallowed, frequently resulting in stoppage or stomach trouble, as many a veterinary surgeon will tell you. Poultry, game and rabbit bones must never be given to any dog large or small, in any circumstances whatsoever.

WATER

All dogs need plenty of water. Springers like to take long drinks, and so a bucket should be used and, like all kennel utensils, be cleaned daily, and refilled whenever needful. This bucket should be hooked to the wire of the run so that it cannot be knocked over or carried about. It is no use worrying too much about the way Springers use their water buckets or troughs. They are usually very fond of water and swimming and, particularly in warm weather, they will stand with their forefeet in the bucket and thoroughly enjoy splashing the water about, a simple pleasure and why should we deny it them!

BREEDING

If a stud dog is kept it is essential that he should always be in the pink of condition, but beyond an extra ration of meat and the regular addition of wheat-germ oil to his food it need not differ from that of the rest of the kennel. He should not be used too frequently—in the spring, usually the busy time for matings, twice in one week is reasonable, but this should not continue for too long a period.

Unfortunately, owners can never be quite sure when their bitches will come in season; some are very regular at six-month intervals, others at seven, eight or even longer periods, and not even the same length of time then. Even if they have booked a service to your dog, the bitch may need to come earlier or later and perhaps just when one or two other bitches are booked to come. One cannot disappoint an owner who has very likely written months before, and as an emergency an extra bitch may be fitted in, but afterwards try to arrange at least a week's interval before the dog is used again. It is much better to have spring puppies. They get the benefit of the warm weather and sunshine and can be put in the fresh air to play instead of being cooped up in a kennel because of damp and rain. Sunshine is worth all the infra-red lamps and other artificial aids.

A bitch should be wormed about three or four weeks before she is expected to be in season and it is wise to worm her again about three weeks, but not longer, after mating. If it is decided to breed from a bitch it is no use to leave the provision of special foods and vitamins until after she is mated. She should have a regular dose of wheat-germ oil and cod-liver oil for some time beforehand, together with extra meat. She needs to be well supplied with proteins but must not have too much of any food that will make her over-fat. A fat bitch may have trouble whelping, while an active, well-muscled-up one in hard condition will give birth to her puppies easily.

From the time a bitch is mated give her five drops of Radiostoleum daily in her food, increasing this to ten drops in the last three or four weeks of pregnancy, for then the foetus increases in size and make greater demands upon the bitch's reserves. During this time it is well also to give her a daily ration of glucose D. Extra meat and milk should be fed, but care should be taken that she does not get fed to the extent of getting fat.

For the last ten days before she is due to whelp withhold all hard food and give her only gentle exercise.

A bitter experience of many years ago leads me to give a very serious warning. After a bitch has been mated do not allow her to jump, under any circumstances whatever, and if she is a bitch who is keen on jumping, never let her be in a place where she can do so, as, for instance, on or off a table or bench or over a fence, however low. Jumping may cause the death of the puppies in the womb, a fact that may not be known for quite a time, and then only when a putrid discharge is observed, by which time the only thing that can save the bitch's life is a hysterectomy operation—that is, removal of the womb and other generative organs, so that there will be no possibility of any puppies in the future and, too, however successful a career she may have had in the past in the show ring, she cannot, under Kennel Club rules, ever be shown again. A double tragedy!

However, trouble of this sort is the exception, and I do not want to frighten the novice breeding his first litter, so that he spends the weeks before the puppies are due in a state of nerves and anxiety; but forewarned is forearmed. There are, of course, other reasons for this condition occurring, but I think jumping is the most likely to cause it: it happened in my kennel only once, but I learnt my lesson. Still, there is no reason to wrap the bitch in cotton wool; let her lead her normal life with normal conditions and exercise until about the last three weeks—four, perhaps, if she is very heavy—but take precautions against untoward happenings.

The bitch should sleep in the kennel in which she is to whelp for a while beforehand, and not be thrust into a strange place just when she most wants tranquillity and reassurance.

I have described the puppy kennel I used in the chapter on kennels and now, before the bitch is due to whelp, I recommend that a rail, on the lines of a farrowing rail, be attached to the two sides and the back of the section of the kennel in which it is intended she should whelp. This, raised about 3 in. above the sleeping bench, is screwed to the walls of the kennel so that if a puppy should get behind the dam while she is concerned with the delivery of other pups, or later when they begin to crawl about, there is a space behind the mother which will prevent their getting squeezed, and perhaps killed by her weight, against the wall. When the pups are big enough to be safe the rail can be unscrewed and stored away for future use.

Sixty-three days is the normal period of gestation, but a bitch may whelp up to five days earlier or five days later. Puppies born more than five days before the due time rarely survive, in spite of the utmost efforts to save them.

If a bitch is straining, and yet no pup is produced after a reasonable time, I strongly recommend calling in one's veterinary surgeon to make certain that all is well. If his help is asked for in good time both bitch and pups can be saved, otherwise one or all may be lost.

A bitch usually becomes restless a day or so—or sometimes only a few hours—before she whelps, and generally refuses food, though this cannot be expected as a certain indication, for I have known bitches who have eaten a good meal and then returned to their kennel and started to pup. When it is obvious that a bitch will whelp within a few hours I always recommend that she be given a teaspoonful of Radiostoleum.

Often a bitch will seek a place of her own fancy in which to have her pups, even to the extent of digging a deep hole, and being persuaded from it only with difficulty. That is one reason why she should be put to sleep in the kennel where she is to whelp for some time beforehand, so that she is not agitated by being taken to a place to which she is not used or upset by being removed, however gently, from the possibly unsuitable place she has chosen for herself.

I like to have a big supply of newspapers at hand and a good layer already spread on the whelping-bench floor. Sometimes the bitch will tear up this first lot in an instinctive desire to make a nest, but more can very easily be slipped on to the bench. As the pups are born the papers can be renewed and so the mother does not lie, as she would otherwise do, on a wet floor or sodden straw, getting thoroughly chilled.

Always have a basket in which there is a rubber hot-water bottle well covered by old, soft woollen material into which to put any pup that seems to need particular care or, if it is a big litter, to place some of the pups while the dam is engaged in producing others.

Each puppy is enclosed in a membrane bag, and the dam's first action is to remove the pup and bite through the cord attached to its navel. The afterbirth may come away as the puppy is born; if not it will, as a rule, follow shortly and be cleared up by the bitch. This again is a survival of ancient instincts from the time when there were no anxious humans to stand by and feed and help. This afterbirth, or placenta, seems to have some sustaining value to help the bitch through the strain of whelping. Some breeders do not like to give any food during the actual whelping period, but I always found that a bitch took a little drink of warm milk, to which a spoonful of glucose D had been added, very gratefully, often between the arrival of each pup unless they came very rapidly. If the whelping is protracted and the bitch appears at all exhausted a teaspoonful of brandy added to the milk is a great help.

After the bitch has finished whelping take her outside for a minute or two if she is willing to go, but do not force her in any way. Remove all the papers and spread a thick clean sack, that has previously been well washed in disinfectant water and then most thoroughly rinsed and dried, over the bench, fastening it firmly at the four corners, so that the dam will come back to a clean dry bed. This sacking gives the pups something into which their nails can take a hold as they move their legs back and forth when suckling, and if fastened down the bitch cannot scratch it up when moving around. If the puppies are on bare boards their feet get no hold, and they constantly slip away as they try to feed. Some clean dry straw should be put into the bed; it will soon be pushed away from the centre and form a nest round the edge. Both sacking and straw should be changed daily. It is well to have a good supply of sacking—old biscuit-meal bags are excellent—then if the weather turns wet there need be no hurry about the necessity of getting the 'clean sheets' dry.

Care should be taken to watch each puppy's navel to see that no infection develops and that there is no sign of a hernia. Some bitches are inclined to bite the umbilical cord off too short, and then trouble may ensue. For this reason it is often wiser to have a pair of nurse's scissors (blunt-pointed) handy and cut the cord oneself about two inches from the navel; it will soon wither and drop off.

The bitch should be given plenty of milk and brown bread and milk during the first day after whelping, adding to one feed a teaspoonful of Radiostoleum, and to a second a teaspoonful of cod-liver oil, and to each glucose D. Afterwards she should have three meals daily of finely cut-up meat, brown bread and milk and, if she appears at all short of milk, Benger's Food. Ten drops of Radiostoleum should be given daily while she is nursing the puppies, as well as cod-liver oil and glucose D. For the first week or two she should be kept quiet and be attended to and visited by only those people she knows well. The eager visitor who comes saying 'Please may I see the puppies' must be sternly refused.

Springer bitches frequently have large litters and it is difficult to decide how many puppies to keep. I always said to my bitches, 'Now, six, or, at most, seven nice puppies, please.' But they rarely listened to me and produced nine, ten or even twelve pups. Many people say pick the six best and destroy the rest, but how, at a day old, can one be sure of the best? I remember that, in her first litter, when mated to Mr David MacDonald's Ch. Little Brand, my Ch. Reipple of Ranscombe had ten puppies. Two were slightly smaller than the others and so were the ones it was decided to put down, but they were such lovely puppies that I could not bring myself to have them destroyed. I decided to keep the lot and to augment the bitch's milk by giving all the puppies two or three feeds daily of a special puppy milk from a baby's bottle. After the first time they needed no coaxing but drank eagerly and the whole litter thrived and Reipple remained in beautiful condition. One of the litter became Int.Ch. Li'le Buccaneer and one of the little dogs I reprieved was Reuben of Ranscombe, a Challenge Certificate winner and a prize-winner at field trials, sire of many good workers and good lookers. Among his descendants was Triple F.T.Ch. Wakes Wager, the only English Springer ever to become a Field Trial Champion in three continents: Europe, Asia and America.

So, remembering the past, I hesitate to be drastic and get rid of puppies hurriedly. I have noticed that nature very often decides the matter and the weaklings die off in the first day or two. This must not be confused with 'fading puppy' trouble, quite another thing, when the whole litter fades out, or possibly, after tremendous efforts to save them, one puppy survives. This is dealt with in another chapter.

If the litter is a large one and all the puppies are strong, or if for any reason a bitch is unable to nurse her puppies, it is sometimes desirable to obtain the services of a foster-mother. Should it appear likely that the litter will be very large, arrangements for a foster-mother can be made beforehand with a firm advertising in the dog papers, being sure to say that the puppies will be English Springers, so that neither a St Bernard nor a toy dog size is sent!

Very generally the foster-mothers are quiet, clean, healthy bitches and arrive with two or three puppies in the box with them. After feeding and exercising her, examine her very carefully to see that she is entirely free from fleas and lice and that her skin is quite healthy; this is usually the case but it is as well to be quite sure. Put her in her kennel, let her own pups remain for the moment, then add one or two of the Springers. Watch carefully, and if she accepts them without any fuss and begins to wash them add one or two more and, very quietly and without upsetting her, remove one of her own pups and so, in turn, give her the rest of the Springers she is to foster and remove the unwanted pups.

Springers are usually easy whelpers. Fortunately for them they have not been bred, as have Bulldogs and Pekingese and some other breeds, for flatness of face and big heads, so that, for them, whelping is a natural affair and very rarely difficult and not an anxiety for their owners. In my own experience I have had only one bitch who was a bad whelper and although her puppies were good, after a second litter, when there was no improvement, I retired her from maternal duties and she spent the rest of her life very happily at work.

Should a bitch, after the labour pains have started, continue to strain continuously and no pup be born, do not wait too long or attempt to do anything yourself; above all never use instruments, but ring up your veterinary surgeon. After examining her he may give her an injection which will set things moving, or his examination may indicate that there is a puppy wrongly placed and so impossible for the bitch to deliver without help. This help the veterinary surgeon can give. He is skilled in using both his fingers and instruments, for as one of them once said to me: 'I rarely see an easy whelping. The breeders see all those, but there's very little I don't know about difficult ones after all those I've been called in to help with.' But these, happily for Springer owners, occur very, very rarely in our breed.

There are times when a Caesarian operation may be necessary; these are usually quite successful and both dam and pups can be saved by this method. If the veterinary surgeon suggests it, agree at once. He has the knowledge and experience to decide if it is needed, and then no time should be lost.

If the pups are strong and healthy, and feeding well, the tails should be docked; any time between the fourth and sixth day after they are born will do. The most important thing is to get the length right. I have seen so many Springers quite spoilt by having too short a tail, and this is the one matter on which I have a grievance against some veterinary surgeons. Those who live in towns, do not go to shows and do not shoot, take it for granted that all Spaniels must be docked as short as Cockers; I have seen some docked even shorter. This very often happens with a novice breeder who, with a first litter, and never having had any experience of how a Springer's tail should be docked, calls in a veterinary surgeon to do it, with implicit faith in his knowing exactly the right length. I saw a litter that had been docked in exactly these circumstances recently, and my first comment was: 'Who ever cut these puppies' tails? They've spoilt them for show and work.' And when I could bring myself to look at the puppies without thinking of the tails I found them to be really lovely and yet they will have to go through life with such a handicap!

A Springer tells so much by its tail action, particularly when at work, and to leave only a stump an inch or two long deprives it of its way of showing pleasure or telling you that it is on a hot scent and will soon flush a bird or get on the line of a runner or that it soon hopes to make a retrieve.

A Springer's tail goes down level so far, then begins to taper and should never be cut shorter than at least two joints after

Ch. Northdown Donna

Ch. Higham Tom Tit

Boxer of Bramhope

(Mrs Jones)

Ch. Stokeley Lucky

the taper begins. Personally, I like about half the tail left. On the other hand, it is essential to dock the tail, and when docking not to leave it too long. When working, a Springer moves its tail very fast, so that when it is in thick briars it beats it against the thorns to such an extent that it will actually tear the skin of a too long tail, which will drip with blood. I have seen this happen, and though the dog, in its enjoyment of its work, seems to take no notice at the time, when it goes home it must have a very sore tail, which may take a long time to heal. This, of course, is the fundamental reason for docking Spaniels' tails.

When the puppies are to be docked it is a good idea, if the bitch is willing to go out, to put her on a leash and send her out with someone she knows and trusts. If she does not want to leave the pups, leave her in the nest, quietly put two of the pups in a basket and take them out of earshot of the bitch. Directly they are docked return them and remove two or three more, and so on until all have been dealt with.

Docking is a very simple operation. Have ready a *sharp* pair of scissors, a pair of curved scissors, small forceps and a supply of cotton wool with which to make swabs to put on the forceps. Orange-sticks, round the ends of which swabs can be rolled, do equally well, and a box of powdered permanganate of potash into which the swabs can be dipped quickly.

Hold the puppy under your left arm and, with the left thumb and forefinger, press the skin up the tail towards its body, holding the tail very firmly. Select the joint at which it is decided to cut the tail and then cut through quickly, an easy matter as it is only gristle. Dip the forceps into the permanganate and rub the swab quickly and hard on the end of the tail. Not one drop of blood should be lost. If the puppies have dew-claws, these must be removed on both front and back legs. The small, sharp, surgical scissors should be used for these. Hold the leg just at the point of the dew-claw, cut in and out quickly with a curving action, so that you get right down to the bone attachment to the leg and then apply the permanagante in the same way, and, again, not one drop of blood should be lost.

Dew-claws should always be removed; they are unsightly, and, more important, they can catch and tear when a dog is either jumping or getting through a fence. Sometimes, too, if not watched and cut regularly, the nail grows and curves round into the flesh of the leg, when it will cause the dog to go lame,

E

and if cut then will often leave a painful wound to be dealt with.

The bitch usually gives the pups a lick over after they are returned to her after being docked, but she rarely does more, as the permanganate has an unpleasant taste. It is wise, however, to keep an eye on the pups to see that the dam has not started any bleeding by licking; in that case a further application of permanganate should be used.

After the pups are docked, and if the bitch is herself in good fettle, eating and sleeping well and with plenty of milk for her family, it can be reasonably anticipated that she will take full responsibility for them for the next three weeks. The only things you will be called upon to do will be to keep the kennels and sleeping quarters scrupulously clean, to provide the bitch with good nourishing food and to exercise her regularly. And one more thing. To slip in extra boards on the front of the sleeping apartment as the puppies grow and become active, so that none can climb out and perhaps get lost wandering round the kennel. Some bitches, hearing a lost puppy's lament, will pick it up and carry it back to the nest, but not all of them do this, so that it is wise to build up the front to prevent straying, particularly at night. After a time the puppies are strong enough to get about the kennel and know the way 'home', then all but the lowest board can be taken out. This lowest board should be really low, only a couple of inches high, as it is bad for puppies to struggle to climb in at a height. It is a thing that may well cause bad fronts if done frequently. For the same reason, once the puppies are old enough to leave the kennel and go into their run, a ramp should be fixed from the kennel entrance to the ground, so that there is no question of their going up or down steps too high for them or jumping from the kennel level to the ground and trying to climb back afterwards.

At between the third and fourth weeks a start should be made in feeding the puppies. To begin with, each should be given a teaspoonful of scraped raw beef. If they are at all uncertain about it, place a very little in the mouth. The pups will suck at it, soon realise that although it is a new taste it is a most pleasant one, and will finish up their spoonful with gusto.

In the next few days, in addition to the meat meal, give each pup two little drinks of milk with five drops of Radiostoleum in one of them. If goat's milk can be obtained, it is much superior for puppies than cow's milk. A good brand of puppy milk is to be preferred to cow's milk. The pups will then be on the way towards weaning and the dam will get some relief from their constant and rapidly increasing demands. At five to six weeks old let one of the milk meals have brown bread added to it, so that at the end of the sixth week the puppies can become entirely self-supporting and the bitch able to leave them. During the last week she might sleep with them; after that, for a day or two, visit them for a short period night and morning, then only in the morning for a very short time. During the last week or two in which a bitch is feeding her puppies, many bitches, if left with them after being fed, will bring up their food and encourage them to eat, nature's way of teaching the pups to eat solid food. Although the intention is admirable it is, perhaps, not the best diet for tinies, and so I recommend keeping the mother away for a time after she is fed.

At six weeks old, with the puppies no longer receiving sustenance from their mother, six meals a day should be given much as follows:

8 a.m. Breakfast. Brown bread and milk, five drops of Radio-stoleum.

11 a.m. Elevenses. Milk with Bemax or Farex.

2 p.m. Dinner. Scraped raw beef, crumbled Vetzyme tablet and orange-juice.

5 p.m. Tea. Puppy meal soaked in milk or good stock, cod-liver oil (Saval or Weatmeat are very good starting meals).

7.30 p.m. Supper. Scraped beef.

10 p.m. Nightcap. Milk or egg-and-milk, with glucose D.

These times may start earlier if they fit in better with kennel routine and the demands of other work in kennel and home, but the times should be kept to.

At eight weeks old the meals can be reduced to four in number, but increased in size; the milk feeds can be added as extra to two others. The supper should be given shortly before the puppies are put to bed for the night; the meat can be minced, and, after another two weeks, cut up. One of the bread-and-milk or soaked-meal meals can have rusks or not-too-hard puppy biscuits (broken to start with) substituted, followed by a drink of milk.

At twelve weeks old three larger meals may be given, rusks or biscuits and milk, meat and a third meal of either meat and biscuit meal or rusked brown bread, fish being given as a change from meat at times, but all the 'trimmings'—Radiostoleum, cod-liver oil, orange-juice and Vetzymes—should be continued.

At six months all normal puppies should need only two meals a day. Their bones, helped by the Radiostoleum and cod-liver oil, should be strong, and a solid meal of meat and meal should not prove too heavy. At a year old the youngsters should go on to the times and diet of the older dogs in the kennel.

Puppies should never be fed from a communal dish. The greedy ones will push the slow feeders out and get too much, so that there is a risk of their getting too fat and so going over on their legs, spoiling their shoulders and fronts and blowing out their little stomachs, while the others will be undernourished.

Even if puppies are given separate dishes, some will swallow their own food and rush to the dish of any other pup who has been eating like a little lady or gentleman. To prevent this, and to make feeding quick and easy, I made a set of 'stalls' from orange-boxes. Placed lengthways, I divided each box into three compartments and put it on a bench or on the top of the cover of the sleeping compartment. A dish of food was placed right at the back of each 'stall' and a puppy pushed in nose first: it could not see its neighbour and when it backed out, having finished its food, it was lifted down, the dish refilled and another pup picked up. It is wonderful how quickly quite a large number of pups can be fed in this way, and one can be sure that each gets its fair share. Be careful, however, not to pick up a puppy twice if two should be very alike—better slip the fed ones outside in their run or into another compartment of the kennel. Springer puppies are capable of looking at you with the most innocent eyes that assure you that not a morsel of food has passed their lips for days.

It is a good thing to train Springer puppies to sit down while waiting their turn to be fed. Nothing is more irritating than to have them all scrambling round one's legs and jumping up, added to which it is the first step in their training. If the word 'sit' is used every time food is brought into the kennel, and first one pup and then another is pushed gently down, they learn remarkably quickly, as they realise that no food is forthcoming until they are sitting quietly. This is a help, too, when they are too big to use their 'stalls', as by then they have learnt to sit still and will come forward only when their names are called.

Do not use bowls that will tip easily, as saucer-shaped dishes do if an eager puppy puts its foot on one side. The food will be spilled and wasted. For little puppies the empty tins in which one buys tinned dog-meat, etc., are excellent. If opened with the patent winding cutter made by Henry Squire & Sons of Willenhall, Staffs., which cuts the lid off cleanly, an absolutely smooth edge is left inside the tin. Later, use the patent bowls made by Spratts' and other food or equipment firms. Some firms make a special bowl for Spaniels, much deeper but narrower than the ordinary bowl at the top, and these do prevent the Spaniel getting its ears in the food. Tiny puppies can get their ears very messy, and though their brothers and sisters are always very willing to lick their faces and ears it is not a good habit for them to get into because sometimes, later, they will actually chew the hair on another dog's ears. An excellent plan is to cut the tops off woollen socks, so that you have circles which stretch over the head and hold back the ears on the neck. Larger 'feeders' can be used for grown dogs, and in the case of show dogs their ears can thus be kept immaculate.

At six weeks, earlier if there are indications that it is necessary, the puppies should be wormed, and this should be repeated at about eight to ten weeks, according to whether it has been found that they are badly infested with worms or not. At this age puppies seem to suffer only from round worms, but these, if neglected, could cause death, and in any case are a very serious drawback to a puppy's growth and well-being. There are numerous remedies for worms on the market, but for many years I have used one made up by a veterinary surgeon. It acts most efficiently and I have never known it upset a puppy; it has the added merit of not requiring castor oil or any other aperient.

One last point when rearing puppies. Do have a cat around the kennels. If you can bring a kitten of about the same age up with a litter of puppies, so much the better. They play together and as they grow up the Springers accept cats as part of the family and have no desire to chase them, not even strange ones. Nothing is worse than to see any dog, particularly one of a gundog breed, chasing a cat until it takes refuge in a tree, and if there are several dogs around and one starts then away they all go! Should a cat turn it may use its claws and perhaps really injure a dog's eyes or give it a nasty tear down its face. As one dog said to another, 'Cats don't fight fair, they use claws, no gloves and no holds barred.' And then went off to lick his wounds!

Two other good reasons for having a cat about: first, never having chased 'fur' in the shape of a cat the Springer is less likely to chase fur when at work, either a rabbit or that most tempting and provocative 'puss' the hare; second, a good cat round the kennels will keep down mice and rats, and anyone who has seen a Springer suffering from rat jaundice will know the value of keeping the whole place clear of these disease-carrying vermin.

Notes on Milk and special foods for puppies

Very good puppy meals are made by Spratts', Spiller's, Lowe's and other firms. Phillips' Yeast Products, in their supplement products, are also good: Stress, with its mineral elements, calcium, phosphorus and bone-forming minerals; Kenadex which supplies vitamins A and B, proteins and fats; and Vetzymes, a yeast product which also contains calcium, phosphorus and magnesium and is a valuable addition to the diet of dogs of all ages.

Ordinary cow's milk is very much less rich in protein and fat than that of the bitch. Goat's milk is somewhat richer in both than that of the cow, but is still less than a third as rich in proteins, and not quite half as rich in fats, so that both should be augmented with cream or eggs once the puppies have left the bitch. On the other hand, there is no calcium or phosphorus in a bitch's milk, and these should be added to the diet of a nursing mother.

Excellent milk compounds for puppies are made such as Lactol, Delimil, Lintomilk, etc., but one of the finest foods for a nursing mother and for puppies and also for sick dogs is Benger's Food. I have used it continuously since the 1920s with most excellent results. Many years ago a friend came to me in great distress. He had a very beautiful Wire-haired Terrier bitch, but had lost her puppies three times because, however he fed her, she had no milk. He had seen my Springer bitches with simply wonderful 'milk bars', and their puppies fat and flourishing, and he begged us to have his bitch for her whelping. Miss M. A. Brice, who for a number of years shared the care of the Ranscombes with me, and I were very doubtful taking this on. I consulted my veterinary surgeon, and he advised us to feed the bitch on Benger's Food, morning, noon and night, and this we did. She had a litter of five lovely pups and she had an ample supply of milk for them. Since then I have recommended Benger's for all such cases and have found it a wonderful stand-by in nursing sick dogs.

WHELPING TABLE

Served	Due Whelp	Served	Due Whelp	Served	Due Whelp	Served	Due Whelp	Served	Due Whelp	Served	Due Whelp	Served	Due Whelp	Served	Due Whelp	Served	Due Whelp	Served	Due Whelp	Served	Due Whelp	Served	Due Whelp
Jan.	March	Feb.	April	March	May	April	June	May	July	June	Aug.	July	Sept.	Aug.	Oct.	Sept.	Nov.	Oct.	Dec.	Nov.	Jan.	Dec.	Feb.
1	5	1	5	1	3	1	3	1	3	1	3	1	2	1	3	1	3	1	3	1	3	1	2
2	6	2	6	2	4	2	4	2	4	2	4	2	3	2	4	2	4	2	4	2	4	2	3
3	7	3	7	3	5	3	5	3	5	3	5	3	4	3	5	3	5	3	5	3	5	3	4
4	8	4	8	4	6	4	6	4	6	4	6	4	5	4	6	4	6	4	6	4	6	4	5
5	9	5	9	5	7	5	7	5	7	5	7	5	6	5	7	5	7	5	7	5	7	5	6
6	10	6	10	6	8	6	8	6	8	6	8	6	7	6	8	6	8	6	8	6	8	6	7
7	11	7	11	7	9	7	9	7	9	7	9	7	8	7	9	7	9	7	9	7	9	7	8
8	12	8	12	8	10	8	10	8	10	8	10	8	9	8	10	8	10	8	10	8	10	8	9
9	13	9	13	9	11	9	11	9	11	9	11	9	10	9	11	9	11	9	11	9	11	9	10
10	14	10	14	10	12	10	12	10	12	10	12	10	11	10	12	10	12	10	12	10	12	10	11
11	15	11	15	11	13	11	13	11	13	11	13	11	12	11	13	11	13	11	13	11	13	11	12
12	16	12	16	12	14	12	14	12	14	12	14	12	13	12	14	12	14	12	14	12	14	12	13
13	17	13	17	13	15	13	15	13	15	13	15	13	14	13	15	13	15	13	15	13	15	13	14
14	18	14	18	14	16	14	16	14	16	14	16	14	15	14	16	14	16	14	16	14	16	14	15
15	19	15	19	15	17	15	17	15	17	15	17	15	16	15	17	15	17	15	17	15	17	15	16
16	20	16	20	16	18	16	18	16	18	16	18	16	17	16	18	16	18	16	18	16	18	16	17
17	21	17	21	17	19	17	19	17	19	17	19	17	18	17	19	17	19	17	19	17	19	17	18
18	22	18	22	18	20	18	20	18	20	18	20	18	19	18	20	18	20	18	20	18	20	18	19
19	23	19	23	19	21	19	21	19	21	19	21	19	20	19	21	19	21	19	21	19	21	19	20
20	24	20	24	20	22	20	22	20	22	20	22	20	21	20	22	20	22	20	22	20	22	20	21
21	25	21	25	21	23	21	23	21	23	21	23	21	22	21	23	21	23	21	23	21	23	21	22
22	26	22	26	22	24	22	24	22	24	22	24	22	23	22	24	22	24	22	24	22	24	22	23
23	27	23	27	23	25	23	25	23	25	23	25	23	24	23	25	23	25	23	25	23	25	23	24
24	28	24	28	24	26	24	26	24	26	24	26	24	25	24	26	24	26	24	26	24	26	24	25
25	29	25	29	25	27	25	27	25	27	25	27	25	26	25	27	25	27	25	27	25	27	25	26
26	30	26	30	26	28	26	28	26	28	26	28	26	27	26	28	26	28	26	28	26	28	26	27
27	31	27	1 (May)	27	29	27	29	27	29	27	29	27	28	27	29	27	29	27	29	27	29	27	28
28	1 (Apl)	28	2	28	30	28	30	28	30	28	30	28	29	28	30	28	30	28	30	28	30	28	1 (Mar)
29	2			29	31	29	1 (July)	29	31	29	31	29	30	29	31	29	1 (Dec)	29	31	29	31	29	2
30	3			30	1 (June)	30	2	30	1 (Aug)	30	1 (Sept)	30	1 (Oct)	30	1 (Nov)	30	2	30	1 (Jan)	30	1 (Feb)	30	3
31	4			31	2			31	2			31	2	31	2			31	2			31	4

Chapter VI

AILMENTS OF THE SPRINGER SPANIEL

FIRST and foremost I would say, when considering the diseases a dog may contract or the accidents that may happen to it, always call in the veterinary surgeon directly for anything more than the little upsets a simple remedy or treatment will put right.

A dog's temperature, taken in the rectum, is 101·4°F., three degrees higher than that of a human. Should it fall much below 100°F. or rise above 103°F., be prepared for trouble. The owner of even one Springer should also be the owner of a clinical thermometer, a half-minute one, and it should be used immediately if a dog appears to be off colour. Temperatures may rise, of course, after violent exercise or unusual excitement, but taken in conjunction with any other symptoms a rise or fall in temperature is a direct warning to take care.

This chapter is not meant to be an extensive treatise on the diseases a Springer may contract. They are a strong and hardy breed and an outline only is given of the main troubles for which we should be prepared and which, if simple, can be dealt with by the owner, or if the symptoms are in any way disturbing or unfamiliar should mean the immediate calling in of the veterinary surgeon.

Before going further, however, I feel I must pay a tribute to the work done in the 1920s at the *Field* Research Station at Mill Hill by Messrs Laidlaw and Dunkin, who first isolated the filter-passing distemper virus, and to the Canine Research Centre of the Animal Health Trust at Kennet, Newmarket, with its wonderful team of veterinary scientists, who have perfected vaccines not only for distemper but also for many of the other ills to which the dog is heir.

Perhaps present-day dog owners do not realise how very much they owe to this research, but those of us who remember how, time after time, we suffered the heartbreak and devastation due to distemper epidemics know that we cannot be too thankful for what has been done to stop this ever recurring scourge.

It was a terrible and terrifying disease, and we of the older generation who nursed dogs suffering from it will remember how helpless one felt, for in spite of the best veterinary advice and the most careful nursing, day and night, the rate of mortality was very high. It was a six-weeks infection and one never knew what new developments might occur. It was often said that distemper never killed a dog, but only the complications that almost invariably followed, and if the infection was of the virulent type no amount of good nursing could stop pleurisy, pneumonia, meningitis, enteritis, chorea or paralysis. In spite of the utmost care any one, or several, of these fell diseases would appear with absolutely no warning.

Occasionally a mild type of distemper went round the country, but generally it seemed to be of the virulent type—the killer type. Hard-pad, a closely allied virus, did not appear till later, but it, too, was a killer of the worst kind. When one heard the clatter of the dog's paws across a kennel floor as if they were shod with iron one rarely had much hope of its recovery. Fits ensued and generally increased in violence, until the unhappy animal went from fit to fit without a break and the only kind thing was to have it destroyed.

The work of the Animal Health Trust is entirely dependent on voluntary support and, remembering what it has done in the past and the continuous research going on now at the Canine Research Station at Kennet, it is incumbent upon all who love and in return receive the love of their Springers to do all in their power to help a cause which has done so much to relieve suffering among our dogs and is endeavouring to do even more in the future.

Only the common ailments are dealt with and a bare outline given here. In many cases treatment is not mentioned because it is beyond the scope of the owner. Anything serious, beyond immediate first-aid and nursing techniques, should be under the care and direction of a veterinary surgeon.

Common ailments may be classified in three divisions:

1. Infectious and contagious diseases.
2. Non-infectious conditions of a general nature.
3. Diseases of various systems, e.g. digestive system, nervous system, etc.

INFECTIOUS AND CONTAGIOUS DISEASES

1. *Canine Virus Hepatitis. Rubarth's Disease.* This is a common fever of all dogs, caused by a virus, which may be rapidly fatal in

acute cases, showing temperatures up to 104°F., marked prostration, depression, loss of appetite and intense thirst. Damage is principally confined to the liver and blood-vessels. In the less acute cases the mortality is low, but this disease in recent years has been implicated in 'fading' in puppies, and so is a serious hazard in breeding kennels. There is an effective vaccine.

2. *Coccidiosis.* Occasionally this is met with in individual dogs, but more often as an outbreak in kennels. This parasite, similar to that affecting poultry, causes chronic diarrhoea, sometimes with blood in the motions, poor condition and a developing anaemia. Treatment must not only be directed towards the curing of the bowel condition but, as infection is spread via the motions, thorough cleansing and disinfection of the quarters is essential.

3. *Distemper and Hard-pad Disease.* These are only too well known to dog owners and still constitute the biggest hazard to the life of his dog. Hard-pad disease is caused either by a different strain of distemper virus or by a closely related virus. The recently developed vaccines protect against both diseases.

Symptoms are well known. Nowadays, with modern drugs it is possible to control the symptoms of pneumonia, enteritis, etc., which formerly killed many dogs, but there is still the ever present danger of nervous symptoms developing, i.e. convulsions, chorea, paralysis. Nursing treatments, such as a quiet life along with anti-convulsant drugs taken over a long period of time, may help to avoid these disastrous symptoms developing.

4. *Leptospirosis.* Two varieties of this bacteria affect dogs. One causes yellow, or rat, jaundice. This condition shows as marked prostration, vomiting, injected membranes of the eyes and mouth and intense thirst. Within two or three days of the first symptoms jaundice appears. This is an extremely dangerous condition, with a high percentage of deaths, and hunting dogs like the Springer should always be vaccinated against it.

The dog may gain contact from rats or from another affected dog, and the normal route of infection is by contact with infected urine. In a kennel where a case has occurred, attention must therefore be given to the elimination of rats andalso to general cleansing and disinfection.

The other variety of leptospira affecting dogs gives a much milder picture of a fever and depression for a few days, generally with spontaneous recovery. However, it is thought that the damage done to the kidneys during an attack in a young dog may eventually show in chronic kidney disease in the middle-aged or old animal. A single vaccine covers both types.

5. *Tetanus or Lockjaw.* The dog is relatively resistant to this infection, which gains access to the body through wounds and elaborates a poison which affects the nerves, causing spasm of the muscles. Symptoms are very characteristic, the dog moving stiffly like a jointed toy soldier. A good result may be expected with proper treatment and nursing. Quiet, easily swallowed food, sedatives or tranquillisers to avoid nervous upset and dim surroundings are necessary.

PARASITES (INTERNAL)

Worms

All dogs, especially hunting dogs, have great opportunities to pick up worm-eggs, and if with other dogs in a kennel the chances are increased. It is therefore recommended that puppies should be dosed regularly during the first six months of life and thereafter at least once yearly, as a routine.

1. *Round Worms, Ascarid Worms.* Most dogs are affected, but symptoms show only in puppies, unless infestation is very heavy. Puppies get worm-eggs from their mother, in some cases very early in life. Care should be taken to use a suitable worm remedy for the age and condition of the puppy and, when heavy infestation is present, re-worming should be done after an interval of two weeks. The dam should be dosed against round worms two to three weeks before whelping, using one of the more gentle remedies.

2. *Tape Worms, Flat Worms.* Usually affecting older dogs. Again routine worming is necessary, some dogs having to be dosed twice yearly where the reinfestation chances are great. This is easy to tell, as the worm segments are seen round the anus and in the dog's motions.

3. *Hook Worms and Whip Worms.* These parasites are not so common in this country, but in certain kennels can become a serious nuisance, as they are resistant to the usual worm remedies. However, recently an effective remedy has become available.

Control of worms in the dog depends on:

(1) Elimination of worms from the dog's bowel.

(2) Destruction of worm eggs and larvae from the kennels by

cleansing and disinfection, the latter preferably by a naked flame, e.g. a blow-lamp.

PARASITES (EXTERNAL)

Lice and fleas, sometimes picked up from grass where hens, rabbits and other infested animals have been. Gammexine, thoroughly rubbed into the coat, particularly round the ears and neck, will provide a rapid and complete cure: it must be used also on all bedding and in kennels. Harvest bugs, a mite picked up more generally in the autumn in stubble fields, are very irritating, and again Gammexine is the cure. Ticks are most often found in neighbourhoods where there are large numbers of sheep. A tick digs its barbed proboscis into the dog's skin and sucks blood until its body is swollen, often to the size of a hat-pin head. It is no use trying to pick the tick off; the head will probably be left in the skin, causing a swelling and a sore. Dab a lighted match or cigarette-end on the body of the tick and quickly twist off. The shock of the burn causes the tick to protract the barbs on its proboscis and the whole head comes out.

NON-INFECTIOUS GENERAL CONDITIONS

1. *Vitamin Deficiencies.* These conditions point to deficiencies in feeding. Prevention involves a good varied diet, supplemented when necessary by compound vitamins, i.e. tablets or capsules containing all the known vitamins in balanced form. This is much more sensible than giving supplements of individual vitamins.

2. *Mineral Deficiencies.* Prevention again involves a good diet. Compound, balanced, mineral supplements should be given when necessary, e.g. to the lactating bitch.

3. *Growths.* Apart from the common old-age benign growths, and the commonly seen mammary growths in bitches, these are not so common in Springers. They may be benign growths, which grow slowly and do not spread throughout the body. These may be surgically removed with small risk of recurring.

They may be malignant or cancerous growths, which grow and spread rapidly, i.e. in a few weeks. These cases are incurable.

4. *Congenital Conditions.* In this category come monster and deformed puppies, those with overshot and undershot jaws, cleft palates, hare-lips, small eyes, etc. If these animals are allowed to survive they should not be bred from.

PHYSICAL INFLUENCES

1. *Heat Stroke.* Caused by excess external temperature and humidity. Prevention is ordinary care in hot weather, especially in not leaving dogs shut in cars during extreme heat—this can cause death. Treatment consists of cold water applied to the body and saline solution given to drink in small quantities.

2. *Motion Sickness, Car Sickness, Air Sickness,* etc. This is partly due to nervous reaction. When necessary give sedatives or tranquillisers before a journey.

DISEASES OF THE DIGESTIVE SYSTEM

The Mouth. Ulcers of the tongue, cheeks, etc., occur and may be part of a general condition, giving rise to offensive smell and difficulty in eating.

Treatment. Mouth washes, soft food and a high intake of vitamins.

The Teeth. Broken teeth are commonly found in those dogs who carry sticks and stones. Regular scaling of teeth is essential to stop decay. Occasionally an abscess in the root of the 'gnawing' tooth of the Springer results in a running fistula which erupts just below the eye. The tooth must be removed.

Epulis. This is a hard fibrous growth of irregular shape, originating at the tooth and gum margins, mostly in older dogs. It may be surgically removed if necessary.

Hare-lips and Cleft Palates. These conditions often go together, and affected pups do not often survive, because they cannot suckle efficiently.

Inflamed Throat and Tonsillitis. Often occur together, perhaps part of a general disease, e.g. distemper or Rubarth's disease. Nursing measures include soft food, etc., which should be given, along with treatment to destroy the infection

Foreign Bodies in the Throat or Oesophagus. It is quite common to have a bone in the throat or gullet. If in the throat, it is best to try to get it back via the mouth. If in the gullet, try with a tube to push gently down into the stomach. If this is not possible an operation may be necessary. A general anaesthetic is normally necessary for either of these procedures.

Gastritis, Inflammation of the Stomach. This is very common in dogs. The symptoms are vomiting, pain and thirst. A high temperature is usual. There are various causes, perhaps infections or having swallowed irritant material.

Treatment. Antidote if a definite poison is suspected along with something to make the dog sick. Otherwise give nothing, neither food nor drink, as the stomach needs time to rest. Fluids can be given by injection if necessary.

Foreign Bodies in the Stomach. Quite common, caused by swallowing various objects—balls, bones, safety-pins, etc. Generally an operation is necessary.

Enteritis, Inflammation of the Bowel. There are various degrees of this complaint, from a mild diarrhoea to the picture of a very ill dog, with blood in the motions, injected membranes, prostration, etc. Various causes of an infectious or non-infectious nature. The treatment depends on the cause, but generally, if severe, the dog is in pain and sedatives are indicated.

Intestinal Obstruction, Blockage of the Bowel. If this happens suddenly it may be a foreign body lodged in the bowel, and purges will worsen the condition. An operation is necessary. If partial blockages keep recurring at short intervals, the cause may be a developing growth in the bowel.

Chronic Colitis, Inflammation of the Larger Bowel. The cause of this condition is unknown. Diarrhoea becomes persistent and the dog becomes wasted and anaemic. Treatment is not very effective, cortisone being promising although expensive.

Anal and Rectal Prolapsis. This condition is due to straining from any cause. Most often found with puppies with worms, occasionally with older dogs.

Treatment. Replace the prolapsis under general anaesthetic and stitch round anus to keep in place. Remove the cause of straining.

Anal Gland Impaction. The openings of the anal glands often get blocked and require to be opened by squeezing the glands. The condition may progress so that the glands become infected, giving suppuration and an abscessed condition. It is often necessary then to remove the glands.

Anal Tumours. In older dogs it is common to find benign growths arising from small glands surrounding the rectum. These may be removed, and seldom recur.

Liver Disease. Disturbance of liver function is shown by dullness, depression, occasional vomiting showing bile and yellow, evil-smelling motions. Laxatives and a light diet are recommended.

Disease of the Pancreas. Diabetis. Very occasionally occurs.

Confirmation of diagnosis is by urine analysis. Treatment is not recommended if the dog shows any symptoms of illness.

DISEASES OF THE URINARY SYSTEM

Nephritis, Kidney Disease. Chronic nephritis is common in older male dogs. The outset is gradual; appetite is poor, the coat dull and great thirst develops. Later stages show vomiting, breath smelling of urine, coated tongue and extreme weakness. Advanced cases should be destroyed. Early cases can be controlled by encouraging drinking and giving a light diet, low in protein, in small feeds three times daily.

Acute Nephritis. This may be brought about by stress factors, infection or poisoning by an agent damaging the kidney tissues. The picture here shows a fast, weak pulse, vomiting, injected membranes, high temperature and a dog in a state of pain and collapse.

Glucose saline solution should be given, along with specific treatment if possible. Good nursing here is very essential.

Cystitis, Inflammation of the Bladder. This is generally an infectious condition. Treatment is required to kill the infection, along with large quantities of fluid to flush out the system.

Stones of the Bladder and Urethra. Normally the reaction of the dog's urine is strongly acid. If it becomes neutral or alkaline the urine tends to sediment out in the bladder and form into stones. These may work their way partly down the urethra and form a blockage. Prevention is to give a diet to ensure an acid urine, i.e. one high in meat. Treatment is surgical.

DISEASES OF THE GENITAL SYSTEM

The Dog

Inflammation of the testicles is rare. Occasionally cuts and damage occur to the scrotum from barbed wire. Inflammation of the penis and sheath occurs and this is handled by irrigating the sheath with antiseptic or antibiotic douches.

Monorchidism and Cryptorchidism. These congenital faults are well recognised now and, whilst it is permissible to show a dog with these defects, it is desirable that such a dog should not be used for breeding.

The Bitch

Ovarian Diseases. Tumours of the ovary are rare. Cysts on the ovaries are not uncommon, giving rise to suppressed heat periods and false pregnancy.

Acute Metritis. This may occur after protracted labour or where afterbirth is not properly passed. Specific treatment is necessary and urgent.

Chronic Metritis, Pyometra. Occurs in middle-aged or old bitches, more generally but not always in maiden bitches. Symptoms: gradual onset of thirst, lassitude, poor appetite, sagging abdomen, sometimes a purulent discharge from the genital passage. Medical treatment does not normally effect a permanent cure and surgery is indicated.

DISEASES OF THE NERVOUS SYSTEM

The Brain. Local affections of the brain are very uncommon, but may be linked with a general condition. For example, hysteria may be linked with worms, bad diet, etc. Eucephalitis may be linked with distemper or poisons like dieldrin or strychnin.

Epilepsy occurs occasionally in the dog. If the attacks occur at long intervals they may be controlled by sedatives, but if frequent the dog should be destroyed. Where convulsions occur, and the cause is not known, heavy doses of sedatives should be given until the condition is accurately diagnosed.

DISEASES OF THE SPINAL CORD

Partial or complete paralysis may occur as an after effect of distemper or may be due to an accident from damage to and pressure on the spine. Prolapsed and ruptured discs can also give a partial or complete paralysis. Great care is necessary in the early stages to prevent more damage. As it is impossible to immobilise the spine, sedatives must be given until healing is advanced, then stimulants given and exercise encouraged to get the nerve fibres functional again.

In severe cases of paralysis from any of these causes it is a long and difficult job. Very careful nursing is necessary because, often, the dog has no control of bowels or bladder and bed-sores are liable to develop, also burns from urine irritation. Control returns later as function returns to the nerves.

Damage may also be done to various nerves by accidents, cuts, etc.

Ch. Larkstoke Ptarmigan

Eng. Sh.Ch. and Ceylon Ch. Hazel of Stubham

Ch. Whaddon
Chase Snipe

(*Alan Lambert*)

Whittlemoor Flicker reading *The Training of Spaniels* to her
grandchildren

Radial paralysis of the foreleg results from a blow in front of the shoulder, and shows in dropped shoulder and inability to draw the leg forward. Damage to the facial nerve on one side results in lips being pulled to the opposite side, giving a lop-sided appearance.

DISEASES OF THE SKIN

General Considerations. Glandular conditions, composition of the diet, vitamin and mineral intake and handling and exercise have a marked effect on the skin, even when a specific disease of the skin is involved. In treating skin complaints these factors must be attended to as well as specific treatment.

Eczema or Dermatitis. This starts as a raised red patch, rapidly shows blisters which rupture and give rise to raw weeping areas, later becoming encrusted. It is essential to clip the hair from the area, also two inches around it. Clean off discharge and dress with antiseptic, antibiotic and drying dressings. The cortisone group of drugs, given by mouth and locally, shows a marked soothing effect. In eczema due to allergies, anti-histaminic drugs are also helpful.

Ringworm. Shows as small round patches where hair is thin and broken—there is a typical ring formation. This disease can be transferred to humans. New antibiotic called Griseofulvin is effective, along with local treatment of the skin and hair.

Mange. Extremely common in all breeds. It is of two kinds:

1. Sarcoptic.   2. Demodectic.

1. Sarcoptic mange, caused by a mite, results in intense itching, and the dog scratches and rubs continuously. The skin becomes thickened, dry and wrinkled and complete or partial loss of hair occurs. In puppies it is often first noticed as pink pupules on stomach and inner thighs, then spreads to other parts.

2. Demodectic mange is also caused by a mite, and may be transmitted through particular strains, i.e. it appears to be hereditary. It is distinguished by the relative lack of scratching. The lesions often show first as partially bald patches, developing around the eyes and on the head, and later spreading. There is a slight thickening of the skin, which is covered by a fine whitish scale.

Treatment. (1) Sarcoptic mange. Clipping the dog helps initially, particularly long-haired dogs, such as the Springer.

F

Medicated baths have the advantage over local treatment in that early lesions are not missed. Agents used are sulphur compounds, benzyl benzoate, benzene hyachloride, etc.

(2) Demodectic mange. Many agents are used with varying degrees of success. The new antibiotic Griseofulvin may be useful.

Measures for control should be taken at once by completely isolating all dogs suffering from mange and by the most careful inspection of other dogs, to whom it is advisable to give a medicated bath as a precaution. Cleansing and disinfection of kennels, burning of bedding, etc., is most essential.

Alopecia or Baldness. This is not common in Springers. Occasionally it is associated with over-feeding, lack of exercise or glandular unbalance. Treatment is directed to the cause.

Interdigital Cysts. These are very common. Sometimes several cysts erupt at one time. They make the dog lame and they can be very painful. In the stage before they burst, poultices are helpful, and afterwards frequent bathing. When cysts persist in recurring it is often necessary to remove them surgically and cauterise the area.

Foreign Bodies in the Skin. Often a flint or thorn penetrates the foot or pad and it is sometimes very difficult to see where the opening is. It is then necessary to shave away the pad carefully. Perforating thorns in other parts of the body may give rise to a small local abscess.

Grass Seeds. Common places for these are in the ear and between the pads and toes. The seeds can penetrate and travel up the leg under the skin, where they are shown by a soft swelling or a weeping place. It is often very difficult to find the seed and remove it.

Skin Cysts. Found on various parts of the body, skin cysts should be removed if they grow to any size.

Growths of the Skin. Warty growths are common in old dogs and should be removed only if causing trouble. Benign growths are fairly common, especially mammary growths in the bitch. These may grow very large and commonly become ulcerated and unpleasant unless removed.

Wounds. Springers are liable to be wounded from tears, bites, shot wounds, etc. First aid consists of clipping the skin from the area, applying antiseptics to sterilise the skin and adding a dressing of sulphonamide antibiotic cream. Other measures, such as stitching, shock treatment, etc., should be taken as soon as possible.

Bites. Springers are a most friendly and pacific breed, but this is not the case with all the other breeds they may meet. Should a Springer have been involved in a fight, go over it very carefully afterwards to see what damage has been done; with their long coats it is sometimes difficult to see bites easily. Particularly examine the ears, throat and chest. Wash all wounds with antiseptic in the water. Should there be a long tear or a bite on the face or near the eyes it may require to be stitched and this should be done immediately one can get the dog to a veterinary surgeon.

Scalds and Burns. Fortunately scalds and burns are not of common occurrence with Springers, but very distressing if they should happen. Use antiflavin smeared over the surface, which should then be lightly covered with a gauze dressing. Treat for shock and telephone the veterinary surgeon asking for immediate help.

Stings. Wasps do not leave their stings in the skin. Bees do, and these should be squeezed out as quickly as possible A solution of bicarbonate of soda or ammonia in water should be applied. If the sting is in the mouth or on the tongue use bicarbonate, and watch carefully that the swelling does not cause obstruction in the throat.

Snake-Bites. In this country the adder is the only poisonous snake, and Springers hunting in thick heather and bracken can get bitten on nose, mouth or legs. A cut should be made across the puncture and the poison, which is harmless if taken orally, sucked out. The cut should then have powdered permanganate of potash well pressed into the wound. This is the best first-aid treatment. An injection of anti-snake serum should be given as soon as possible.

DISEASES OF THE BONES AND JOINTS

Various congenital conditions occur, e.g. incomplete skull closure, imperfect formation of the hip joint.

Rickets. Not so common nowadays, prevention and treatment of rickets depend on adequate and balanced amounts of calcium, phosphorus and vitamin D.

Fractures and Dislocations. Commonly caused by car accidents, the fractures most common are in limb-bones, pelvis and ribs. It is very important to move the dog as little as possible until examined. Warmth and mild stimulants are indicated as first aid.

Hernias. These are of four types:

(1) Umbilical. These vary in size. Those in small puppies often resolve themselves.

(2) Inguinal. Hernia in the groin. This is always a hereditary condition.

(3) Scrotal. Again hereditary.

(4) Diaphragmatic. Occasionally seen due to accident. A very serious condition.

All these hernias may be corrected by surgery.

CONDITIONS AFFECTING THE EYE

The Eyelids. (1) *Entropion.* In-turning of the eyelids, usually the lower lid. This irritates the eye and, if left, will cause damage to the cornea. Treatment is surgical.

(2) *Ectropion.* Out-turning of the eyelids, giving a bloodhound look, which is not only unsightly but exposes the eye to dust and dirt. Again, treatment is surgical.

Bliphanitis. Inflammation of the eyelids, which generally goes with conjunctivitis. Soothing and antibiotic creams are the treatment.

Blockage of the Tear Ducts. This generally occurs due to the very small tear-ducts swelling. Tears spill over from the eye, giving, in time, loss of hair and irritation of the skin below the eye.

Conjunctivitis. Inflammation of the membrane surrounding the eyeball. This condition is caused by dust, grit, chemical irritants or infection and can be very painful. Treatment should be directed to eliminating the cause and soothing the inflammation. Ointment or drops containing cortisone are very helpful.

Keratitis and Corneal Ulcer. Due to inflammation or damage to the sheen of the eye. A bluish-white opaque area shows the affected part. If an ulcer develops on the cornea, great care must be taken to avoid mechanical irritation to the eye while healing proceeds, i.e. keep away from dust, grit, strong winds, bushes, etc. Bathing the eye in milk, soothing lotions, antiseptic and anti-biotic dressings is the treatment.

Glaucoma. Enlargement of the eyeball, due to increased fluid, hence pressure, inside the eyeball. It is a serious condition and may affect one or both eyes. Treatment is directed to the cause, which is often part of a general condition.

Cataract. Opacity of the lens. Often met with in the older dog, with consequent diminishing of vision. In complete blindness, surgical removal of the lens is possible in selected cases, with fairly good results.

CONDITIONS AFFECTING THE EAR

Aural Haematoma. Very large blood-blisters on the inside of the ear flap, due in most cases to shaking the head sharply or scratching the ears. Lancing and stitching of the haematoma is necessary, together with treatment of the cause of irritation.

External Otitis. Inflammation of the ear canal. A very common condition, showing a reddened, inflamed ear canal with exudate forming, and with symptoms of itching, painful ears and restlessness. The cause of the trouble varies from foreign bodies in the canal, i.e. grass seeds, pieces of straw, etc., or bacterial infection, mite infestation of the ear canal, etc. Canker is the name commonly given to an ear badly infected, with purulent exudate, and a raw, ulcerated ear canal.

Treatment varies according to the causes and symptoms. The ear must be carefully washed and dried first of all, then dressings applied: (1) to remove the cause, i.e. infection, mites, etc., (2) to soothe the irritation, prevent scratching, rubbing, etc., (3) to dry the ear and prevent exudate forming.

Otitis Media. Inflammation of the Middle ear. The cause is nearly always an extension of infection from the outer ear, so creating further infection in the middle ear. The treatment is by sulphomonides and antibiotics by injection.

CONDITIONS AFFECTING THE NOSE

Epistaxis, Nose Bleeding. Damage by a blow is the commonest cause; others are foreign bodies in the nose, growths and ulceration of the nasal membrane.

First-aid measures to arrest bleeding are crushed ice-packs placed on the nose and injections of adrenalin and calcium.

Rhinitis. Inflammation of the Nasal Membrane. This shows as a discharge, often part of a general infection like distemper. The nose should be cleansed daily with antiseptic solution and the nostrils gently smeared with a soothing ointment to prevent raw and cracked areas developing.

FIRST AID AND NURSING

First-aid treatment in emergencies such as accidents with motor-cars, dogs accidentally shot and injuries from jumping from heights should be conservative. In particular the dog should be moved as little as possible because if bones are broken the risk of dangerous displacement of broken fragments is always present, e.g. perforation of the lung from fragment of broken rib. Again, where internal haemorrhage is present, bleeding may start up again through excessive movement.

Warmth should be applied by rugs, hot-water bottles, etc., and glucose solution given if possible. Where wounds are bleeding badly, an antiseptic pack and bandage is indicated, but care must be taken when bandaging a limb not to make the bandage too tight, otherwise the blood supply to the leg is interfered with.

Nursing a sick dog is largely common sense. A light, nourishing, appetising diet, encouragement to drink as much as possible and a pleasant, even temperature are all very essential. Often, in gastric cases, everything is vomited, and then water must be removed until the stomach inflammation has subsided. If this persists over a period of days, then glucose-saline must be given by injection to prevent dehydration developing. This is a most valuable procedure in these cases.

Where the dog is restless, in discomfort or pain, the aspirin compounds are very helpful. The dog is tolerant to aspirin and quite large doses may be safely given.

GERIATRICS, CARE OF THE AGED DOG

The old dog, it should be remembered, has become very much a creature of habit and the daily routine should be varied as little as possible. The times of meals and times of exercise should be kept constant. A common fault is over-feeding. The diet should be light, but nourishing, containing less protein than that of an active working dog. Vitamin intake must be watched and a compound vitamin-and-mineral supplement is recommended.

Grooming is very important. Cleaning of ears, scaling of teeth, nail-clipping, bathing of eyes and expression of the anal glands when necessary, should be carried out regularly.

Exercise should be carefully watched and the length of walks governed by the dog's state and inclination. Signs of breathlessness may indicate a failing heart, when a little heart-tonic daily may correct the balance. A warm, comfortable sleeping place at night is important, preferably at the fireside.

The Springer is, happily, among the breeds that retain their youth and vigour well into double figures, and thirteen or fourteen is a very general age for them to attain.

Chapter VII

SHOWING

THE novice has now bred his first litter and hopes that in it he
has been fortunate enough to have bred one or two puppies
who he thinks may bring him some measure of success in the
show ring, and, unless he is a position to keep all the litter until
they are about six months old, the time has come for him to
look at them very critically and to choose the one or two that
seem the most promising. Do not rely entirely on your own judgement this first time. As you will have attended a number of
shows, you will, I am sure, have become acquainted with Springer
owners who have had experience in both breeding and showing,
and I can assure you that there are very few who will not do all
they can to help you. Ask their opinion and listen carefully to
any advice they can give you.

Sometimes a puppy, even at a few weeks old, will stand out
in a litter, and sometimes the whole litter is of such equal merit
that you could put your hand down and pick any one and not be
far wrong. Still, a decision has to be made, and it is above all
essential to pick a bold, active puppy with no sign of nerves. It
must be remembered that these puppies have known you all
their lives and so will take you for granted, never showing nerves
or shyness with you or the people who come about the kennel
daily. But watch the puppies' behaviour when a stranger comes
in. The whole lot may come forward, pleased to welcome all and
sundry, but it may be that one or more of the litter will stay at
the back of the run or even retreat into the kennel. These latter
puppies may, in time, show reasonbly well, but they will always
go into the ring with an expression on their faces which, as the
judge looks at them, says as plainly as any words, 'I loathe the
whole of this business and you in particular; be quick and get it
over and let me go home!' Some others will not be shy or nervous,
but always bored, never putting all they could into showing, and,
however good, often losing to an inferior dog which is showing
its very best. A gay, happy temperament is most important, and
must be a first consideration. My old Ch. Reipple was one who
adored shows: she went into the ring and stood, swinging her

tail, head up, eyes bright and saying quite clearly: 'What are we waiting for? I've come for that prize, please hand it over,' and she brought it off an amazing number of times. In those days when, very often, I was unable to get to shows Mr H. S. Lloyd very kindly took her for me, and the combination of the greatest Spaniel showman of our times and the Springer that loved showing off was often irresistible.

After deciding on temperament take each puppy and examine it critically. Is the head clean through from the muzzle? Is there promise of fluting (division) between the eyes? Is there a good stop but no sign of 'apple-head'? Are the ears well set? What shape and colour are the eyes? If the eyes are light with a chalky, hard expression they will never darken, but will entirely spoil the outlook of the dog throughout its life. A certain breeder many years ago used a Merle Collie to obtain something he wanted particularly in his strain, and the eye, which is quite good in a Merle Collie, became established in his Springer strain, where it was frankly hideous. This breeder also used Setter blood, and the combination of Setter-cum-Springer type with Collie eye were so marked that a dog of this breeding could be picked out anywhere—at a show, in the field or in the street. Liver-and-white puppies sometimes have a lightish eye, but if there is a dark brown rim round the iris the eye will almost certainly darken with age. Still the best eye of all is the one that is a good brown to start with. Black-and-white Springers nearly always seem to have a very dark eye, almost black. I can remember very few exceptions and, of course, the darker the better with this colour coat.

After examining the head look carefully at the body. See how the pup's forelegs are set into the shoulders and that the bone is flat, round bone, straight and clean. At three months one cannot expect a big spring of ribs, but a shapely body with a loin which looks likely to be strong and not too long, going off into a good rump and with the tail set low and never carried gaily, should be looked for. Even at this age one can judge the bend of stifle, and a puppy which walks stiffly and with no promise of drive should not be the one chosen. Feet matter a lot, and a close, neat foot—never an open, loose one—is important.

If you can find all these perfections in one puppy, keep it and rear it with the utmost care, and, if possible, keep two puppies; they do so much better playing and exercising together.

Since all the litter is not to be kept, sell the remainder as soon as you can. In my experience one gets very little, often no more, for a five- or six-months puppy than for one of eight to twelve weeks old, and if one does get a few pounds more it has probably cost all the extra money in food during the longer period.

A word of advice here. When a prospective buyer is coming, put all the pups that are for sale in a run together and the ones you have decided to keep in another place. The visitor may have as good an eye as you for the best puppies—and, if an experienced breeder, perhaps better—and seeing them all the visitor may not be satisfied with any of the others. Replica was a very attractive puppy, though a number of others were perhaps equally good. A buyer came and had almost decided on a puppy when he caught sight of Replica coming into the run and said at once, 'That's the one I'll have.' No explaining that Replica was not for sale was any use; he was prepared to pay whatever I liked to ask, but as I was determined not to sell he just turned round and went, saying, 'If I can't have that one I won't have one at all!'

The chosen puppy must next be taught to walk well on a leash. The best thing is to put a collar on for a short time for a few days, then, attaching a light leash, coax it to walk with you. If it 'jibs' don't pull, but just stand still and let it play around until it gets used to the restraint of collar and leash, then if it will come a few paces pat and pet it and to begin with, perhaps, give it a titbit. Then, each time it is put on a leash it will probably go farther, the reward can be dispensed with and a word of praise will be sufficient. Often a puppy will go well on a leash almost at once, if taken with an older dog who will walk steadily and take no notice of the puppy's antics.

Directly the puppy goes well on the leash it should be taken first on quiet roads (in the country if possible) and later in village or town, where it will see strange people, other dogs, cars, horses, etc., and so become thoroughly accustomed to meeting people and to seeing and hearing traffic. I have many times seen really good puppies, who have never before been in contact with the world outside their home surroundings, so upset by the unusual conditions when taken to their first show that they have absolutely refused to show.

Do not take a puppy either into a town or anywhere where it could come in contact with other dogs (and this applies particularly to shows) until it has had its epivaxplus and its leptovaxplus inoculations to protect it against distemper, hard-pad and the other diseases dealt with in the chapter on ailments.

Before being taken to a show a puppy should be practised in going up and down a distance relative to an average ring, turning at the end and coming straight back to the point at which it started. It is a good thing to have someone else move the puppy at times, so that you can see its action, both coming and going. You cannot see this while you are walking *with* the puppy, but if you have a long mirror in which you can watch the forward action as you approach you get a very good idea of how it looks to the judge.

Start training the puppy to stand well by itself without having its head and tail held, its legs arranged, its neck stretched out, its handler kneeling or stooping beside it. This can be done if owners will give the time to a little daily training. Lead the puppy up an imaginary ring, stop and say 'Stand' and give, perhaps, a little jerk on the lead to pull it back into a good stance. It won't be exactly right the first time or, maybe, not even at the twentieth; some dogs come to it more quickly than others, but it can be attained with patience. Once a puppy has really learnt this lesson there should be no need to worry about his position; he will fall into it naturally, just as he learns to go easily up and down a ring to show his movement.

Continue this training right up to the time the puppy is old enough to be taken to a show, and do it both in a grass run and on a floor so that it is used to both surfaces, depending on whether the show is an outdoor or an indoor one. When he is made to stand, see that his position is correct and keep him interested. Stand behind, but a few inches beyond, the dog's head, so that you can see that his position is right and also that he can see you and be quick to do what you want. Be sure to see that his front legs go down at right angles to his body and are not angled forward. This spoils the outline, and yet again and again I have seen handlers take infinite trouble to arrange the back legs effectively and leave the front legs in this ugly position. Once more the use of a mirror, in which you can see the exact position of the dog as he stands, is very valuable.

It may take a long time to get the dog moving and standing perfectly, but once it is achieved it is worth all the time and trouble. Anyone who ever saw Mr H. S. Lloyd in the ring with one of his Cockers will realise what I mean, but do not think that even he could take a dog into a ring where it would show perfectly without training. He told me that with some dogs he has given hours and hours to teaching them exactly what he wants, but I am sure the result repaid him.

The earliest age at which a dog can be shown is six months, but unless a Springer puppy is very well advanced for its age I do not recommend showing it until it is at least eight or nine months old. To plunge a young puppy into the hurly-burly of a show, particularly one where there is no benching and the dogs, perhaps noisy breeds, have to lie about on the floor, possibly in close proximity to one another, is asking a lot of it. A benched show is really less disturbing.

Obtain a schedule from the secretary of the show to which it is decided to go and fill in all the particulars required very carefully *in block letters*. Entry forms always ask for this and it is a tremendous help to the secretary and the printers in preparing the catalogue, but it is surprising how often this instruction is ignored, with the result that sometimes most remarkable names appear. I speak feelingly about this as I have wasted endless time trying to decipher most curious scripts. Incorrect names and mistakes may lead to disqualification later if a prize has been won at a Show.

Be sure to post your entry in good time. It is a strict rule of the Kennel Club that late entries must not be accepted: the postmark must not be later than the day given in the schedule for closing of entries. Entries may, however, be sent by telephone or telegram if despatched before midnight on the closing date, provided the entry form itself follows immediately.

Much must be done well before entries close and the dog is taken to the show. Hurried preparation of his coat at the last moment is hopeless. A Springer has a silky top-coat with a dense undercoat to resist all weathers, and this coat needs thorough brushing and combing regularly. This will bring out dead hair and allow the new top-coat to lie smooth, and any dead, fluffy, faded hair that still remains on head, ears, flanks, etc., must be taken out with finger and thumb. This is done by bringing the thumb-nail down on the hair to be removed—a few hairs at a time on to the first finger and giving a little jerk. The hair comes out quite easily and it does not hurt the dog at all. I have seen many go to sleep while I have trimmed in this way; it takes a little time, but if the coat is cared for every day it is soon free from the dead hair which looks like a soft, untidy down.

I do beg all Springer owners to use this method and not to cut the coat, either with scissors or a knife. Coats that have been cut develop a curl, and the sleek, smooth, silky coat, so much admired at shows and which, I must admit, allows the judge to see the shape of the dog, is gone, often for ever. If anyone has any doubt about this they have only to look at Dr Wilson's Australian Dual Ch. Curtsey George. He left Australia with a flat coat, as can be seen in all the photographs taken of him there, but he came out of quarantine here in England with a wavy, even a curly, coat, the result of trimming with a knife.

The hair against the head in front of the ears (that is the thick dead hair) should be removed with finger and thumb. This lets the full length of the head from the muzzle be seen, allows the ears to lie flat against the head and prevents any appearance of cheekiness. Dead hair must be trimmed from the top of the ears, but whatever you do, don't cut it, and remember that Springers' ears are not set low like those of Cockers. Nothing is uglier than to see a Springer's ears and head shaved down low; all Springer character is lost, and after a time the hair stiffens and sticks out, and however cleverly it is cut or shaved it can always be seen. Any untidy hair on the flanks, and superfluous feathering on front legs and above the hocks, must be removed. This is easily plucked out, but must not be cut.

The feet, however, do need tidying up, and here a pair of curved scissors should be used to trim the hair round the shape of the foot, taking great care not to nip the nails. Springers grow a lot of hair between the toes and this should be trimmed down very carefully with sharp scissors. The hair between the toes should be brought down to the bottom of the foot between the nails and cut to match the line round the pads, and the hair underneath the foot trimmed back to the pads. The long hair at the back of the front leg should be trimmed at the bottom for an inch to an inch and a half, according to the length of the leg, showing a clean line from the foot to the pastern. To finish off the foot the hair should be levelled down to a neat line all round with a sharp knife, so that no uneven hairs stick up, and the foot should have the hair lying as smoothly down to the edge of the toes as the naturally smooth short hair along the front of the legs. The hair on the back legs from below the hock to the foot should be trimmed off short; this gives a good line when the dog is standing and shows the placing of the foot and leg when moving.

If Springers get plenty of exercise, and at times are walked on hard roads or pavements, their toenails rarely need cutting. Should it be necessary, use a pair of dog nail-cutters; be very careful not to cut the quick, which shows a darker colour through the nail. If the end of the nail is at all rough after being cut, file it smooth with an ordinary nail-file.

If one lives in the country, well away from any industrial area, Springers are easily kept clean with good brushing, but in or near a big town or a mining area the smoky atmosphere will form a deposit on the ground and grass; dogs living in such places can get to look very drab, and then it is necessary to bath them a few days before a show. Not only does it militate against their chances of success, but to bring dirty dogs into the ring is an insult to the judge. When they have to travel by train, or in any other public conveyance, I know that it is most difficult to end the journey with the dogs in the pristine condition in which they started, but a clean rug on which they can lie and a thorough brushing with a stiff brush on arrival at the show will remove this surface grubbiness and bring up the bloom which makes a Springer's coat so attractive. Application of a chalk-block if he is very dirty helps, but this chalk *must* be brushed out afterwards.

Normally Springers do not need frequent baths. If you have a clear, running stream or a clean pond near, a good swim and then a gallop over grass will in summer keep them beautiful, but if you have no such facilities a bath is essential.

Place the dog in a bath in which there is plenty of room for him to stand comfortably, then plug his ears with cotton wool so that no water can get into the inner ear, wet him with fairly warm water, a portion at a time, and apply a good dog-shampoo, rubbing well into the skin. Starting with the legs, go on to the body and finish with the head and ears, being very careful not to get soap into the eyes when doing the face. If the weather makes it at all possible take the dog out of the bath, stand him on the grass and rinse thoroughly with warm water poured from a can. All the water then drains off and he is not standing in a bath full of dirty, soapy water. Give a second thorough rinse, then dip a good-sized chamois leather in hot water, wring it out as dry as possible and rub the dog down. Directly the leather is wet, dip it again in hot water, and wring and rub until the dog is dry. This will be in a remarkably short time, for it is quite the quickest way in which to dry an animal.

If your dog is not a good traveller in a car, and is inclined to dribble, tie a big, thick sheet round his neck so that his head lies on it and it is well spread in front of him; his neck and legs are protected and he will arrive clean and dry. If he is one that suffers from car-sickness have plenty of newspapers ready! Quells, Sea-legs and other remedies for humans for seasickness can be tried, but it is wise to enquire into their constituents as some are not suitable for dogs, so chemists have told me.

The very best thing is to train a puppy to travel in cars from the earliest age possible. Give it short journeys first, held on someone's knees and kept interested; increase the journey gradually, give it a short run before the return journey, and gradually car travel becomes a sought-after pleasure. Very few Springers are bad travellers if started early, and to many car-riding is a real joy. Those to whom it means going shooting will leap into a car directly they see it come out of the garage.

The theory that a chain attached to the back of the car, so that it trails on the ground, prevents car-sickness is widely held. I have tried it only once, so cannot offer any definite opinion, but that once it did not work! Anyhow the chain must be watched, as it wears and breaks, and if dangling above the ground it is quite useless; without contact with the ground there is a break in the electrical circuit.

Always have a special bag for taking what you require for the show and check over the items to see that nothing has been for-gotten. You will need a show-chain with three swivels so that the dog does not get twisted up on the bench, a slip-lead that will fall back loosely and so show the length of neck, a brush, comb and hound-glove, a piece of soft chamois leather or an old chamois-leather glove to give a final polish, a small, unupsettable dish for food and water. I always take a bottle of water, for, unless one is near a place at an indoor show where water can be obtained from a tap, it is most difficult to carry a bowl of water across any distance and arrive at one's bench with enough water for the dog to drink. At outdoor shows where there may not be a standpipe near the tent I very much dislike the idea of dipping my bowl into a tank into which all and sundry bowls have been dipped, after they have been used by other dogs. One cannot be too careful. If you are taking a puppy, and he is used to a drink of milk, take milk as well as water. Have a specially nice dinner of fresh meat packed in a polythene bag, and if he is likely to fancy biscuits take a small supply, but at most of the big indoor championship shows and at many of the outdoor ones, like the W.E.L.K.S., Windsor, etc., the dog-food manufacturers usually have stands, and it is possible to get the brand of biscuit or meal that your dog likes best, and this saves carrying. For a puppy, or for a dog difficult to show, a few Vetzymes or a piece of very hard-baked liver to keep his attention in the ring is useful, kept in the hand so that he can smell but not eat it. A rug for the bench completes the equipment.

Have your pass and the dog's numbered entry-card handy in a pocket to show quickly at the gate.

Have your dog ready for his first class. Do not rely on the steward coming to fetch you, and if Springers are not the first in the ring do not assume that it will be safe to go off to lunch or to talk to friends. Be at the ringside well before you are needed, go in quickly and *do* remember your dog's number. It is very trying for a busy steward to have to ask your name and that of your dog and look up the number in the catalogue. Keep your puppy interested in what is going on, and if you have taken the trouble to train him for the ring, as I have suggested, all should be well. If you should win a place in your first class, stand in the order of your award on the side of the ring for dogs already seen. Don't worry the steward and exasperate the judge by wandering about or getting in the way of the new dogs in the class. And, above all, accept the judge's placings graciously. If you are first this is easy, but if you are Reserve or V.H.C. take your award-card with a smile and a 'thank you'. If you get nothing, remember that you entered for the judge's opinion, and go out of the ring looking satisfied and as if you knew that your dog's day would come later, even if he hasn't fulfilled your hopes this time.

I shall never forget the first Challenge Certificate I ever won. It was at Worcester in 1921, under Mr E. C. Spencer, one of the great Spaniel breeders and judges of the pre- and post-World War I period. I won the Limit Class with Ranger and went on to the Open Class, in which were, among others, Mr David MacDonald's Ch. Little Brand from Scotland and another well-known winner. I was placed first with Little Brand second, and I was so astonished that I turned to Mr Spencer and gasped, 'But I haven't beaten Little Brand.' He assured me that I had, and

my day was made for me when Mr MacDonald, great sportsman
that he was, put out his hand and congratulated me heartily,
though I believe that was the only time his dog was ever beaten
on English soil.

Some Show Springers of the Past and Present

It is impossible, in a book of this length, to record all the
winning Springers of the period between the two wars. I can
mention only a few who stand out in my memory as exceptionally
good dogs. Since the last war a very great number of new exhibitors have come into the breed and, again, I cannot include them
all. I have, therefore, taken the winning dogs whose owners
began to exhibit very soon after shows were resumed and who
have continued up to the present time, although I have included
some few of the more recent exhibitors whose dogs have been
outstanding.

I cannot remember when I first saw Mr A. MacNab Chassel's
very handsome Inveresk Springers. It was, I know, in my very
early days as a Springer owner, and still winning 'Inveresks'
continue to appear at shows, following a long line of Champions
who won during the years between the wars. Int.Ch. Inveresk
Chancellor went to the United States and made a great name
there. Among many others were Ch. Inveresk Cocksure, Ch.
Inveresk Careful, Int.Ch. Inveresk Cashier and Int.Ch. Inveresk Coronation. Coronation stands out in my memory as one
of the most beautiful Springers of her day. She was born in
1925, and she could win today, competing with the best of our
modern bitches.

The 'Carnfield' prefix of Mr G. A. Taylor perhaps reached
its peak of success in the 1920s with such dogs as Carnfield King,
Queen, Cassie and, most notably, Ch. Standard and Ashborne
Stroller, both of whom went to India, while after the last war
further winning dogs appeared, headed by Ch. Carnfield Chick,
Ch. Carnfield Florrie and Ch. Albvic Legioner.

It is impossible to name all the winning Springers during the
1930s but the Shotton Kennels of Mr M. D. Withers must be
mentioned, if only for two outstanding dogs in Ch. Showman of

(*F. W. Simms*)

Ch. Winch Starturn

(*C. M. Cooke*)

Ch. Brandyhole Diadem

Inverruel Sheila

F.T.Ch. Layerbrook Michelle

Shotton and Ch. Jess of Shelcot. Mrs Travers also bred a number of typical Springers, Totonian Finder and Sportsman of Toton among them, and carried on in post-war days with a very attractive bitch, Totonian Biddy, and a dog that ran successfully at trials, Totonian Swift. The 'Worthern' dogs, Surprise, Sunshine, Supreme and several others, had great quality, while Ch. Pleasant Peter and his son, Peter's Benefactor, were handsome dogs and their names appear in many present-day pedigrees.

When one realises that before her first marriage to the late Captain Selby-Lowndes Lady Lambe, as she now is, was a Miss Arkwright, a member of the family of which Mr William Arkwright is famed as having arranged the first Spaniel field trial ever held, it is not surprising to know that Springers have always been one of her greatest interests, and in pre-World War II days the show winners Whaddon Chase Ticket, a field trial prizewinner, and Sh.Ch. Whaddon Chase Robin were Captain Selby-Lowndes's favourite shooting dogs. Lady Lambe did not start showing her Springers until 1932 but soon had a long list of winners to her credit. Perhaps the very best one was Ch. Higham Tom-Tit (Ch. Marmion of Marmion ex Ch. Higham Teal), who was certainly one of the ousttandingly beautiful dogs of the 1930–40 period. After the last war Lady Lambe showed a son of Tom-Tit ex Butter (Int.Ch. Dry Toast ex Int.Ch. Balgray Joy), and this dog, Ch. Whaddon Chase Bonny Tom, a worthy son of his distinguished father, proved one of the leading winners and sires for many years. In 1947 Lady Lambe bred the famous litter by Higham Tristram ex Ch. Whaddon Chase Snipe in which were Ch. Whaddon Chase Bracken, Ch. Whaddon Chase Prince and Ch. Higham Topsy, with Whaddon Chase Duke a Challenge Certificate winner as well as a field trial prize-winner. Three other Champions were Whaddon Chase Grouse, Bonny Lass and Swift, followed by a number of Show Champions and Challenge Certificate winners.

Another kennel where the dogs had to work as well as look handsome was the Northdown Kennel, owned by the late Mr W. Manin. With the limited time he could spare from business he won awards at trials with Northdown Susie and Northdown Jabez, who were also winners at shows. He had his first Springer 50 years ago.

Early in the 1930s he bought a grandson of F.T.Ch. Banchory Boy out of a bitch going back to the Highams and Horsfords, and he proved not only an excellent worker but was so good looking that his master showed and won with him. As this dog went back in his breeding to F.T.Ch. Rivington Sam, Mr Manin bought a bitch also descended from Rivington Sam and so started his strain. He purchased Northdown Maquis, which sired North-down Style, dam of three Champions in two litters, and he bred Ch. Northdown Donna, which won the Challenge Certificate at Cruft's in 1958 and again in 1959.

Mrs Mary Scott, who had had Springers since she was very young, and in the 1930s had owned Boghurst Berry, a litter sister of Ch. Boghurst Bristle, did not think of showing until 1944. Undoubtedly her best-known dog was Boxer of Bramhope (by Peter's Benefactor ex Bramhope Suzette), which proved an exceptional sire, as he had fourteen Champions to his credit in addition to numerous Show Champions and Challenge Certificate winners, among the best known being the Champions Alexander of Stubham, Clintonhouse George, Studley Major, Bramhope Bathsheba, Bramhope Belarosa and Peter of Lorton Fell.

Mrs Scott was a founder-member of the Midland Springer Spaniel Club and from 1947 was the honorary secretary for ten years. She judged in many countries, including the U.S.A., Denmark, Ireland, Scandinavia and other parts of the world. In 1958 she brought the American Ch. Melilotus Shooting Star back with her from Mrs Gilman Smith's kennel in the States.

The late Mr D. C. Hannah must be included in the list of show exhibitors, although his real interest was on the working side of the breed. He bred the Champions Stokeley Bonny Boy, Stokeley Gay Boy and Stokeley Lucky, all three in turn winning Challenge Certificates at Cruft's, and since then he bred a number of Show Champions.

Miss C. M. Francis is also keenly interested in field trials, but again combines looks and work in her strain, for both Ch. Higham Teal in the 1930s and Ch. Higham Topsy in 1955 were Best of Breed at Cruft's.

Mrs I. Davies had been devoted to dogs all her life, so that the one wedding present that pleased her most was the English Springer given to her by her husband, and a puppy from this present (by Carnfield King) was the beginning of their interest in shows. Showing brought them in touch with Mrs Thomson, with whom they formed a great friendship. When she became too ill to show her dogs herself, Mr and Mrs Davies took charge of her bitch, Clintonhouse Hazeltong Judith (Replica of Ranscombe ex Judy of Hazeltong), and her two puppies by Boxer of Bramhope, Clintonhouse George and Clintonhouse Greta. They bred a litter by Carnfield Field Marshal ex Coates Park Enterprise in which was a handsome dog, Colmaris Toreador, and with this dog, winner of two Challenge Certificates, mated to Judith, bred Ch. Colmaris Contessa. George and Contessa proved a wonderful brace, as in the year 1953-4 they took the Challenge Certificates, either singly or both, at every championship show they attended. Then occurred a tragedy for Mr and Mrs Davies, for, with less than twenty-four hours' illness, George died on the morning of Cruft's Show, 1955, at just over four years of age. He had won in that short time eighteen Challenge Certificates, ten Reserve Challenge Certificates and had been Best of Breed fourteen times. The loss to the breed cannot be estimated, for he was also a good gundog and an excellent retriever. Ch. Contessa, winner of eleven Challenge Certificates and fourteen Reserve Certificates, is fortunately still an inmate of the kennel and has bred some very good stock. Two of George's puppies, Ch. Northdown Donna and Int.Ch. Print of Ardrick, are well known, and even in the short time he lived he sired a number of Show Champions and other winners, and his grandchildren are winning well today.

Another wedding present of an English Springer, a bitch called Pixie of Larkstoke, given to Mr and Mrs I. B. Hampton by Mr M. D. Withers, who owned the Shotton Springers, so well known before the war, resulted in the small but very successful Larkstoke Kennel being started. Incidentally, what a very fortunate thing this gift was for the English Springer Spaniel Club, for had Mr and Mrs Hampton not been given Pixie they might never have known the fascination of owning our breed and the club might never had had its present indefatigable and enthusiastic honorary secretary and honorary treasurer. Misfortune seemed to dog the Larkstokes for a number of years but the Hamptons refused to be discouraged, athough Showman, a Best in Show winner and an outstanding worker, was poisoned; Sandpiper, a Reserve Challenge Certificate winner, died after hard-pad; and Sugarcandy, who had won two Challenge Certificates, and her qualifier, died whelping. The one puppy surviving, the hand-reared Larkstoke Sweetwilliam, has proved an excellent sire and his grand-daughter Larkstoke Barley Sugar was a Best in Show and a Best of Breed winner. This bitch, Larkstoke Aprilstar and her mother Larkstoke Higham Tidy (ex Ch. Higham Topsy) were three winning bitches followed by Ch. Larkstoke Ptarmigan. In addition to the bitches all being first-prize winners at championship shows they all work up to the standard required on a rough shoot.

As very often happens with English Springers, the first one owned by Mrs G. G. Crawford was bought in 1941 for work. This bitch, Winch Ruby, a grand-daughter of Renrut Jock, was mated to Good Hunting (Bircher of Yelme ex Grock of Blair), and a grand-daughter of this mating, Winch Jewel, was sent to be mated to my Replica of Ranscombe. I was so struck by this bitch's good looks that I suggested to her mistress that she was well worth showing, and Jewel certainly justified my opinion of her by winning at a number of shows, including Cruft's. Her son, Winch Agate, in addition to being a good gundog, won a great many prizes. He was the first of a long list of successful Springers of Winch-Ranscombe breeding: Replica and his grandson, Rollicker of Ranscombe, being brought in on both the dog and bitch lines, so fixing a very definite type of much quality. Ch. Winch Starturn, Winch Flint, Winch Azurite, Winch Fluospar and Winch Enargite being shown now are the eighth generation of Winch breeding and, like their predecessors, all take their turn when Mr and Mrs Crawford go shooting. Winch Springers have gone abroad to a number of countries and at least four have become Champions in their new homes.

In 1943 Mrs F. Sherwood came to see me and returned home with two puppies by Replica of Ranscombe ex Uspup of Tarbay, and this started her breeding and showing under her 'Woodbay' prefix, which has become one of the leading strains at shows. She was the joint owner of Ch. Northdown Donna with Mr Manin. Donna's daughter, Woodbay Prima Donna, became a Sh. Champion. Another noted winner was Ch. Woodbay Gay Charmer owned by Mr N. Jenkins.

Mrs F. O. Till started her kennel of show Springers in 1947 and has won success on the bench with a large number of dogs, pride of place, of course, going to Ch. Alexander of Stubham, her first full Champion. She also owns Ch. Royal Salute of Stubham, Ch. Studley Diadem and Ch. Hyperion of Stubham, and bred Ch. Duchess of Stubham, owned by Mrs Spence, and Ch. Dinah of Stubham, owned by Mr Grant. In addition she has bred a number of Show Champions, the latest being Sh.Ch. Scarlet Ribbons of Stubham, and she has exported dogs to all parts of the world, where they have won distinctions on the bench, including a number of championship titles.

Though it is comparatively few years since Mrs J. Spence bred her first litter of English Springers she has since built up one of the best-known winning strains on the bench today. In this litter, by Replica of Ranscombe ex Cani of Brandyhole, was a dog which proved a very good worker and a successful show dog too, as he won over seventy awards, including a number of firsts at championship shows. This encouraged Mrs Spence to take up showing seriously and she purchased a puppy, Duchess of Stubham (Boxer of Bramhope ex Susan of Stubham), from Mrs Till, and after winning several Challenge Certificates trained and handled her herself to win her qualifying certificate for her title. Ch. Duchess, mated to Ch. Clintonhouse George, and later to Studley Brave Buccaneer, bred her a number of winners in each litter, and now Mrs Spence has four generations in her kennel: Ch. Duchess, Brandyhole Bellflower, her daughter, Ch. Brandyhole Diadem, her grand-daughter, and Brandyhole Grand Duchess, her great-grand-daughter. The list of Challenge Certificate winners she has bred is impressive, and she has sent her Springers to many countries abroad, where they are all winning.

The Crosslane Springers owned by Mr E. A. Anderson were winning before the war and, headed by Sh.Ch. Beauvallet of Crosslane, a very successful team continues to win now. Two most attractive youngsters, Night and Transpots of Crosslane (Beauvallet ex Higham Trim), combine show and field trial blood and should go far.

Mr J. C. Hanning is the owner of Ch. Peter of Lorton Fell and Mrs Hare-Dinsley of Ch. Camdin Chief: both own a number of typical young Springers. Mr D. P. B. Campbell has come from Scotland to win at Cruft's with Ch. Inverruel Raider and Ch. Inverruel Pacemaker who was BOB in 1971. Mrs Hancock, so well known to us before her marriage as Miss J. Robinson, owns the two Champions Hawkhill Brave and Floravon Silverstar, and besides owning a team of promising youngsters is the breeder of Ch. Hyperion of Stubham. Mrs M. Smithson is the breeder and owner of Ch. Studley Major and Sh.Ch. Studley Brave Buccaneer, and a very attractive young dog in Sh.Ch. Studley Oscar.

Mrs Broadley owned several Champions soon after the war and recently made Sandylands Suzannah a Show Champion. Another exhibitor who makes an occasional appearance in the Springer ring, where he always shows a good one, is Mr A. B. Nicolson. His latest, Sh.Ch. O'Malley's Tango of Glenbervie, won the Bitch Certificate at Cruft's in 1962. Mrs Dobson was the owner of the beautiful Ch. Tyneview Margaret and her 'Teesview' prefix includes the home-bred Champions Teesview Titus, Tarmac and Telstar. Another very enthusiastic exhibitor is Mrs I. Campbell Durie, who had considerable success with her Kildusklands.

Within recent years, the Hawkhill prefix of Mrs Judith Hancock, the Moorcliff prefix of Mr Ernest Froggatt and the Cleavehill prefix of Mrs Jean Taylor have established themselves at the head of the Show Bench winners.

Mr Jimmy Cudworth, in partnership with Mrs Hancock, has piloted Sh.Ch. Hawkhill Royal Palace to close on a record number of Challenge Certificates, whilst a litter sister Sh.Ch. Hawkhill Derby Daydream has won a large number of Challenge Certificates for her young owner Miss Frances Bagshawe. Sh.Ch. Hawkhill Connaught is current winning dog. Mr Froggatt's Ch. Moorcliff Dougal of Truelindale, bred by Miss M. Alder, has many top wins to his credit. These two dogs have taken the breed to top honours at Championship events.

Black/white colouring has become increasingly popular and many Challenge Certificate winners have come from Mrs Taylor's Cleavehill Kennel. Perhaps the best known is Sh.Ch. Dulcie of Kennersleigh, bred by Mrs M. Keighley, for this bitch has produced her fair share of winning off-spring.

Mr Colin Muirhead of the Shipden prefix has also bred and shown a large number of winning black/white Springers. His current winning dog is Ch. Swallowtail of Shipden.

A rarer but most attractive colouring is black/white/tan. At the present time there are two full Champion bitches carrying these markings; Ch. Woodbay Gay Charmer owned by Mr N. Jenkins and Ch. Larkstoke Ptarmigan owned by Mrs I. B. Hampton.

I.B.H.

Winning Springers in the Channel Islands

The Channel Islands come under the Kennel Club just as do Great Britain and Northern Ireland, but, with the greater difficulty of reaching the main shows here, the islands tend to have their own interests and shows.

During the occupation the Channel Islands were practically depopulated of dogs, and Jersey still has very few Springers, only two having been shown in the last four years. By contrast, in Guernsey there are about 100 Springers, some two-thirds of these being used for shooting only, but there is considerable interest in both showing and working the other third. This is largely due to Mr F. C. A. Church, whom we remember here as a Springer owner and field trial supporter before the last war.

The Jersey and Guernsey Dog Clubs operate separately, but with a happy spirit of co-operation; both are affiliated to the English Kennel Club. Three open shows are held in each island in the spring and autumn, but there is no championship show. Sanction and members' shows are also held. Jersey excludes Champions from competition, and to be eligible to compete at a show in either island dogs must have been in the Channel Islands at least two months before the date of closing of entries.

In 1948 Mr Church bred Mutali Flicker (Replica of Ranscombe ex Dinsdale Bijou) and showed her for some years, later giving her to Mr E. W. Hunt who continued to show and win with her: in 1952 Mr Church bred Mutali Fly (Simon of Vallon ex Dinsdale Bijou) but has kept her entirely as his shooting dog.

Fired by Mr Church's enthusiasm for the English Springer, Mr Hunt added Lady of Karberlee (Bramhope Bellboy of Empshot ex Banzai of Bramhope). This bitch he mated to Whaddon Chase Granger, and puppies known as Balm, Bloom and Basil of le Jaonnett are now winning well in the ownerships of Mrs F. S. Roussel and Mrs L. V. Firth respectively.

Recent importations have been Silverbirch of Stubham (Ch. Alexander of Stubham ex Hawkhill Bella Donna) by Mr D. Tosterin, Bostonian of Bramhope (Am.Ch. Melilotus Shooting Star ex Blakarstan of Bramhope) by Mr T. W. Oliver and Whaddon Chase Granger (Ch. Whaddon Chase Prince ex Ch. Whaddon Chase Grouse) owned by Mr H. J. Renarf.

These Channel Island owners are keen enough to fly to shows in England. No field trials are held in the islands, which, considering their small area, is understandable.

Chapter VIII

JUDGING AND STEWARDING

JUDGING

'IT IS most important for a judge, both for his own peace of
mind and for the quality of his decisions, that he should not
worry about them. He should do his very best to get them right,
but, having done so and delivered his judgements, he should
not be tormented about their correctness. A judge should be
able to make up his mind and, having done so, he should give
his decisions and go to the theatre.'

Mr Henry Cecil in *Alibi for a Judge*

The time will usually come when the exhibitor, having served
his noviciate as an owner and breeder and shown successfully for
some time, will begin to be recognised as having knowledge and
experience of Springers sufficient to warrant his being invited to
judge the breed. He will probably be put on the English Springer
Spaniel Club list of judges for open shows and in due course may
be asked to officiate at a small show, at which perhaps some three
or four classes for Springers are scheduled.

The secretaries of all breed clubs have a list of judges approved
by the club, and if approached by the secretary of a show for the
name of a judge are able to send a copy of the club list from which
a judge may be selected. Frequently clubs make a rule that they
will give support to a show, in the shape of special prizes and/or
guarantees for classes, if a judge is chosen from their official list.
In addition to this list club secretaries have a further list of judges
their committees have approved for championship shows. The
Kennel Club also issues its own list of approved judges for championship shows in every breed. It does not always follow that these
two lists are identical. A club committee may not always approve
all the names on the Kennel Club list and then the remedy
is in its hands, as the club secretaries are empowered by their
committees not to offer special prizes or guarantee classes if
the judge proposed is not on their list. This is the case with the
English Springer Spaniel Club for both ordinary and championship shows and their lists are very carefully compiled and then
revised at regular intervals.

As a general rule a person must have judged during a period of five years before he is approved by the Kennel Club to judge at a championship show and award Challenge Certificates. The secretary of every show at which Challenge Certificates are to be awarded has to submit a list to the Kennel Club of the proposed judges in every breed, and these names are considered by the Kennel Club Shows Regulation Committee. If the name is already on the Kennel Club list approval is automatic, unless the person concerned has judged the breed within six months previous to the date of the show, as no one is allowed to award Challenge Certificates in the same breed twice within six months. If the name is not on the Kennel Club list, that body sends the proposed judge a questionnaire, asking for a list of the names of all the dogs he has bred and/or owned, which have qualified for entry in the *Kennel Club Stud Book*, a further list of other dogs bred and/or owned by him, giving names and registration numbers, the names and dates of all shows at which he has judged the breed, with number of classes and number of entries and, in addition, the names and dates of shows at which he has judged any breed. He is further required to state: (1) if he is on any club list of judges and if so he must give the names of the clubs; (2) if he has ever received reward or expenses for preparing dogs for show; if so, details must be given; (3) if he has ever handled any dogs other than his own at a show and if so he must give the registered names of such dogs and say whether he has received any reward or expenses; (4) if employed at the time of the questionnaire in any kennel and if so he must give full particulars; (5) if he owns or takes any part in management of a dog shop; and, again, if this is the case, full particulars must be given.

This questionnaire, however, will cover five years in the future when a novice Springer judge takes his first step into the middle of the ring, and during those years he should be able to gain much experience and confidence.

The quotation at the head of this chapter is full of wisdom. All who have read Mr Henry Cecil's books, with their delightfully whimsical humour, will know that under the amusing situations he devises for his characters and with which he sometimes develops his plots there is much common sense, and this paragraph certainly gives serious and most sensible advice to our newcomer to the centre of the ring. If he will take it he should feel satisfied with what he has done during the course of his judging, be prepared to uphold his judgement against criticism that may be levelled at it, and afterwards refuse to allow himself to worry.

It is fatal to go into the ring to judge without an absolutely definite idea of what you want in a Springer. It results in what I call 'here and there' judging—one dog put up for one specially good point, a second for another good point, a third for something else that attracts and so on. In the end the prize-winners in the middle of the ring are just a mixed assortment.

Think carefully of the standard for the breed and then think of the Springer, among all those that you know, that conforms most closely to that standard and affords you the most satisfaction in looking at it, and then add good movement as an essential: finally add quality above all else. You will have seen many Springers by the time you are first invited to judge, and probably have decided on one in particular that is nearest to your ideal. Keep that Springer in your mind's eye and pick as many dogs as you can of that type, then consider each one of them in detail and place them according to how near your ideal they come.

From the day I first judged Springers, right up to the present time, when I go into a ring I have the picture of my first dog Ranger before me mentally. I hope always to find his equal—I never have found one that satisfied me so completely, but I still hope, and I put up the Springers that satisfy me most. His quality was so great that he glowed with it, and his head and expression were perfect. Those few people remaining now who knew him still talk of him as a really beautiful Springer and I endeavour to judge to that ideal.

Sometimes a dog will come into the ring who has no fault on which you can pick specially, if judged strictly by the club standard, yet the whole effect is 'common'. It has no quality, and though its head is the right shape and it has a good body and legs and feet and moves properly, it is not a dog of whom you could honestly say (as one has to do in signing a Challenge Certificate) that you consider it worthy of the title of Champion or even feel that it will do the breed any good, and this simply and solely because it had a common look. Quality, I feel, matters almost more than anything else, and I would rather put up a dog with a fault than one lacking quality. Consider movement carefully, and if other things are equal decide finally on the dogs that move best, the dogs with straight action in front, and plenty of drive behind—no pin toes, no cow hocks and no hackney action —and then if they have real quality, in addition to the other merits you see in them, give them their places as the winners.

To the beginner, as a judge, I say most emphatically, Get the exhibitors to move their dogs on a loose leash. You cannot judge movement if the dog is strung-up and almost 'conveyed' across the ring on a stranglehold. In judging movement it is important to see not only the action as the dog moves towards and away from you, but also as you see him from the side. I recommend that you ask each handler to take his dog across the ring diagonally from the corner in which you are standing, then across the top of the ring and back, and finally to return to you. You can move a few paces from your corner to watch the side movement, and back to your corner to see the front action.

I shall hope that as a novice exhibitor you have trained your own dogs to stand in the ring without being held by head and tail, and that you will now, as a judge, wish to see the dogs shown under you standing naturally. You will realise that you can see the outline right through from nose to tail if no hand is put over the muzzle or under the throat. If exhibitors insist on holding a dog in a particular way the judge gets the impression that they may be trying to hide a fault—lack of breadth, or depth of fore-face, or throatiness, perhaps. It may not be so, but it puts the idea into the judge's mind and he looks to see if the fault it suggests to him actually exists.

It is much harder to judge a class of poor dogs than a class of good ones. In some small shows, with perhaps a number of local and novice exhibitors, one sometimes gets a class where one feels that the only thing to do is to pick out the dogs with the least faults. That is all one can do, and then, as Mr Cecil says, make your decisions and do not be tormented about their correctness.

Temperament should carry quite a lot of weight. In the U.S.A. there is a definite Kennel Club rule that no bad-tempered dog shall be placed in the awards, and shyness and nervousness, except in the case of puppies, are also penalised. A Springer which is at all vicious is useless as a gundog to take shooting in company, as it may pick a quarrel with another dog or behave badly with other members of the party than its owner. Equally, a dog that snaps when a judge attempts to handle it has a nature so utterly alien to Springer character that it should not be included in the awards. Bad temperaments breed bad temperaments, just as a nervous disposition reappears in future generations, and so, if you find this bad temper or nervousness in a dog in the ring, you must think very, very carefully before giving it a place among the winners.

'A good horse cannot be a bad colour' is a very sound axiom, and a novice judge must not be led away by flashy markings— these certainly make a dog noticeable as it stands in the ring, and the judge, however experienced, instinctively looks at it a first, second or even a third time unless it is obviously faulty. It may, of course, be a very good dog and then any place given it is justified, but beware the 'flatcatcher' dog! Very often a dog with an almost all brown or black head and body is dismissed as not typical. The conventionally marked Springer with an attractive blaze is so easy to pick out, and the good points of the head are so quickly estimated, but anyone who has had much to do with a dark-faced Springer will know how charming and how good these heads can be; indeed, some of these are very often among the best-headed ones in the breed.

Among Springers there must never be any 'colour bar'. Whatever the personal preference of a judge it must never be given any weight in the ring. Liver and white; liver, white and tan; black and white; or the tri-colour (black, white and tan), should all be considered equally by a judge. Make and shape, movement, temperament and quality must be the deciding factors. The only colour not allowed is the red and white of the Welsh Springer.

Finally, be patient with your exhibitors, particularly those who are obviously novices, and give them a second or even a third opportunity to show the dog's movement if it is clear that lack of experience on the part of either the dog or the handler is spoiling their chances. Do not handle a dog without a preliminary pat and word to it, and do let the owner open its mouth for you to see the teeth. Although water and towel are provided on the table in the ring, you cannot rinse your hands between the examination of each dog, and to have owners do this is such an easy way in which to prevent the possible spread of infection.

When you have picked out the dogs you think you will want for your final decision, be kind in your dismissal of the others. It takes very little longer to say, 'Thank you, I shall not want you again in this class,' than a curt, 'Finished with you,' as I have sometimes heard, and it makes a lot of difference to the feelings of the beginner who has perhaps brought his cherished ewe-lamb out for the first time.

After making your final decision on your winners, place your four dogs in order from left to right, with the first-prize winner at the top, and keep to this placing through all your classes. If sometimes you start from right to left and in another class reverse the order from left to right, as I saw happen at a recent championship show, the onlookers at the ringside will be left guessing, and the exhibitors will certainly be left in suspense until the cards are in their hands.

One hears criticisms sometimes from ringsiders, and also perhaps from disappointed exhibitors, of a judge who puts up a dog bred from one of his own dogs or bitches, or with a great deal of his breeding in its pedigree, but such judging is understandable, for he has presumably bred a type he likes and so naturally picks out dogs of the same type, even though they may be two, three or more generations from those of his actual breeding.

The ringsider will also at times criticise a judge's placings, but it is only when one actually handles a dog that one realises all its good points (and sometimes the bad points too!).

If all judges judged alike there would soon be an end to dog shows.

And so I come back to Mr Henry Cecil's very wise advice at the head of this chapter: if you follow this you must go home satisfied and content.

STEWARDING

Good stewards are essential to the success of a show and to keep the classes running smoothly, so that there is no delay for the judge at any point in the proceedings. Two stewards are necessary for every ring.

An early arrival at the show is important, so that the steward can go to the secretary's office, obtain his catalogue, the ring-numbers and the award-cards. If information has been received by the secretary that any dog or dogs will be absent this will be reported to the stewards so that they can mark their catalogues accordingly and not spend the time seeking on the benches for dogs that are definitely not to be found there.

The steward should next go to his ring and check that all

necessary equipment is ready: a table, three or four chairs behind it in such a position that the spectators will not assume that they are for general use, a bowl of water and towel for the judge's use, a card for award-slips, award-board, chalk and duster. If it is an outdoor show he must then ascertain the whereabouts of his wet-weather ring and visit it so that he knows exactly where it is and can ensure that no time is lost in getting his exhibitors to it if it has to be used from the start, or if a hurried change to it has to be made in case of a sudden downpour.

I always think that one steward should be in the ring before the judge arrives in order to introduce himself, if he does not already know the judge, as may be the case if he is stewarding for a breed other than his own. If the judge is known it is pleasant to have a few words with him, and in either case the steward must tell the judge of any dogs that he knows will be absent, so that he can mark his judging book accordingly.

One steward should have visited the benches and checked the dogs off in his catalogue, making a note of any dogs that the owner or other exhibitors tell him will be absent, and before the time for the start of judging a steward should again visit the benches, make a final check and announce in a *loud* voice that judging of the first class will begin, and that all dogs for it must be taken to the ring.

Novice exhibitors are often at a loss as to how to find their ring and are grateful for instructions from the steward, while old exhibitors are sometimes so busy giving finishing touches to their dogs or exchanging news with other friends in the breed that they do not notice the call to the ring and have to be 'woken up'. It must be admitted that these offenders are comparatively few, but, as it is a steward's duty to see that all dogs are taken into the ring, the dawdlers must be rounded up.

When the exhibits for the first class enter the ring their handlers must be given their ring-numbers and be checked off in the steward's catalogue. If exhibitors would realise what a help it can be to the stewards, and what a lot of time is saved by their knowing their numbers and being able to ask for them without the steward's having to ask their name and that of the dog, and then look them up in the catalogue, I am sure they would all take this very little extra trouble.

It must not be forgotten that it is a steward's duty to see that all the dogs in the breed for which he is responsible are brought into the ring, if present in the show. If an exhibit is missing, the steward must visit the benches. If it is there, but its owner is absent, he must take the dog to the ring and see that it is shown; if both dog and exhibitor are not to be found, the judge must be informed, and the dog marked as absent from the class.

Once the first class is in the ring the judge must be told that it is ready for him, but usually the judge will himself be waiting and probably be noticing the dogs as they arrive. The steward must see, if the judge wishes to move the whole class round the ring, that the dogs are well spread out, using the whole space available. After that the steward can retire to the table and wait until the judge has picked his winners and is ready to make his final decisions. Then he should come forward, stand behind the judge with the award-cards in his hand ready to give them out and, as he hands the cards, he should call the number of the dog, so that the ringsiders can mark their catalogues—it is not always easy for everyone round the ring to see the exhibitors' numbers.

One steward should then write the numbers on the awards-board, attach one of the judging slips to the award-card, and place the other in his award-clip ready to be collected by the office: he must be sure, too, to see that the judge has initialled all award-slips.

When the second class is called the steward, after giving out the number-cards for the new dogs, must see that they are all together on one side of the ring and that the dogs from the previous class, who are also in this class, are in the correct order of their placings and are well away on the other side of the ring, leaving plenty of room for the judge to move his new exhibits.

This procedure must be followed throughout all the succeeding classes.

A steward should never go to a show without a specially ruled card—a stiff piece of cardboard on which it will be easy to write as he stands. This should be marked across the top 1, 2, 3, Res., V.H.C. and on the left the class numbers, and name of each class, written downwards. (See table, p. 112.)

As each class is judged the steward fills in the numbers of the winning exhibits, and afterwards crosses through every number in it which has been beaten by an exhibit in another class. By the end of the judging the steward can see at a glance which dogs remain unbeaten, and can give their numbers to the judge if he wants them brought into the ring to compare with his final, or top-class, winners.

Class		1	2	3	Res.	V.H.C.	V.H.C.	H.C.
55 Puppy	D	87	~~83~~	~~91~~	~~99~~	~~93~~	94	~~72~~
56 Novice	D	~~83~~	~~96~~	~~89~~	~~108~~	77	~~91~~	
57 Under Graduate	D	104	~~88~~	~~83~~	~~89~~	~~106~~	77	
58 Minor Limit	D	~~110~~	~~116~~	~~83~~	~~89~~	~~106~~	~~93~~	
59 Limit	D	112	~~110~~	~~116~~	~~88~~	~~106~~		
60 Open	D	112	~~117~~	~~116~~	~~101~~	~~88~~		
61 Puppy	B	80	~~82~~	~~95~~	~~107~~	~~76~~		
62 Novice	B	~~82~~	~~103~~	~~109~~	~~95~~	~~107~~	~~76~~	
63 Under Graduate	B	~~104~~	~~111~~	~~103~~	~~81~~	~~107~~		
64 Minor Limit	B	127	~~124~~	~~126~~	~~111~~	~~103~~		
65 Limit	B	~~84~~	~~97~~	~~126~~	114	~~111~~		
66 Open	B	86	~~84~~	~~97~~	~~126~~	~~114~~ ~~124~~		

In the example given the steward sees that there are three un-beaten dogs and three unbeaten bitches that have not met, and he can give the judge these numbers and the classes, should he ask for them and wish to have them brought into the ring when deciding on his Best of Sex and Best of Breed.

There is no actual 'right' to challenge for the certificate at a championship show. The judge can, if he wishes, ask for any exhibit to be brought into the ring and can then give the certifi-cate to whichever dog he pleases and, in the same way, can make the award of the Reserve Best of Sex as he likes. Should the winner of the Open Class be passed over for the certificate, he may be awarded the Reserve Certificate for Best of Sex, or it may go to any other unbeaten dog who has not met the Challenge Certificate winner. The steward should be most careful to know what dogs in the lower classes are unbeaten. In one instance the steward, without being asked by the judge, erroneously told him that there was no unbeaten dog except the winner of the Dog Open Class and accordingly that dog was given the Challenge Certificate. After the bitch classes were over the steward informed

F.T.Ch. Willy of
Barnacre
(winner of the
Kennel Club
Spaniel Cham-
pionship 1959)

(*C. M. Cooke*)

F.T.Ch.
Markdown Muffin
(winner of the
Kennel Club
Spaniel Cham-
pionship 1962)

(*C. M. Cooke*)

(*C. G. Goodall*)

T. J. Greatorex with (from left to right) F.T.Ch. Spurt O'Vara, F.T.Ch. Spark O'Vara and F.T.Ch. Sarkie O'Vara

(*C. M. Cooke*)

F.T.Ch. Streonshalh Comet retrieving to handler Mr J. Chudley

the judge that there were two unbeaten bitches besides the Open Class winner and he was told to bring them into the ring. The owner of a young unbeaten dog asked why, if unbeaten bitches were asked for, his dog was not, and was told by the judge that the steward had informed him that the Open Class dog was the only unbeaten one, otherwise he would have wanted to see this dog. Had the steward kept a chart this could not have occurred. Of course it is the responsibility of the judge to know what dogs are unbeaten, but with a very large entry and a number of classes, perhaps eighteen or twenty at a big show, a judge may overlook an early winner—it is the steward's business to help a judge in this matter, *if asked*.

Another thing about which a steward must be absolutely sure before he gives out the award-cards is the judge's placings. I once saw a steward give out the cards from the wrong end. The judge had in all previous classes placed her winners from right to left, and in this class, saying, 'These are my winners,' turned to write some notes at the table. The steward, apparently thinking that the dog at the right, which was smaller than the other three, could not possibly be the one the judge had placed first, gave the cards out from left to right. In the next class the small dog was still placed at the right-hand end and again the steward went to the left. The judge was watching this time and exclaimed, 'But my winner is the same as in the last class, No. ——. Explanations followed and some disappointed exhibitors had to give their award-cards back.

Stewarding is always interesting. One sees the dogs at close quarters and, being able to stand at vantage points in the ring, which one cannot do when seated at the ringside, it is possible to watch movement and see how the dogs look as the judge handles them. It may be a first step towards occupying the ring as a judge, for stewarding can well serve as an apprenticeship to judging. A good exercise is to note the numbers of the dogs you think best and then, after the judge has made his final placings, see how yours compare with those of an experienced judge.

Finally, be patient with, and courteous to, the exhibitors and kindly and helpful to the obvious novices. Do not sweep the unsuccessful exhibitors out of the ring with a curt word—I have seen this done—but remember they are probably disappointed, and a pleasant dismissal may give them courage to try another time.

H

Chapter IX

THE KENNEL CLUB AND CRUFT'S

The Kennel Club

THE first dog show ever held in England was at Newcastle, in 1859, with two classes, one for Pointers and one for Setters, with thirty-six and twenty-three entries respectively; later the same year another show was held at Birmingham, where classes were provided for Pointers, Setters, Retrievers, Clumber and Cocker Spaniels and some few other breeds, but it was not until 1873 that the Kennel Club was founded after a number of shows had been held during the preceding fifteen years. By then it was felt that definite rules were needed, with a governing body to control the conduct of shows and to insist that they were carried on on satisfactory lines. Mr S. E. Shirley, M.P., was the founder and first chairman, a committee was formed and the first Kennel Club Show was held at the Crystal Palace. A stud book was published, containing the pedigrees of the winning dogs at the most important shows held till then—4,027 dogs in forty breeds—a code of rules for shows, and the manner in which field trials should be conducted; altogether a monumental work, for those times, of 600 pages. One particular rule stated that dogs could not be exhibited at any show held under Kennel Club approval unless it was registered under a definite name at the Kennel Club, though it was not till 1900 that feeling against the bad conduct of unrecognised shows resulted in the decision that dogs shown at unrecognised shows would be disqualified from exhibition at any show recognised by the Kennel Club. In 1904 all shows, with the exception of hound shows, had to have Kennel Club recognition and a set of rules was formulated for shows. These, generally, are considered to work very satisfactorily, and they certainly militate against sharp practices, as fewer cases seem to come before the Kennel Club Disciplinary Sub-Committee every year.

Last year 1,985 shows were held under Kennel Club rules and very few complaints were brought before the committee.

As stated earlier, before a dog can be shown it must be registered under a distinctive name and that name, once accepted by the Kennel Club, cannot be used again for another dog for ten years. If a dog, by virtue of its winning (a first, second or third in Limit, Open or Field Trial Class at a championship show, or a Certificate of Merit or higher award at a field trial), is given a stud-book number, that name can never be used again, even by the addition of the new owner's prefix. At one time the purchaser of a dog already registered at the Kennel Club could change its name to whatever other name he liked, even if it bore the previous owner's registered prefix, so that considerable confusion could arise if a stud dog's name were changed after he had already sired pups, or a bitch's after she had had a litter. Son of Merry might become Happy Sportsman and a bitch called Sporting Echo might become Duskie Delight. Now, the only alteration that can be made in a name is the addition of the new owner's prefix, and for this a fee of £5 is charged, and the addition, of course, is conditional on the name not being already in the stud book.

The necessary form for registering a dog can be obtained from the Kennel Club, 1–4 Clarges Street, London, W.1, and should be carefully completed, giving four names in order of preference, the names of parents and grand-parents, with their stud-book numbers, or, if not in the stud book, their registration numbers and the signature of the breeder as well as the owner, should he not be the breeder. If desired a litter registration form can be used if all the puppies in a litter are being registered; this saves quite a lot of writing. A fee of 50p. must accompany the form for each dog to be registered, if applied for by the breeder; if sent in by any other person the fee is £1·50 for each dog.

If the breeder's declaration is not signed, the fee for registration is £2. Increases in the registration fees tend to encourage the registration of each generation in the first case and certainly discourages the use of non-pedigree stock in the second case.

The registration card received from the Kennel Club should be kept carefully, and if the dog is sold should be handed to the purchaser, together with a transfer-of-ownership form, duly signed by the seller. This form has to be completed by the new owner and sent to the Kennel Club with a fee of £1 and the dog cannot be shown in its new ownership until this transfer is recorded, though if the purchaser wants to show the dog and entries for the show close before the transfer card is received the show entry may be made with T.A.F. (transfer applied for) after the name, just as if the registration card has not been received the entry may be made with N.A.F. (name applied for) after the name.

When one considers that, in March 1972 alone, applications for 15,229 registrations were received and that each one has to be checked in the vast card-index system at the Kennel Club, it can be understood that cards cannot be expected by return of post.

Should a special word or name, known as a prefix or affix, be desired, for the sole use of one person, application must be made to the Kennel Club, and after the proposed word has been advertised in the *Kennel Gazette* if no objection is made by any other prefix-holder it is granted on payment of a fee of £3 plus a maintenance fee of £1 per annum. This maintenance fee may be compounded by a single payment of £7.

Should a person for any reason decide that he wishes the name under which he has registered a dog to remain unchanged—that is that no prefix or affix other than his own should be added—the Kennel Club charges an extra 50p fee, while if a stud-book entry is desired, other than that obtained by a win at a show or a field trial, for which no charge is made, the fee is again 50p.

The Kennel Club will also make further special restrictions on a registration if desired. Should a dog be sold on condition that it should not be shown, or that its puppies should not be shown, or that it should not be bred from, the registration card must be sent to the Kennel Club and will be marked accordingly. It is much better to have this done than to leave it to a 'gentleman's agreement'. It is surprising how often these 'gentleman's agreements' can go wrong.

Another service which the Kennel Club will undertake is the registration of the loan of a bitch for breeding purposes. It may be that you would like to breed from a bitch owned by someone else, or that you yourself would be willing to lend a bitch for breeding; this can be recorded at the Kennel Club for a fee of £1.

While dealing with this I would draw attention to the question of parting with a bitch on breeding terms. These can be exactly what the two parties agree to make them. Very generally they may be that the bitch goes to the second party on condition that a certain number of the puppies in the first, or in the first and second, litter should be taken by the owner of the bitch and that he shall be the breeder of the puppies, the ownership of the bitch passing to the second party when the conditions agreed upon are fulfilled.

Provision should be made in the agreement for the possibility of there being only one puppy, a very unusual occurrence with Springers, nevertheless one to which thought should be given. The method of picking the puppies should also be agreed upon. Very often this is pick and pick about, the owner having the first choice.

An export pedigree is required for any registered dog going abroad. This the Kennel Club will issue, together with a transfer form made out to the name of the new owner. An export pedigree for a dog going to the United States of America must be sent with it; to all other countries it can go with other documents through the post. If a bitch is mated before being despatched abroad it is desirable to ascertain whether a Stud Service Certificate and a copy of the dog's pedigree are also required.

A veterinary surgeon's certificate of health is required for dogs being exported. A recently made Kennel Club rule prohibits the exhibition of any dog which is a monorchid or cryptorchid, and since this rule was passed any dog suffering from this condition must have what is called a certificate re mono or cryptorchidism, signed by the veterinary surgeon at the time he completes the export bill of health, if it is being sent abroad. Without it no export pedigree will be issued by the Kennel Club.

The fee charged by the Kennel Club for an export pedigree is £2·50 for all countries except France and Germany, where special information as to colours, markings and registration details are demanded, and then additional fees may be payable.

The Kennel Club controls the definition of certain classes at shows, and the exact conditions under which dogs may enter for each class are given in the schedules issued by every show secretary, so there is no need to detail them here. The qualifications for the different classes vary according to the type of show.

The four types of shows are as follows:

The championship show, either general or specialist, where Challenge Certificates are offered. There are about twenty-three general shows at which any number of breeds are scheduled, and the specialist shows are usually run by a club or society for its own breed only. English Springers have Challenge Certificates offered at twenty-one general shows and at two specialist shows, those of the English Springer Spaniel Club and of the Midland English Springer Spaniel Club.

The open show is one where there is no restriction as to exhibitors or area from which they come; conditions are similar to those of a championship show but there are no Challenge Certificates.

A limited show is one where only members of the club or society organising it can show and are restricted to a limited number of classes.

A sanction show is limited to a maximum of twenty classes, to members of the club or society organising it, and it has certain restrictions on the entry of dogs that have won prizes previously.

A match is a meeting arranged for dogs owned by members of a club or society, or between two clubs or societies, where each dog is given a number and dogs are drawn against each other in pairs in the first round, the winner of the pair going into the second round on another draw, this process continuing until all the dogs but the last two are eliminated. The best of this final pair is declared the winner of the match.

An exemption show is one held in aid of some charitable object and at which, by special Kennel Club permission, the dogs exhibited need not be registered at the Kennel Club, though there is no restriction on registered dogs competing. There can only be four regular classes, such as Any Variety Gundog, Any Variety Terrier, Any Variety Non-sporting and Any Variety Toy, or any variation of these that the promoters wish. In addition, a number of extra classes may be allowed, such as Prettiest Puppy, Best Conditioned Dog, etc., and entries are usually accepted up to the time of the beginning of the show.

There are four advisory councils which meet to discuss various aspects of the show, field trial, obedience and working sections of the dog world.

The Kennel Club Liaison Council is an advisory body which can send recommendations on show matters to the Kennel Club Show Regulation Committee. Until a few years ago representatives were sent to it from most of the show societies, but the number grew so large that the council became unwieldy, and now the country is divided into areas with three representatives for Scotland, one for Northern Ireland, and twenty-five for England

and Wales. In addition there are five group representatives and two championship-show representatives.

The Obedience Council and the Working Trials Council are formed by representatives from societies interested in these sides of dog activities and send recommendations to the Working Trials and Obedience Committee. Very few Springers seem to take part in these tests.

The Kennel Club controls all field trial activities, as it does those for shows. Dogs must be registered before they can run at a field trial and all trials are held under Kennel Club rules. The Field Trial Council came into being in 1923 largely through the good offices of Mr Lewis D. Wigan, and now every field trial society sends a delegate to the Field Trial Council meeting held at the Kennel Club about March each year. The agenda consists of items which must have been passed at either the Annual General Meeting or at a committee meeting of the society in whose name it appears, and the delegate of that society must be present to propose and speak for it, otherwise it cannot be considered. As with the other councils, the Field Trial Council sits in an entirely advisory capacity and only items on the agenda that are duly seconded and passed at council meetings can go forward as recommendations to the Kennel Club Field Trial Committee, which will accept them or not as they deem best. If accepted they are added to the Kennel Club Field Trial rules.

In 1950 The Kennel Club accepted a proposal that eleven members of the Field Trial Council should sit on the Kennel Club Field Trial Committee, and now two representatives for Pointers and Setters, five for Retrievers and four for Spaniels sit on that committee. They are elected annually by the Field Trial Council.

The Kennel Club grants the title of Champion to any dog who has won three Challenge Certificates under three different judges, but in the case of gundogs a qualifying certificate, obtained at a field trial, is required before it can assume the title. Any dog who has won an award in actual competition at a field trial can assume the title of Champion directly it wins a third Challenge Certificate. Since 1958 gundogs winning three Challenge Certificates are allowed the title of Show Champion.

The title of Field Trial Champion is given to a Springer winning two open stakes for Any Variety Spaniel at trials at which a win qualifies a dog to run at the Kennel Club Spaniel

Championship. The Spaniel winning the Spaniel Championship takes the title of Field Trial Champion.

CRUFT'S SHOW

For gundog people Cruft's Show is different from any other championship show in that on the day that gundogs are exhibited not only the regular show exhibitors are there in larger numbers than at any other show, but it is the only one to which shooting men, field trial enthusiasts, gundog trainers and gamekeepers from all parts of the country come, as well as many visitors from overseas.

At Olympia, as in the days when the show was at the Agricultural Hall, all the leading game food manufacturers and pheasant-egg farms and hatcheries have stands where owners of shoots and head keepers can place their orders for the coming breeding season, and this is the reason for so many of them coming to Cruft's. It is held just after the end of the shooting season and before work on the rearing field starts, and it is a real day out for keepers, who also have their own classes for gundogs, arranged by Mr P. A. Gouldbury, the secretary of the Gamekeepers' Association.

The origin of Cruft's Dog Show is for many of the present generation shrouded in the mists of time. Mr Charles Cruft was assistant and traveller to Mr James Spratt, who began to manufacture dog biscuits in 1860, and he first took an interest in shows when he had to arrange for the show benching which Spratt's had added to their other activities. He organised a show for Terriers in 1880 and a series of further shows in the years that followed, but it was not until 1891 that he formed Cruft's Dog Show Society and held the first 'Cruft's Great Dog Show' at the Agricultural Hall for all breeds of dogs. At this show there were 2,500 entries and 2,000 dogs. All the different varieties of Spaniels were entered simply as Spaniels, and Springers were not classified until the Kennel Club gave them separate registration in 1902.

Cruft's Show continued with a break of only three years, 1918–20, and when Charles Cruft died in 1938 Miss Hardingham, his secretary, organised and ran the 1939 event, which was the last held at the Agricultural Hall under the Cruft banner. After the last war the Kennel Club took over the Cruft's Dog Show Society and as the show had completely outgrown the Agricultural Hall it was transferred to Olympia, where it has been held ever since. Up to 1917 the show was a three-day event, as were a number of other championship shows. When resumed in 1921 it was for two days only, and puppies were not required to be at the show on the second day. I wonder sometimes, when I see some present-day exhibitors packed up and ready to start off for home at about four o'clock in the afternoon, and grumbling because they have to stay till five o'clock at least (actually eight o'clock at Cruft's, where no early removals are allowed), what they would have said to staying two, let alone three, days. There were, however, some advantages: we could really look at and study one another's dogs on the first day, and on the second day chat with our friends and attend club meetings, without feeling that we were missing seeing many friends who would come to the benches and find us absent as happens now. Life was more leisurely then, and, too, expenses in travelling and putting up for the night were very much less than they are now.

Sometimes at the Agricultural Hall, where ring-space was at a premium, some breeds did not get judged until the second day, though a very strict rule of the Kennel Club was that puppies *must* be judged on the first day. I remember one year, when Springers were still waiting for a ring long after 6 p.m., the appointed judge gave up hope and went home, saying that he would start early the following morning. The owners of puppies who did not want to submit them to the strain of a second day held an impromptu meeting, found that Col. F. H. B. Carrell was at the show and, Kennel Club approval having been obtained, the authorities asked him to judge the puppy classes. This he did and many of us took our puppies home, leaving the prize-cards, if we had been lucky enough to win any, over the empty benches. The next morning the original judge arrived, judged what puppies were there, mostly those of exhibitors from a long distance who could not get home and back, and a second set of prize-cards went up over the benches. This meant another telephone call to the Kennel Club. Colonel Carrell's awards were upheld, as of course they had to be, for the Kennel Club had to keep its own rules about the attendance of puppies. This was a great disappointment for the owners of the morning winners, but their puppies had already been in the ring the evening before and not succeeded, and with many puppies absent the competition was very different.

In the early years, when Cruft's Show was resumed after World War I, Springers, in spite of big entries, were often treated very much as the poor relations of the gundog world. On one occasion, having no hope of getting a ring by late on the first evening, we took our dogs up into one of the galleries where we improvised a ring. The Horse Show was following Cruft's within a day or two, and stalls for the horses were being built in this gallery. Every few minutes judging was suspended while great baulks of timber were carried across the 'ring' by men who were working to a schedule to get their work done, and who were not at all pleased or interested in seeing our dogs. This, of course, was not the only time when we were forced to find a corner for Springers to be judged, but in view of the huge entries in very many breeds from the 1920s onward it was a masterpiece of organisation that so many rings could be available at any one time. How, I wonder, would present-day exhibitors of Springers, with the big rings at Olympia and the great tented shows, react to the difficulties we took almost in our stride and certainly with very little grumbling?

At Cruft's, in the Agricultural Hall days, one saw the best and the worst Springers in the country; for, situated as it was right in the east of London and advertised as no other show had ever been, it struck the imagination of the one-dog and the pet-dog owner and they were proud to say, 'I showed my Springer at Cruft's.' It did not matter that it had not won—to have been shown at Cruft's was the distinction.

On the Saturday evening, when admission was reduced to a shilling, it seemed as if the whole of East London was pouring into the show, and Springers attracted so much attention that movement along the gangways between their benches was almost impossible. Now that Cruft's is held at Olympia, Springers always have a good entry and a big ring, and the judging is watched by crowds of very interested spectators, including, as I said earlier, many shooting men, trainers and keepers. I wish very much that some of them who own quite good-looking Springers would take courage and show them, particularly those who own Springers which have won a prize or Certificate of Merit at trials, and so could enter them in the Field Trial Class. With all the working Springers there are in the country it is sad that in the last few years seven is the highest entry we have had in this class, and for the last two or three years there have been only twos and threes.

I do know, however, that at one Cruft's Show some very discouraging remarks were made on dogs in this class by the judges, who completely ignored any good points and emphasised the bad ones, and so discouraged the field trial owners that they vowed never to enter a dog at a show again. Equally, I know, show dogs get unfavourable comments made on them, at some trials, for being too big and slow. The great need is for much more effort to be made to find a happy mean between the two types.

As from 1st January 1973, the Kennel Club is introducing a completely new scale of charges which concern breeders, purchasers of stock and the Secretaries of Canine Societies. This text has been amended to suit the new scales but owing to administrative changes at the Kennel Club, breeders and others are recommended to consult the complete scale of fees as detailed on page five of the July 1972 issue of the *Kennel Gazette*. This is published monthly by the Kennel Club and is really the only method of keeping up to date with all the changes which concern the administration of canine affairs. The current price is 20p. per copy but it is better to apply to the Kennel Club for annual subscription rates. These increases are a revision of the new scales introduced in January 1971.

The Kennel Club has recognised the problems arising from breeding with stock affected by hereditary diseases and in consultation with the British Veterinary Association has established a joint scheme for the certification of freedom from Hip Dysplasia, Hereditary Cataract and Progressive Retinal Atrophy (PRA). The latter disease leads to complete blindness but in the earlier stages the dog shows signs of difficulty of seeing in the dark. Many breeders are taking advantage of these schemes and the prospective buyer would be well advised to check that a puppy has been bred from 'certified' parents.

I.B.H.

Chapter X

THE WORKING SPRINGER

SELECTION AND TRAINING

IN ENGLAND the same name is used for the working Springer and the show Springer. Both own authentic Springer pedigrees, although during the last twenty-five years they have developed on distinctly different lines, but in the pedigrees of forty or fifty years ago all go back to the same strains: Denne, Rivington, Beech-grove, Aqualate, Caistor, Foel and Tissington. Yet now, in looks, size and style often they are worlds apart.

This I regret, and I could wish that the show owners would have the courage to mate their bitches with a field trial dog and, similarly, that the field trial owners would use, just once, a show mating, so that the big, handsome but slow show dog could breed pups with something of the keen intelligence, quick movement and style of the trial dog, or, on the other side, so that the small, very often plain-headed working dog could acquire a more recognisably Springer appearance.

I am glad to say that in many cases the very small trial dog of pre-war days has disappeared and a number of the leading trial dogs are no disgrace to the breed in head, make and shape. The trouble is, however, that the show-dog owners will not risk breed-ing even one generation that does not have a chance of going right to the top on the bench, while the trial people regard with apprehension the result of breeding with a show dog who has, perhaps, forbears that have not worked. Very few on the show side, and none on the trial side, have had the courage to experi-ment.

English Springers are gundogs and if, generation after genera-tion, they are not given at least some training, the instinct for work will be lost. This is why I am so emphatically in favour of all Springers receiving at least elementary training, even if they cannot work regularly throughout the season. Personally I make no secret of my regret that the Kennel Club has allowed gundogs to take the title of Show Champion, for many exhibitors at shows, who previously made an effort to get their Springers trained up to the very simple standard required for a Qualifying Certificate, are now quite content to accept the Show Champion title.

So little is required to qualify a Springer. The judges must sign a certificate that it will hunt, face cover, is not gun-shy, will retrieve and has a light mouth, but it need not be steady, either to shot or fur or feather, and there is no question of its having to show speed and style.

If the show and trial Springers are too far apart in Springer type, there are very many Springers throughout the country which are kept solely for work, and are often quite good specimens of the breed. Their owners are definitely not interested in shows and would call a day at a show a waste of time, but they have dogs who can certainly give a good account of themselves at a long day's shoot, and it is these dogs who account for the popularity of the breed among sporting people, for the Springer is the gun-dog above all others who can do everything—the handyman or the general servant of the gundog world. It can hunt, put up (often pointing its game first), retrieve, face the thickest of brambles with tremendous courage and swim like an otter.

One cannot ask a Pointer or Setter to do more than point—it is a dog for the wide open spaces of the moors, and nothing is more delightful than to see one staunch on point with its fellow backing it.

The Retriever is a pleasure to watch as it follows at heel or sits at a drive, marking the birds as they fall and then going out to retrieve, ignoring the tempting hare that may get up on its way out or back; but it does not hunt up the game.

The Clumber, of whom we see too few nowadays, is a charming dog. He goes steadily out on his methodical hunt, he retrieves well and will face the thickest briars, but he is not a fast dog by any means. For that reason he is ideal as an 'old gentleman's dog'; the two can spend many happy hours together working quietly on their own, but he is not considered fast enough for general purposes.

The Field Spaniel, unhappily, has practically ceased to exist as a shooting dog; there have been very few at trials since the war. Rothley Bruin, owned by Mr J. B. Taylor and trained and handled by Mr J. MacQueen, Jnr., was a brilliant worker, the only Field Spaniel I have ever seen who could compare with, and who did win stakes in competition with, Springers.

I remember delightful working Sussex Spaniels, early after

World War I, when the Rosehill strain—smallish dogs, with coats of the colour of bracken in autumn with a golden glint—ran at trials and were used for work, but it is many a year since I have seen more than a few used for shooting.

The working and trial Cocker, for which I have the greatest admiration, is a wonderful little dog, though often as far away in appearance from the show Cocker as is the working from the show Springer, but unless it comes of a big strain it cannot retrieve a big hare or pheasant with the ease and speed with which a Springer can do so.

So we come back to the English Springer, the handyman of the gundog breeds, a compact dog who can live quietly and contentedly in the house and takes up little room there or in a car and will do all the work that any shooting man requires.

There can be no question as to the Springer's supremacy in the Spaniel world, when it comes to work. At the Kennel Club Spaniel Championship Field Trials, for many years past English Springers have been the only variety to qualify for the stake for Any Variety Spaniel except Cockers, and the Springers that qualified became so numerous that it was found impossible to test them all adequately in the time available, so that, instead of first, second and third prize-winners at qualifying trials being eligible to run, it was decided that, from the 1960 championship onwards, only first and second prize-winners should be allowed to compete, thus making the competition even more keen.

The newcomer who decides on a Springer, and that he wants a dog for work and/or field trials rather than for shows, if he has friends who own Springers over which they shoot, should watch their dogs at work, ask their advice as to good working strains, endeavour to see some of the professional trainers with the dogs they are preparing for the shooting season, and then study the pedigrees and records of the strains that consistently produce Springers which, generation after generation, are keen workers, dogs that have intelligence, courage to face the thickest of covert, enjoy retrieving, have tender mouths and good noses, are quick and stylish and, above all, are 'kind'—that is, have a desire to please.

To elaborate these points I feel I cannot do better than to quote the words of that great owner of Springers in the past, Mr William Arkwright, on whose Sutton Scarsdale estate in Derbyshire the very first Spaniel trial ever held was run in 1899 by the

Sporting Spaniel Society. They appear in the preface he wrote for Mr H. W. Carlton's book *Spaniels, Their Breaking for Sport and Field Trials*, in 1915, from which I am kindly allowed to quote by Mr Wilson Stephens, editor of *The Field*, which published the book.

Mr Arkwright starts by reminding us of the old French proverb, '*Bon chien chasse de Race*'—the good dog comes from hunting stock. He insists that the pup should have a first-rate dam —one that excels in natural talent and one who is the favourite shooting companion of her master. He is sure that a man who values his bitch's working abilities so highly will be certain to choose a sire of outstanding ability as a worker.

Secondly, he tells us to choose a puppy with a big round skull, well filled over the temples and with a look of dauntless curiosity in his well-opened eyes. (I am sure he would have had nothing to do with the long, narrow, houndy-headed dogs or those with the deep, flapping, St Bernardish muzzles that we sometimes see on the bench.)

He then goes on to speak of 'natural qualities', which, he says, 'are those qualities that the most capable master cannot put into his pupil and without which no Spaniel can become a first-rater'; he enumerates them as follows:

'1. Docility, which is the wish to learn—the desire to please his master.

2. Courage, which makes a dog unconscious of fatigue— which will crash him through thorns and brambles and gorse, which will force him across a river in flood.

3. Nose, which really stands for keenness of scenting power, combined with the sense to apply it aright.

4. Style, which is chiefly merry bustle with flashing, quivering tail and head ever alert, now high to reach body scent, now low to investigate a track, attributes that are most precious to a tired man or to one vexed at a bad shot. Style exhibits itself also in working of a decisive, dashing kind: for instance, in springing a rabbit with such vehemence as to frighten it into leaving its covert post haste.'

Mr Arkwright concludes this section of his advice by saying that he believes that all these natural qualities are hereditary and are certainly impossible of inculcation by any breaker. (This word 'breaker' has ceased to be used—we talk now of a trainer, a much happier suggestion.)

Finally, Mr Arkwright adds two additional qualities, 'that are often natural, but if not natural, that may be to a certain extent acquired'.

'1. Retrieving is often inherent in a Spaniel puppy and is exhibited by a partiality for lifting anything that is handy and carrying it about. Such a puppy usually has, in addition, a soft dry mouth and will make the best retriever of all. But many good dogs require some schooling in the retrieve. . . .

2. Water work. Most Spaniels take to this naturally, but not all of them. Some do not by instinct know the way to swim, others do not care for the shock of cold water. They can one and all be taught by firm kindness and perseverance but these artificially made swimmers are never *great* water dogs, with their cork-like abilities of dealing with rock and surf and whirlpool. It is probable that a remote strain of English Water Spaniel is responsible for the wonderful powers of some strains, and it is well to remember that a *thick, wavy, oily coat usually goes with proficiency in swimming.*' (The italics are mine.)

And now, over half a century later, I do not think I can improve on the advice Mr Arkwright gave in 1914. If you can find a puppy or young Springer which appears to have all these attributes, take your courage in your hand, make it your personal companion and friend and proceed to train it to the best of your ability.

The picture I would draw of the ideal Springer for shooting is that of a not too big or heavy dog, with a skull wide enough for brains, a foreface not too deep in flew, with a dark, well-set intelligent eye, not hampered for work by too long ears, a long, reachy neck, a strongly built, muscular body, well-sprung ribs, strong loin and powerful quarters, which together will enable him to move fast and jump well, good legs with close, round feet on which he can keep going all day, and a fairly long tail, never carried above the level of the back and which, when at work, has a very quick, lively motion.

Higham Tit Bit

(*C. M. Cooke*)

F.T.Ch. Pinehawk
Sark

(*C. M. Cooke*)

(*C. M. Cooke*)

Stokeley Higham Tonga

(*C. M. Cooke*)

Int.F.T.Ch. and American National Ch. Carswell Contessa

Training a Springer for Shooting

To begin with I must acknowledge a debt of gratitude to the authors of three books on training gundogs, all books published in the early days of this century: C. Mackay Sanderson's *Practical Breaking and Training of Gundogs*; H. W. Carlton's *Spaniels. Their Breaking for Sport and Field Trials*, 1915; and R. Sharpe's *Dog Training by Amateurs*, 1924. I read them many times and found them the greatest help in directing the education of my early 'Ranscombes'.

I write now defininitely for the novice trainer and handler, and in doing so I write of how, starting as the veriest novice, I trained my own puppies.

I do this with the utmost deference when I consider the wealth of knowledge and experience of such people as the late Lady Howe, Mr John Kent, Mr John Forbes, Mr T. J. Greatorex, Mr T. Gaunt, Mr R. Hill, the late Mr J. Scott, Senr, Mr T. Ellis, who were winning trials before World War I, and Mr A. Wylie, Mr J. Wylie, Mr A. E. Curtis, Mr T. B. Laird, Mr J. Chudley, Mr K. Chudley, Mr J. W. Scott, Jnr, Mr W. Edwards, the late Mr W. D. Edwards, the late Mr David MacDonald and the late W. G. Sheldon, who, together with Major H. Peacock, Mr Hal Jackson, Mr W. G. Fiske, Mr and Mrs R. B. Weston-Webb and many others too numerous to mention were winning between and/or after the two wars and all of whom I have seen handling their Springers and other Spaniels at trials and from whom I have learnt much. In some cases I have been privileged to watch them actually at work training their young entry, and shall never cease to be grateful for the advice and help they have given me.

Field trials can be so much more interesting than shows in that the dogs are at work *doing something* all day, instead of moving up and down a ring for a few minutes.

In another respect, also, field trials are much more enjoyable than shows; instead of the hurry homewards at the first possible moment that one is allowed to remove one's dogs, a Spaniel field trial is generally a two-day affair, and at the hotel in the evening not only is there a great feeling of friendliness and fellowship but the 'battles of many days afore' are fought over again and the reasons for this or that success or failure are discussed. One can learn a lot from listening to the wisdom of the giants.

One cannot start too young with the training of Springer puppies, once they have left their mother and are self-supporting. If they are taught to sit to await their turn to be fed, the word 'sit' being used continuously for this, they soon know it and realise that the more quickly they obey the sooner they get their food. Once they sit almost automatically at the word, start raising the hand as you say 'sit' and soon the pups will recognise that the action means the same thing as the word and it will be possible to get them to sit by raising the hand without speaking. After achieving this, begin to teach the puppies the meaning of a whistle. A soft low whistle when the puppies are near, and the holding out of a piece of biscuit or other titbit so that they come racing to get it, is the start. Praise the puppy that comes quickest. After they have learned to recognise the whistle as the signal for return, dispense with the bribe; not all at once, but more and more often give praise instead of food. The next thing the puppy can learn is to return to its handler by signal, the hand being brought down two or three times against the leg with a patting or slapping action. Always whistle the pups to their kennel at bedtime and then give them their final meal.

Next start the puppies on getting used to loud noises and bangs. A paper bag blown up and burst, so that it makes a little bang, is a good idea, especially if the bag is then shown them and they can see that it is quite harmless. After this a small practice pistol, firing blanks, can be used, starting at a considerable distance from the puppies, but just near enough to attract their attention. In using this pistol, always lift the hand holding the pistol as you fire, and after they become used to the sound come nearer to them by degrees and use the word 'sit' as you fire. With steady practice (a few bangs a day) these two lessons can be combined: in time the bang will mean sit just as much as the word or raised hand.

At the same time as these lessons are going on, retrieving can be practised. Any Springer puppy from a good working strain will pick up a dummy and, if called by name, will probably bring it back. Take it gently, holding the hand under the mouth, hoping that the pup will just drop the dummy into your hand. If it does not return, don't run after it, but walk away and the pup will very likely follow you. If it does this, let it walk beside you for a little distance, then very quietly put down your hand and say 'Dead', when it will probably give you the dummy. Should it not come to you as you walk away, fetch another puppy and make a fuss of it and the first one will very likely come back to get its share of interest.

It is very much better, when starting to practise retrieving, to do so in a narrow 'lane' about 4 ft. wide, perhaps between two kennel-runs, and with no outlet at the far end, so that there is no possibility of the pup's running off, as in a big field or run.

First show the puppy the dummy, an old fur glove or small woollen bundle, and get it interested in it. Then throw it a short distance; be sure that the puppy sees it go. But hold the puppy, using the word 'sit', and after only a little interval, during which it sits and watches the dummy, let it go, using either the word 'fetch' or the word 'bring', but always using the same word. Do not repeat this retrieving practice more than three or four times at once, but if possible finish with a successful retrieve, so that you are able to praise the puppy to end the lesson. If it has not done well it is no use going on and on; better put the puppy back in its kennel and try again later.

By this time you will probably have got a good idea of which puppy shows the most promise and the most style, and will be beginning to make up your mind as to which one to keep; though puppies are just like children, and one cannot be absolutely certain. With some, the early brilliance fades out; with others, like some children that fail the 'eleven plus', they may be 'late developers'. I know that at eighteen months the foundation bitch of a very famous kennel was so apparently dull as to be described as useless, and her owner could not even give her away. At two years she was winning field trial stakes. Another, described by two well-known trainers as the most promising puppy they had had for years when she was twelve months old, was not good enough to run even in a Novice Stake at eighteen months old, while her litter sister, sold just as a shooting dog, was brilliant.

Still, one can't keep a whole litter for years, or, in some cases, even months, and quite often one does pick the right puppy.

If a puppy does not take to retrieving naturally it is better to leave it out of the 'selection list'. There is such a thing as forced retrieving, but I have never used it and to tell the truth do not know how it is done; fortunately for me the 'Ranscombes' have all been very keen retrievers. If a Springer has not an inborn instinct for retrieving it never does it with the style and joy of the dog to whom it comes naturally and one's time is better spent on more promising material.

One needs to teach a puppy to use its nose in retrieving, not merely to pick up the dummy it sees thrown and fall, and one useful exercise is to drop the dummy as one walks forward with the puppy at heel, being sure that the puppy does not see it fall, then proceed for a certain distance and send the puppy back, with a 'find' or 'seek dead'. At first, practise this with the wind coming towards you, and as the puppy becomes quicker increase the distance. Next, after dropping the dummy, move across the ground so that the scent is not coming directly to you and the puppy has to work back and forth until it winds its retrieve. Help the puppy here by signalling it in the right direction, and remember that a dog that will pause, if doubtful, and look for a signal is showing intelligence, though, on the other hand, one does not want a dog that depends too much on its handler and does not use its nose.

Many trainers use a spring thrower. A very simple one is that illustrated in R. Sharpe's book *Dog Training by Amateurs*. I had a very similar one made by a blacksmith. The dummy is placed on a flat holder, which is held down by a catch. To this catch is attached a long cord or wire, which can be led across the grass to a considerable distance from the thrower, and when the cord is pulled the spring is released and the dummy is thrown high into the air, falling well out from the thrower and from the dog and the handler. The puppy must be made to wait for the order to retrieve and sometimes not be allowed to 'fetch', either the handler picking it up while the puppy remains sitting or another dog being sent for it, so teaching the puppy that he is not to retrieve everything that is shot, and that he must wait patiently while another dog hunts and retrieves. Another advantage of using a thrower is that there is no question of a puppy's merely following your foot-scent back, as would be the case if it were sent back for a dummy you had dropped as you walked forward with the puppy at heel.

Before making the final choice, the puppies must be watched very often out in a meadow, and the great thing to observe here is the way they hunt. A really stylish hunter will show it while very young, and style in hunting, good nose, good retrieving, courage and a light mouth are the real essentials to look for in selecting a Springer for work.

A puppy that works about in a field with its nose down, following any scent that there may be, always with its tail moving fast, and as it gets more and more interested by a stronger scent its tail going faster and faster, is the one to consider carefully, especially if it has satisfied you in another important respect, that it is 'kind', which means that it is anxious to please, is willing to do what is required of it and does not sulk if corrected.

Style, like quality in a Springer, is again like that 'public-school something' which can be seen at once but cannot be described. One dog may be altogether worthy and do everything that is required of a good gundog, possibly as well as the other, and yet never give you the pleasure in watching it work that the stylish dog does.

Puppies have to learn that they are out in the open field to hunt, not just to please themselves but to please you, and that is why it is important to have taught them from earliest days to sit on command and to the raised hand and to attend to a whistle.

Use the word 'sit' when the puppy is fairly near, then use the whistle that, in its kennel or run, has meant come back and practise this with the puppy farther and farther away. Should a puppy not attend to word and/or whistle because it is so intent on its hunting (and I sometimes think that, thrilled with hunting and with that one idea in their minds, they really are temporarily deaf and do not hear, or at least they would wish one to believe so), put a collar on it next time it is taken out, with a long, strong but light cord attached to it. Let the cord trail, and if no attention is paid to your command or whistle step on the end of the cord and this will pull the puppy up with a jerk. Slowly gather in the cord, using the word 'back' until the puppy has reached your side. Then, with about a yard slack, walk towards the kennel or gate of the field, not letting the pup's nose come beyond your side. Should it do so, pull it back, using the word 'heel', which it should know from its early lessons in walking on a leash, and so continue until the kennel is reached. I do not, however, like to keep a cord on a puppy any longer than is necessary, for it is liable to have a restrictive effect on its hunting and spoil the freedom of its style. Nothing is more annoying than the Springer that just hunts round one's feet.

A puppy should also be taught the sound of the whistle in a different note or trill from that which means come back, and this whistle should be taught to the accompaniment of the word 'sit' or the raised hand. This is taught so that should the puppy be at a distance, or not in a position to see a hand signal, it will stop at once and sit, as it has also been taught to do at the sound of the practice pistol. At this point, too, it is as well to let the puppies hear the sound of a gun being fired, at first well away in the distance, then gradually nearer. When they are used to it as a sound for 'sit', as the pistol was, they can soon get used to the action of the gun going to the shoulder and expect the sound which means sit.

After thoroughly instilling the real understanding of the words 'sit', 'heel', 'back', and the whistles which mean 'return' and 'stop' in the puppy's mind, so that you can feel that it is really obedient to those commands, the next thing is to teach it to quarter. Sometimes a dog is a natural quarterer and hunts in front, taking in just the right amount of ground, but in most cases it has to be taught.

With the puppy at heel, begin walking across the middle of the field, and start it hunting with the words 'hi, lost', walking slightly to the left so that the puppy goes out in that direction, a little in front of you. When it has gone the distance you think desirable, give a low whistle, but not your return whistle, to attract its attention, and turn in the opposite direction yourself. The puppy will notice this and reverse its own direction, and this can be continued right across the field.

A 'green lane' about 30 ft. wide is an ideal place in which to start a puppy quartering. It will check as it reaches the hedge, and so be more easily attracted by your whistle, and will turn to the open space instead of going on through the hedge. Although a puppy will go quite happily a long distance from you in an open field, where it can still keep you in sight, it may not, at this stage in its training, be happy to lose sight of you altogether.

It is best to start lessons in quartering where you are sure there are no rabbits, hares or birds about at the time, for one does not want to undo the early training in obedience by a wild career after an exciting quarry. When the puppy really begins to quarter well you can cease moving from side to side and walk straight down the middle of the 'beat'.

I was very fortunate when I started training my puppies in being able to take them up to a shoot at Hill Hall, near Epping. A meadow sloped away downhill from the edge of a wood where there were many rabbit-burrows. In the early evening scores of rabbits came out to feed. (This, of course, was long before the vile infection of myxomatosis spread abroad.) Miss Brice and I used to walk our puppies slowly and as silently as possible along the side of the wood, so that they looked down on the rabbits feeding on the hillside. To begin with we kept the puppies on a loose leash, and if possible walked the whole length of the woodside without disturbing the rabbits. If a puppy started forward we stopped it with a very soft hiss and a pull on the leash. Turning back we would get the head keeper, Mr C. Tyler, who was as keen on the training of the Springers as we were, to shoot one or two of the rabbits, and at the sound of the gun the puppies, remembering their previous training, sat down. The rabbits disappeared like magic into the wood or their burrows and the puppies had to sit and watch them run off in all directions. After an interval, if the rabbits shot were reasonably small, and the puppies a fair size, they were allowed to retrieve.

To give Springers a real training in steadiness a rabbit-run is of the greatest help. I wired in a fairly big shrubbery and put in some half a dozen rabbits to start with. The puppies were put on a long cord and invited to hunt the rabbit scent through the brushes and undergrowth. Directly a rabbit moved into the open the check-cord was used to stop the puppy chasing it, and the word 'sit' used very emphatically. After a time the cord was dispensed with and either word or whistle used. If the puppy forgot its previous lessons and gave chase, a loud whistle and 'no', 'no—sit', was used, and it was rated soundly when it returned. If this occurred again it was put on its check-cord for a further period.

When one is reasonably sure that a puppy has learnt the lesson of steadiness it can be taken out into woods or fields, where it may begin serious work. Nowadays it will not have the temptation of so many rabbits as in the pre-myxomatosis days, but hares are fairly plentiful, and somehow they are often even more of a temptation than rabbits

All this takes time. It is fatal for a novice to hurry any one step in the training, and one must not expect to turn out a finished worker in a few weeks, or even months. Even the greatest among our professional and amateur handlers often give months of careful training to most of their pupils, though there are, of course, some exceptional puppies. I remember seeing Mr John Kent's Pat of Chrishall win a stake at the age of seven months, and Mr F. M. Prime's Wakefares Sprigg win a stake at the same age; later both became Field Trial Champions.

I would suggest to the novice trainer that when he reaches the stage of taking his dog out, and hopes he will find something that can be shot in front of it, that he asks someone else to do the shooting, so that he can concentrate on the puppy and act quickly if temptation looks like being too strong for it. The experienced trainer can do two things at once, but the novice handler is learning his own lessons with the puppy, and, however good a shot he is, while he is thinking about his aim he may just miss the pup's first movement towards chasing or running in to shot. The fewer times a puppy does wrong, the stronger grows his instinct for obedience.

At Hill Hall shoot about three thousand pheasants were reared each season. I was able to take my puppies into the rides in the summer when the pheasants were being whistled in for their evening feed. The birds would come flying in and running in from all directions, and it is a real education for a puppy to learn to sit quietly and watch as the pheasants move here and there, picking up food and often coming quite close to the dogs.

When a young dog has had some experience of actual work a very good addition to its education is to take it 'looking up', with a keeper deputed to find birds not gathered before the guns move off, or perhaps the next morning after a big shoot. An experienced dog is always taken along too, in case the beginner fails.

The most important thing of all about a retrieving gundog is that it should have a light mouth. Any Springer that grips a bird so that it crushes the ribs or breaks the skin is one with a very serious fault. I feel sure that this fault is hereditary and strains in which it frequently appears should be avoided.

All Springers should be good water-dogs. In fact it is more important that they should swim and either bring birds from the water or from across water than that they should retrieve what lies on the ground in front of the guns. One can do this oneself if need be, but one cannot go across water of any width and depth, or into the middle of a lake, and to see birds left because a dog has not been willing to swim is frustrating, to say the least.

Most Springer puppies enter water willingly, but it is as well to introduce them to water where the bank slopes gently down to a shallow stream that is not very wide. They will then probably just paddle about, enjoying splashing around, especially if the weather is warm. Throw a dummy across the stream and encourage one puppy to fetch it, praising him for his success if he brings it, but should he fail send the second puppy, if you have another with you. If not, it is as well to have rubber boots on and be able to cross the stream yourself, bringing back the dummy and throwing it again. This time it is almost certain the puppy will fetch it.

Gradually increase the distance and depth of the water the puppy has to cross, and when it has become quite confident teach it to jump into the water from a bank instead of entering from a shelving beach. Very soon it will probably be hard to keep the Springer puppy out of water, and the really keen, grown dog will spring from a bank to a distance of about six feet out into the water. Nothing is more delightful than to see a Springer swimming fast and high in the water, with a duck or other bird in its mouth.

Most Springers can jump well (most of mine have jumped too well at times and had to have extra-high kennel railings). It is, however, a good thing to give the puppies some training in jumping as they will certainly, at some time in their working career, have to jump wire fences to retrieve. I found that the easiest thing was to put up one or two fences in the narrow lane I used for the start of retrieving. If a dummy is thrown over the first fence the puppy, soon realising that there is no way round, will make an effort to jump. When it does this well over one fence then the dummy can be thrown over the two fences. These can be low at first and then, as the puppy improves, and as it grows bigger, they can be made higher.

Springers as a rule have plenty of courage in facing thorns and thick covert, and this again is something that puppies learn, especially if taken out with an older dog. Directly they realise that a rabbit or bird is tucked away inside thick briars and/or heavy bracken they will try their best to get in to push it out. The temptation then is for them to go beyond the covert when they have moved their quarry out. It is very tempting, after having been encouraged to 'push it out', to go after it, and that is a time when the handler must be on the watch and ready with his 'sit' or his whistle, which means stop.

An experienced Springer, when put to hunt bushes, will often run round them, putting his nose in at every break, but then going on to the next bush. If it is a dog known to be good in facing covert one can be fairly sure that whatever was in the first bush has moved on; as a sensible dog it is not going to waste time and energy on what its nose assures it is no longer there.

Nothing, however, is more trying than a Spaniel that runs round and round bushes and, though clearly showing that there is something inside, will not go in. A dog that 'blinks' its covert can rarely be taught to work well in thick briars and thorns, and however much I liked it in other respects I should not want to own it.

After all this preliminary training the novice may be able to go to a shoot and use his dog to pick up for the guns. As this will only mean retrieving and not hunting up, the dog will be very much under the control of his handler and not have the temptations that hunting may mean. The only risk will be if a hare or rabbit gets up while it is on its way in or out, but then the interest of the retrieve may keep its mind on the one piece of work.

Since the war, Springers have been used quite a lot to work with the beaters, getting well into the undergrowth where the birds are sitting very tight. A Springer that can do this really well is much valued. I was told by a friend that her husband used to get invitations, 'Will Colonel —— shoot with us on such and such a date?' He acquired a Springer that is a particularly good hunter and soon after that the invitations came, 'Will Rilla and Colonel —— shoot with us on such and such a date?'

Colonel F. H. B. Carrell had a number of Springers which he used entirely as a team of beaters.

The time comes when the novice trainer feels that he might venture to become a novice handler at a field trial. Certain Spaniel societies run stakes for Novice and Amateur Handlers, the definition of which is that the handler shall not have won a prize handling at trials and in the second stake shall not have trained and handled dogs for gain.

These are the stakes for the real beginner, for they are the ones where he can feel that he is not in competition with handlers, either professional or amateur, who have had long years of experience of training and handling at trials. I have always found that judges are most kindly and helpful to the novice in such stakes, and it must be remembered that the standard of work is not expected to be as high as in a Novice Dog Stake, where only the dog has to be a beginner, and is certainly much below that of an Open Stake which carries a qualification to run at the Spaniel Championship.

A Certificate of Merit in the Novice or Amateur Handlers' Stake will encourage the winner of it to go on to 'higher things'. I have known several people start in one of these stakes and then seen them again a very few years later running a dog at the Spaniel Championship. If there had not been this 'nursery stake' to encourage them to make a start they would probably never have reached the ultimate height, where even to gain a Diploma is an honour.

It is the greatest help to the novice who hopes one day to handle his own dog at a trial to undertake some job, such as that of number-carrier, which will allow him to be in the line, so that he can watch the work of the dogs and the handlers. He will learn much from seeing the experienced handler direct his dog with the minimum of word or whistle, and he will learn, too, what makes the difference between the dog who can get a place in the prize list and a Certificate of Merit dog or an 'also ran', and this will help him to assess the value of his own dog's chances as a trial dog. If he watches the dogs carefully he will be able to remember the ones who have shown pace and perseverance in hunting, never flagging when they have a long hunt on a 'bare patch'; those who have not missed game as they worked, so that a bird or rabbit is put up by people following behind on ground the dog has already quested; the dogs who go *into*, not over, bracken and thorns; those who can mark well the fall of a bird and who when sent to retrieve pick up cleanly and bring back at a good pace, deliver right to hand, not dropping their retrieve on the way back or putting it down a yard or two from their handler and needing encouragement to complete their task; those who, if put on a runner, will go quickly to the fall and take the line, or if asked to retrieve a bird on which another dog has failed succeed in finding it, although it may be a 'blind retrieve'.

The judges at a trial note all these points very carefully, and their final placings are made not on one brilliant piece of work, although that may carry considerable value, but on all-round good performances, carried out with style and speed. A novice, seeing a dog collect a runner, may feel that it has thereby won the stake, but the judges, having seen all the work, put only a certain value on any one point. It must be remembered, too, that dogs that are stylish at work give much more pleasure and put up far more game than the dull, plodding, 'stodgy' dog, however worthy and obedient. A dog that one feels one wants to push can be quite irritating, and it can be understood why, although it has done all it was asked to do and nothing wrong, it fails to get 'into the money', or indeed any award at all.

Chapter XI

THE KENNEL CLUB SPANIEL CHAMPIONSHIP

JUST as Cruft's is the high-light of the show world, so is the Spaniel Championship to Spaniel field trial enthusiasts. It is held in January, just before the close of the shooting season, and is run in two sections: a stake for Cockers who have qualified at trials during the season and a stake for all Spaniels of any other variety than Cockers who have won a first or second at trials of championship status.

The judges are elected by ballot. A list of eight names nominated by the Kennel Club Field Trial Committee is circulated to the secretaries of all the Spaniel societies entitled to qualify dogs for the title of Field Trial Champion, and the members of the committees of these societies vote for the judges, marking their ballot papers in the order of their preference, so that the selection is entirely democratic.

Early in the year the Kennel Club obtains a venue for these championship trials, the endeavour being to get ground which has a large area of very similar type, so that all the dogs get, as far as possible, the same testing. Grimsthorpe, Bourne, Lincs., Blenheim Park, Woodstock, Oxon., and Shadwell, Thetford, Norfolk, are venues which have been visited on several occasions and are excellent for the championship trials.

As the season advances the interest grows, as first one and then another Springer qualifies to run at the championship, and the final words of farewell as each trial ends and the owners, handlers and many very interested spectators go their different ways are, 'See you at the championship.'

The championship is indeed the Mecca of the Spaniel field trial world and the evening before the trials begin the hotel which is the headquarters begins to fill with competitors and other Spaniel enthusiasts from as far away as the north of Scotland, and Northern Ireland, as well as every part of England and Wales. The Irish contingent excites a great deal of interest, as few of these dogs have been seen running in England, they generally having qualified at trials in their own country.

Talk goes on happily till a late hour and then we all retire to bed with one great anxiety on our minds: What will the weather be like in the morning? As the championship must be held in January, at the conclusion of the shooting season, the chances of waking to find heavy rain or the ground covered with snow and perhaps a blizzard raging have to be faced. However, on the whole, these trials have not been too unfortunate as regards weather, and field trial folk are very hardy and always prepared to endure what cannot be cured.

The cavalcade of cars starts out in good time for the meet, and here the help of the A.A. or the R.A.C. is invaluable in 'signing' the route, as they so willingly do for all trials. Without these signs it would often be difficult to find the trial grounds, which are often remote from town or village, and where there may not be anyone about who can give exact directions.

The Any Variety Open Stake and the Cocker Stake alternate in being run first each year. The dogs go down in their order on the card, as at every other trial, and are watched with the greatest interest by owners, handlers and spectators, who, having seen many of them at work before, assess their performances keenly with, 'Never seen it run better,' 'Has never run worse,' 'A beautiful piece of work,' 'Should never have missed that bird,' 'A splendid retrieve of that runner,' and so on; but it must be remembered that at the championship, as at all other trials, the judges see all the work, the rest of us only part of it, and so it is the judges alone who can decide on the best all-round performance.

If the Cocker Stake is run first there may be time for a start to be made on the Any Variety Stake, other than Cocker, on the first day, and conversely, if that stake is large and comes first, with a smaller Cocker Stake, the Any Variety Stake may be completed on the second day. After another evening of talk and, if a stake has been finished, more congratulations to the happy owner of the winner, and, perhaps, the drinking of the health of the winner and his handler, we set out again for the second day.

When all the dogs have had a run under both judges, the judges go through their books together, the real thrill for both handlers and spectators coming when the dogs wanted for the run-off are called for. The judges, walking side by side, run first two, then another two together, sometimes replacing one with another and then calling up a fifth or sixth dog, or possibly even more dogs still. The tension often grows to such an extent that the spectators forget the rule that they must keep behind the red flag and tend to follow the judges, loth to miss a single point. Provided they keep far enough behind so that they do not get in the way of the judges, guns and handlers, and, above all, the dogs, kindly judges, knowing how thrilling this last fight for the 'blue ribbon' of the Spaniel field trial world is, do not object, but it is only during these last few minutes of the trial that judges feel that this is excusable; to have spectators wandering behind the line all through this or indeed any field trial is worse than annoying, and I cannot emphasise too strongly that spectators (and handlers when not running their dogs) should obey the stewards implicitly, and remember that the red flag is there for their safety, as well as to keep the line clear to enable the judges, handlers and dogs to do their work properly. There have often been times when I have felt that a well-trained sheepdog should be part of the equipment of every field trial secretary.

After which digression I return to the great moment when the organiser of the trial, appointed by the Kennel Club, is called up by the judges and given the awards. Pencils are got out, cards placed ready for marking, and we wait to hear which dog has won the greatest event of the Spaniel world, the supreme title of Field Trial Champion at the Spaniel Championship. And as we know that for many years past only English Springers have run in the Any Variety Stake, we know it must be a dog of our chosen breed.

Then follow the second, third and reserve awards and, what are given only at the championship, Diplomas of Merit, and it is a matter of pride to go home with any of these, won in such company.

Sometimes we feel that these awards are exactly what we would have made ourselves; sometimes we wonder why 'Dash' was considered better than 'Dusky', but again I would say the judges see all the work, we see only part of it.

And so, for the stalwarts, a start on the often long trek home, for others back to tea and relaxation after the two long days, and an evening of talk and plans and hopes for another season.

Chapter XII

PERSONALITIES AND SPRINGERS OF THE FIELD TRIAL WORLD

MR JOHN KENT, the *doyen* of the Spaniel field trial world, first won at trials in 1905 and made his first Field Trial Champion in 1906. This was a Cocker, and his first award with an English Springer was in 1909; he continued to run Spaniels, principally Cockers, until the outbreak of World War I. It is difficult to realise that it is fifty-seven years since Mr Kent won his first award at trials, but watching him training his dogs in his wonderfully equipped ground one sees how his skill and love of gundog training has, through all these many years, produced generation after generation of the perfect workers we see at trials.

I have been privileged to see some of the records of the early years of the century, when there were many fewer societies running field trials. Among the leading ones were the Spaniel Club, the Sporting Spaniel Society and the Scottish Field Trial Association, and the judges were men who did much to establish the English Springer as the dog we know today. Among them were: Mr William Arkwright, Mr C. A. Phillips, Col. R. Claude Caine, Mr C. C. Eversfield and Mr James Farrow. It was under judges such as these that Mr Kent, from 1905 to 1913, running in 21 stakes, won 44 prizes and seven reserves, in addition to very many Certificates of Merit. It is interesting to note too that at the only trial during World War I, held in aid of the Red Cross, Mr Kent won the stake with an English Springer, Walhampton Croy, and he repeated this success at the only Red Cross trial during World War II, winning the stake with Teggie of Chrishall. I remember seeing Teggie run at this trial and being much impressed by her. Had it not been for the war I feel sure she would have been a Field Trial Champion. However, she was the dam of many excellent workers and winners, including F.T.Ch. Silverstar of Chrishall who won seven Open Stakes and with Ringe of Chrishall won the Kennel Club Championship Brace Stake. Silverstar and Ringe running as a brace were never beaten. F.T.Ch. Carlo of Chrishall and F.T.Ch. Speckle of Chrishall are two more recent Field Trial Champions, and

Speckle was third in the Kennel Club Spaniel Championship in 1959.

Mr Kent has won not only with Springers but with Cockers, Clumbers, and Retrievers, and has several wins at the championship to his credit. As a judge at field trials his great experience makes him greatly valued, and his kindness and courtesy is appreciated by all those of us who have run under him. No novice ever goes to him without receiving advice and practical help.

Another 'Grand Old Man' of the field trial world is Mr John Forbes, of the well-known Glennewton prefix, a master in the art of training and handling Spaniels and one whom it is an education to watch as he works his dogs, either at home or at trials. He has, of recent years, run more Cockers than Springers, but he has made both Rossend Prince and Richard of Elan English Springer Field Trial Champions. While he was living in Wales he gave the many Welsh Springer Spaniels owners a great deal of help in training their dogs, and the many fewer entries and successes of Welsh Springers at trials since then show how valuable his assistance was and how greatly he is missed. In addition to being a much-sought-after judge for field trials, Mr Forbes judges gundogs at shows, and has a keen eye for the well-built, active dog that looks as if it can do a good job of work.

I well remember the first time that I met Mr Reg Hill, for it was at the Kensington Society's championship show at the old Holland Park Rink, the first show held after World War I, and for me a most momentous occasion, for it was there that I showed my first Springer, Ranger of Ranscombe. Utterly ignorant of show procedure, I was very grateful for Mr Hill's kindly interest and advice. Before World War I Mr Hill was training and running dogs at trials and he has continued ever since to bring out first one and then another winning dog. He handled Triple F.T.Ch. Wake Wager to his championship status in England and recently brought out a young dog, Templegrafton Hardy, now a F.T. Champion owned by Captain T. L. M. Lonsdale, to win two open stakes as well as Diplomas at two successive Spaniel Championships. A very experienced judge at field trials, Mr Hill occasionally judges at shows and unerringly picks out the best gundogs in the ring.

In the years just before World War I and afterwards, right through the 1920s, Mr William Humphrey had a strain of exceedingly good-working and good-looking Springers. His Dual Ch. Horsford Hetman was the first Dual Champion of the breed and

Triple F.T.Ch.
Wakes Wager of
Greenfair

(*Evelyn Shafer*)

Int.F.T.Ch. Ludlovian Bruce of Greenfair

Curtsey Chiquita (first Australian Dual Ch.)

(Dr M. M. Wilson)

Australian Dual Ch. Curtsey George

had a great influence on the breeding of Springers for many years. Mr Humphrey took several Springers out to the U.S.A., and in 1924 won the first field trial ever held in that country, with Aughrim Flashing first and Horsford Hale second. Flashing became the first U.S.A. Field Trial Champion in 1929, while Horsford Highness became the first U.S.A. Show Champion in 1923. Other winners in England were Horsford Honour, Handy, Heiress, Harebell and Hawk. The Horsford breeding went back to the famous 'Caistor' strain and to the strain bred for many years by Sir Hugo FitzHerbert at Tissington in Derbyshire.

The second person to own a Dual Champion was Colonel F. H. B. Carrell. This was Thoughtful of Harting, by Dual Ch. Horsford Hetman ex Horsford Ho, and bred by Mr W. Humphrey. I must admit that I did not like this dog. He never struck me as a typical Springer and he had a light, hard eye. Colonel Carrell bred a large number of dogs and used them as a pack to beat woods and thick covert.

Dual Ch. Flint of Avendale, owned by the Duke of Hamilton, was the third and last of the English Springer Dual Champions. There have been none since and there has never been a Dual Champion bitch. Flint was a very handsome tri-colour, but Setterish in appearance, style and movement. The Duke of Hamilton rarely showed a dog, but he had a wonderful strain of workers, among them F.T.Ch. Rex of Avendale, F.T.Ch. Reece and F.T.Ch. Prince, all trained and handled by Mr J. Gaunt.

Two of the first dogs that I remember who were owned by the late Mr David MacDonald of Dundee were Ch. Little Brand and Ch. Little Queen. They won both Certificates at the first Cruft's after World War I and were very handsome Springers, as well as being good workers. Little King, their son, was a good-looking dog that was even better known as a trial dog. Mr MacDonald adopted the prefix 'L'ile' and had a long series of Springers carrying his name, among them Merle, Queen, Marquis, L'ile Ladybird, Ch. Brown Lass, as well as Int.Ch. Nuthill Dignity and Int.Ch. L'ile Buccaneer, and all his dogs could be relied upon to give a good account of themselves in the field as well as on the bench.

The late Mr R. R. Kelland trained his first English Springer in 1895 and later judged at many Championship Shows and Field Trials. Later he ran his Springers at many trials, though his interest in Spaniels was not confined to that variety alone. He had Cockers, Fields and Clumbers and won at trials with

K

all of them. Of his Springers, perhaps the greatest trial winner was Nobel Nadir. He also owned a very successful trial dog in F.T.Ch. Downton Bob, which afterwards went to Canada, where it became a Field Trial Champion and then went on to win the title in the United States, thus becoming a Triple Field Trial Champion. Mr Kelland joined the English Springer Club in 1924 and worked untiringly for it, for over thirty years, first as secretary, then chairman and finally president.

The late Mr W. D. Edwards made his prefix 'Pierpoint' famous at trials immediately after World War I, and I first remember him in 1922 as showing a very handsome Springer bitch called Ch. Pierpoint Lass, which was also a winner at trials. He had a succession of excellent shooting dogs that rarely failed to get into the top three or four when running at trials. He was a very popular field trial judge and occasionally judged at shows. He liked a good-looking Springer, but always picked out a dog that looked as if it were capable of a good day's work. His too early death was a great sorrow to his many friends, and a great loss to the breed.

From immediately after World War I the Laverstoke Springers owned by Lady Portal showed that the dual-purpose dog was a definite possibility, for a number of them were among the best being shown, and they were most successful at trials. Ch. Laverstoke Pattern, a very beautiful bitch and a winner of many awards at field trials, was the dam of Ch. Laverstoke Pepper, one of the last bred by Lady Portal. Pepper, mated to Buckshot Jock, a son of Ch. Nuthill Dignity, was the dam of Ch. Marmion of Marmion, a dog which figures in a very large number of present-day pedigrees.

Lorna, Countess Howe's prefix 'Banchory' has been associated for so very many years with Labradors that the present generation do not realise what a brilliant team of English Springers also carried that name and won the Kennel Club Championship Stake several times between 1920 and 1935. Banchory Boy, Banchory Brilliant, Banchory Light were all Field Trial Champions, and Banchory Bright won nine field trials in 1925. Lady Howe also owned Ch. Banchory Tranquil, a beautiful bitch who made a great name for herself on the bench.

A kennel which in the years from 1920 on into the 1930s was famous throughout the field trial world was that of Mr G. Clark with his prefix 'Blair'. F.T.Ch. Bee of Blair was a wonderful little bitch, very quick and with great style—she won, I believe, eighteen

Field Trial Stakes and was the dam of innumerable field trial winners, including F.T.Ch. Beeson of Blair, winner of the Spaniel Championship in 1935. He was a dog I always admired, not merely for his working abilities but as a good-looking, typical Springer. Bee's and Beeson's names appear in very many of our present-day pedigrees, notably in that of F.T.Ch. Silverstar of Chrishall, himself the sire of many winners.

Major Doyne Ditmus's 'Boghurst' Springers were successful both at shows and at trials after World War I; names we remember were Ch. Boghurst Carlo, Ch. Boghurst Bristle, Boghurst Rover, Boghurst Signoretta and Wootton Bramblebush. A number of the Boghurst dogs went to the United States and to Canada, where they earned high praise from field trial supporters. These dogs were good-lookers and won on the bench, but I always wished they had had darker eyes.

Long before the 1914 war Mr Lewis D. Wigan ran his dogs at trials and continued to do so directly trials were resumed in 1920. He had many successful field trial winners, but perhaps the one best remembered is F.T.Ch. Jed of the Cairnies, a son of F.T.Ch. Nithsdale Rover. Trained and handled by the later Mr James Scott, Senr, he was one of the outstanding dogs of his period, and as the grandsire of Mr Edgar Winter's Staindrop Spitfire Jed's name appears in the pedigrees of many present-day Field Trial Champions.

Captain Traherne, for so many years the president of the English Springer Spaniel Club, used the prefix 'Bryngarw', and nearly all his dogs had the word 'Fire' as part of their name. F.T.Ch. Firefly, F.T.Ch. Firearm, Firecrest, Fireworks, Fireflash, Fireside were all well-known trial winners; others Captain Traherne owned and ran were F.T.Ch. Noranby Pelican and Flatcatcher.

Names which are inseparable when one thinks of field trial successes are those of the late Mr Selwyn C. Jones and Mr T. J. Greatorex and the 'O'Vara' prefix. In 1928 Mr Greatorex took over the training and handling at trials of Mr Selwyn Jones's dogs as his sole interest. The first dog was Menaifron Jock, previously owned by Mr Rae of O'Moy Setter fame, and the amazing total of O'Varas that have become Field Trial Champions in England has reached seventeen; a record, I think, not equalled by any other kennel. The Kennel Club Spaniel Championship has been won seven times, and F.T.Ch. Scramble O'Vara won it twice, while the two Field Trial Champions Don and Spy, working as a brace, won the Kennel Club Brace Stakes three years in succession. This wonderful strain has achieved distinction in every part of the world and Mr Greatorex, when I asked him how many O'Varas had become Field Trial Champions in other countries, had to admit that he had lost count. Many of the leading field trial strains have been founded on the O'Varas, for that name is a guarantee of all that can be asked for in brains and brilliance at work. Since Mr Selwyn Jones's death the O'Varas have continued in Mr Greatorex's ownership.

Mr H. S. Lloyd, the 'Wizard of Ware', had for so many years shown his Cockers with such success that I think the present generation of Springer owners actually do not know of his keen interest in our variety of Spaniel, but well before World War I Mr Lloyd owned winning Springers, and immediately after that war ended he bred several litters and showed a number of Springers very successfully. His two greatest dogs were Int.Ch. Springbok of Ware, sire of sixteen champions, and Int.Ch. Jambok of Ware. Others I remember were Ch. Jamson of Ware, Cleon of Ware, Paulinus of Ware and Ch. Nutbrook Boy, while at trials he won with many good-looking dogs, among them Reipple and Ranter of Ware, the litter sister and brother (Nurscombe Prince ex Ch. Reipple of Ranscombe). The former went to India and Ranter to America.

The Eastern Counties Spaniel Society held its first field trial in 1927 and Mr F. Mason Prime made his first appearance there, winning the Novice Stakes with his dog Spanner. Since then he has bred a succession of field trial winners. Thrimley Joe (Reuben of Ranscombe ex Beans) was one of the early successes. He won three open stakes, in the days when three wins were required for the title of Field Trial Champion, but, as only seven instead of the minimum eight dogs ran on one of these occasions, he never achieved the coveted title. Soon after came Triple Int.F.T.Ch. Wakes Wager, whom Mr Prime bred and won with until he sold him to Mr H. S. Lloyd, in whose ownership, handled by Mr R. Hill, he became a Field Trial Champion. He went to India in the ownership of the Maharajah of Patiala and then to the United States of America where he belonged to Mr Quirk. He became a Field Trial Champion in both these countries, and I believe is the only Springer and the only gundog ever to achieve the distinction of being a Field Trial Champion in three continents. Every season Mr Prime has come to trials with a dog that has maintained the honour of the Wakefares, and the latest, F.T.Ch. Wakefares Sprigg (F.T.Ch. Harpersbrook Sammy ex Wakefares Sugar), has won four Open Stakes as well as two Diplomas at the Spaniel Championship Trials. All the Wakefares are home bred and home trained.

Mr A. E. Curtis started his Whittlemoor kennel in 1928 at The Moors, Whittlesford, an absolutely ideal place for training Springers. In 1932 he took charge of the training of Colonel McNeill's Springers, and handling Donna Susie soon made her a Field Trial Champion. A number of other winners followed, and since World War II he has trained F.T.Ch. Whittlemoor George, who in 1950 won the U.S.A. National Championship, and F.T.Ch. Whittleford Record as well as many other winners.

To have bred, trained and owned seven Field Trial Champions since World War II makes Mr T. Laird's name and his prefix Criffel outstanding. Certainly to have produced Daisy Bell, Pamela, Nellie, Prince, Danny, Snipe and Melody—all Field Trial Champions—is a remarkable record.

Mr Andrew Wylie started to train Springers and other gundogs at his Pinehawk Kennels in 1933, and his brother J. S. Wylie joined him a few years afterwards. They have a long list of winners to their credit and to them belongs the distinction of making the first post-war Field Trial Champion in Pinehawk Roger. Since then they have added F.T.Ch. Acheron Trick, F.T.Ch. Ludlovian Socks, F.T.Ch. Pinehawk Sark and F.T.Ch. Pinehawk Spur.

Like father, like son, has come true again in that all the skill of the father in training and the understanding of dogs is apparent in the son of Mr John MacQueen, Senr., for Mr J. MacQueen, Junr, has made a name training and handling at trials. In English Springers perhaps his most notable success is with Mr. F. Thomas's F.T.Ch. Markdown Muffin who was second in the Kennel Club Championship Stake in 1961 and won the Championship Stake in 1962.

The same saying certainly applies to Mr J. W. Scott, son of the late Mr James Scott, for not only is he a successful trainer, but he has a long list of trial winners to his credit, including the winner of the Cocker Championship Stake in F.T.Ch. Brookville Sandy.

Mr G. Curle has owned the Breckonhill Springers for many years and his most recent Field Trial Champions are Breckonhill Bee, Brave, Bridegroom and Bilko.

Major Hugh Peacock is perhaps best known for his many Field Trial Champion Labradors and Cockers, but he has also a great interest in English Springers, F.T.Ch. Greatford Kim and F.T.Ch. Greatford Meadowcourt Stephen being two of his very successful trial dogs.

Another Cocker enthusiast who cannot withstand the charm of the Springer is Lt-Comdr E. A. J. Collard, whose Richard of Elan and Rossend Prince, handled by Mr J. Forbes, have both attained field trial championship status.

To Messrs E. and M. Ainsworth goes the distinction of owning F.T.Ch. Rivington Glensaugh Glean, winner of the Kennel Club Spaniel Championship in 1951 and the sire of eight Field Trial Champions.

It is interesting to notice how many doctors own English Springers and, particularly, how many shoot over them and run them at field trials. Dr Goodwin and Dr Sunderland were great enthusiasts in the 1930s and 1940s, and since then Dr T. K. Davidson, owner of F.T.Ch. Jonkit Jasper and many other home-bred and home-trained winning trial dogs, and Dr D. A. White, owner of F.T.Ch. Posternate Jet and, again, a number of home-bred and home-trained dogs, have been two of the most consistent trial supporters, while Dr D. H. Edmonsdon always has a really good dog, too. Dr J. Hurndall Gann owns F.T.Ch. Harpersbrook Sammy, a dog that ran third in the Kennel Club Spaniel Championship three times, while in 1961 we welcomed another doctor as a newcomer to trials in Dr Diana Bovill, who handled her very good-looking dog Harwes Mark successfully.

Mr R. N. Burton's 'Brackenbank' prefix is again one of the most successful at trials, and his F.T.Ch. Brackenbank Tangle won the U.S.A. National Championship in 1959, having run second to Staindrop Breckonhill Chip in 1958. Chip, bred by Mr G. Curle, had already won the National Championship in 1957. Another dog to win this coveted award twice was F.T.Ch. Micklewood Scud, owned in England by Captain Corbet.

Mr Hal Jackson first ran a dog at trials in 1921, but only after the last war did he go in for trials at all seriously. His reward came when he won the Kennel Club Spaniel Championship with F.T.Ch. Gwen of Barnacre in 1957, and in 1959 he won this stake again with Gwen's son, F.T.Ch. Willy of Barnacre. Among other winners he has bred and owned are Jill of Barnacre, Bess of Barnacre, always a great favourite of mine, and F.T.Ch. Kate and

Mint of Barnacre. To have won the Kennel Club Championship with both mother and son is indeed an achievement.

Mr Talbot Radcliffe, from far-away Anglesey, makes frequent forays into other parts of the country, and since making Saighton's Sentry a Field Trial Champion in 1954 he has, with Mr William Edwards handling his trial dogs, added the title to the names of Scent, Spree and Swing.

Miss C. M. Francis had shot over English Springers for very many years in Norfolk and Bedfordshire, but it was not until 1927 that she purchased Higham Tan, a most attractive tri-colour by Dual Ch. Horsford Hetman, whom she showed with considerable success. Thus began her 'Higham' strain, which has become so well known both for looks and work. Tan, mated to Adcombe Clarice, a grand-daughter of Int.Ch. L'ile Buccaneer, produced Ch. Higham Teal, winner of six Challenge Certificates and Best of Breed at Cruft's in 1933. Teal, mated to Ch. Marmion of Marmion, produced Ch. Higham Tom Tit, undoubtedly one of the best dogs of his period and a dog that could win against the best that we have today. His litter brother, Higham Ticket, won at championship shows and at field trials; both were then owned by Lady Lambe. Tom Tit's son, Higham Tristram, ex Higham Trusty, born in 1938, was prevented by the war years from winning much himself, but proved a very successful sire, for among other good litters he sired Lady Lambe's famous litter ex Ch. Whaddon Chase Snipe, in which were the three champions: Whaddon Chase Bracken, Higham Topsy and Whaddon Chase Prince, with Whaddon Chase Duke a Challenge Certificate winner and field trial prize-winner for good measure. Higham Topsy won six Challenge Certificates and three Certificates of Merit at the only three trials at which she ran, and repeated her great-grandmother Teal's success at Cruft's by being awarded Best of Breed in 1955. Topsy is notable also as the dam of a number of field trial winners; mated to Mr John Kent's F.T.Ch. Silverstar of Chrishall the first to win was Higham Tit Bit who won five stakes, including one Open Stake, and was second in two other Open Stakes, besides winning many other awards at trials and being a prize-winner on the bench. Tit Bit was the only survivor of her litter in the days before hard-pad was conquered; doubtless the other six puppies would have been at least as good. Next with the same breeding came Test, winner of a Novice Stake and numerous other awards at trials as well as at shows. Mating

Topsy to Acheron Spot produced Higham Tell and Higham Turvey, the latter now a Field Trial Champion in Italy, while Tell, after winning here, is now in America. Stokeley Higham Tonga, litter sister of Test, had a distinguished career at trials and was second in the Kennel Club Spaniel Championship in 1958; she too won well at shows. Higham Ted, a good-looking black-and-white by Towser of Chrishall (F.T.Ch. Harpersbrook Sammy ex Higham Test) ex Higham Trim, a daughter of Topsy, has won on the bench and, at the 1961 season, well deserved his Certificates of Merit which he won in very hot competition.

I have given a rather detailed account of the Higham breeding-line because I do want novices in particular to realize that the working and show strains can be combined successfully.

Mrs Margaret Pratt is an amateur who, starting to train a dog, Stokeley Sultan, with whom she had obtained awards at shows, achieved her first success with him in an Amateur Handlers' Stake, which evoked her serious interest in field trials. She purchased a puppy, Higham Tally (F.T.Ch. Harpersbrook Sammy ex Higham Test), and trained and handled it, with the result that in the two seasons 1958 and 1959 she won sixteen awards and finished with a Diploma at the Kennel Club Championship Trials. She purchased another young bitch, Posterngate Jo (Posterngate Jack ex Posterngate Jenny), and in the 1960 season won seven awards with her. Mrs Pratt is an outstanding example of how, by starting in an Amateur Handlers' Stake, enthusiasm can carry a novice handler right on to the Kennel Club Championship Trials, and I am sure that nothing would make the field trial fraternity happier than to see her win the coveted championship.

A brilliant star among field trial amateur trainers and handlers, in the person of Mr Sheldon, rose in 1949, only to set far too soon, to the very great loss to the breed and to the great sorrow of all who had known him during the too brief period he was among us at trials. Ludlow Gyp was first trained by Mr J. Wylie, thereafter Mr Sheldon bred, trained and handled all his own dogs with wonderful success until his death in 1955. In that short period he made Field Trial Champions of Dauntless Monty, Ludlow Gyp, Ludlovian Darkie, Ludlovian Ruby and Ludlovian Bruce. Bruce, now in the ownership of Mr and Mrs Quirk, won the U.S.A. National Championship in 1954 and 1955, while in 1956 F.T.Ch. Ludlovian Socks, bred by Mr Sheldon, was third in the National Championship and second in 1957, with F.T.Ch.

Ludlovian Scamp third in 1957. Quiet, utterly unassuming, very kindly, it was a privilege to have known Mr Sheldon even for so short a time.

A really dual-purpose kennel is that of Mr D. C. Hannah who, having kept English Springers for shooting since 1926, entered the show ring in 1947 with a dog who very soon became a Champion. This was Stokeley Bonny Boy (Ch. Whaddon Chase Bonny Tom ex Clintonhouse Elizabeth). In quick succession came Boy's younger brother, Ch. Stokeley Gay Boy, and Ch. Stokeley Lucky (Ambergris Sportsman ex Clintonhouse Elizabeth); all three, in turn, winning the Challenge Certificate at Cruft's. Lucky also won twenty-four awards at trials, and since then Mr Hannah has won at trials with Stokeley Higham Tonga, who was second in the Kennel Club Spaniel Championship in 1958. Two of her sons, Rogue and Scamp, won well at trials here, and then went to Italy where Rogue won the International Field Trial near Milan in 1960, with Stokeley Speed third. Ch. Stokeley Gay Boy was the first English Springer to go to Italy, where the breed is now well established. Italian Ch. Stokeley Marco won three Open Stakes and two Challenge Certificates. At shows here, Stokeley Sea Sprite and his sister, Stokeley Sea Princess, have each won eight Challenge Certificates.

Mr F. George first competed at trials with Streonshalh Comet, a bitch who very soon became a Field Trial Champion and was second, third and reserve in the Kennel Club Spaniel Championship in three successive years. Then followed F.T.Ch. Harpersbrook Boots, F.T.Ch. Entonlee Cherry, F.T.Ch. Shineradee and a number of other winners, with F.T.Ch. Harpersbrook Reed finishing the 1960 trial season by winning the Kennel Club Spaniel Championship held in January 1961. Mrs George also takes a great interest in field trials, and owns F.T.Ch. Blatherwycke Meadowcourt Hector.

Mr J. Chudley and his brother, Mr K. Chudley, started training dogs at their Harpersbrook Kennels in 1946 and have since then trained and handled many of the most successful Springers of the 1950s. They have trained and handled all Mr and Mrs George's Field Trial Champions and their other winners, as well as Major Peacock's Int.Ch. Greatford Kim, Mr D. Bowlby's F.T.Ch. Bryanston Bess and Dr J. Hurndall Gann's Ch. Harpersbrook Sammy.

Mr P. R. A. Moxon combines training gundogs and writing

about them. He is the Kennel Editor of the *Shooting Times* and, in addition, has found time to write an excellent book on training gundogs.[1]

Mr F. Thomas, whose prefix was 'Markdown', owned a number of good trial winners during the past few years, but pride of place must go to F.T.Ch. Markdown Muffin, winner of the 1962 Spaniel Championship, second in 1961 and one of the most consistently good workers. In addition he is a really good-looking, typical Springer.

Mrs P. M. Badenach-Nicolson, from far-away Kincardineshire, comes south to win at trials with her Carswell Springers, and her home-bred F.T.Ch. Carswell Contessa, a daughter of her F.T.Ch. Carswell Cornelia, who she also bred, made history in the United States by winning the National Championship Stake in 1960, for she was bred by a woman and owned and handled by a woman—Mrs Julia Armour, who is also an amateur handler—a combination which had never occurred before.

Mr R. B. Weston-Webb is an enthusiastic supporter of field trials and has bred and run a large number of very successful 'Meadowcourt' Springers; his F.T.Ch. Meadowcourt Judy was placed second in the Kennel Club Spaniel Championship in 1962. Mrs Weston-Webb, so well known for her Field Trial Champion Cockers, has added Springers as her second interest at trials.

Mr B. B. Dutton entered spaniel trials with his 'Hamers' Springers and his enthusiasm was rewarded when he won the Spaniel Championship A.V. bar Cocker Stake with F.T.Ch. Hamers Hansel.

Mr W. A. Cooke made history with his Hales Smut. This dog was whelped at Keith Erlandson's kennels from field trial stock going back to the O'Vara strain which produced seven winners of the Spaniel Championship. At eight weeks old Smut was sold to Frank Bell and eventually arrived in the kennel of Arthur Cooke. In four seasons he ran in eighteen trials and won seventeen awards. He is the sire of nine Field Trial Champions and figures in the pedigree of many English Springers now running in Trials. At ten years of age, Smut has been described as the greatest force in field trial spaniels yet he never won a Stake.

I.B.H.

---

[1] *Gundogs: Training and Field Trials* (Popular Dogs Publishing Co.).

Chapter XIII

SPRINGERS ABROAD

MISS M. C. FOX, the secretary of the Irish Kennel Club, very kindly sent me a catalogue of the Irish Kennel Club's last championship show. At this ten classes were scheduled for English Springers, with a total of forty-six entries, made up by eighteen dogs and nine bitches; although numbers at this show were not large, the quality was outstanding. The leading dogs at the present time are Mr J. Cranston's Ch. Sir Knight, Mr B. Barker's Ch. Fairey Tail and Golden Crescent, Mrs H. Willoughby's Ch. Mischievous Mac and Mr P. Kinsella's Derryclare Shade of Autumn, which has recently been exported to the U.S.A.

There are from forty to fifty limited shows held each year, but at these no special classes are given for Springers: they have to be entered in Any Variety Spaniel or Any Variety Gundog classes, where they are usually well up in the awards.

There are ten championship shows held each year and at these the award of the Green Star is equivalent to our Challenge Certificate, but before a Springer can take the title of Champion it must qualify in the field.

The English Springer Spaniel Club of Southern Ireland was dissolved some 20 years ago and since then no field trials specially for Springers have been held. Springers are, however, recognised throughout the country as excellent shooting dogs and are in demand and largely used, particularly on rough shoots, and there are, fortunately, a number of enthusiasts who not only insist on good working ability but also on good looks in all the dogs they breed.

FRANCE

A large number of our English Springers has gone to France, and the show and working strains are practically all founded on Springers imported from England.

Madame Guerville-Sevin, the secretary of the French Spaniel Club, tells me that about 350 English Springers are registered at the French Kennel Club each year; she feels this to be a small number compared with the very large registration of Cockers annually, but adds that the quality and general standard is very high.

To become a Bench Champion—'a champion of beauty'—a dog must win three Challenge Certificates under two different judges and a 'very honourable mention' at a field trial, while to become a Field Trial Champion a dog must win three Championship Certificates and obtain a prize and the qualification 'Very Good' at a show.

In order for a win at a field trial to count towards the title there must be at least six runners in the stake (as compared with eight here in England). Field trials are many fewer in number as against the very many we hold here. On the other hand, with no quarantine restrictions, international field trials and shows are held.

There is no doubt that looks and work and work and looks have to go together in France to win either the title for looks or the title for working ability, and so long as this is insisted on neither the slow heavy dog, with nothing but appearance to recommend it, nor the undersized, poor-headed worker will be developed at the expense of the really good-looking type, and the intelligent Springer and the standard of the breed will be maintained.

SWITZERLAND

All matters pertaining to shows and field trials are under the control of the Schweizerische Kynologische Gesellschaft, the equivalent of our Kennel Club.

After a group of English Springers from Frau Luise Richei's kennels were shown at an international show in 1956 an English Springer Spaniel Club of Switzerland was formed in 1957 and recognised by the Swiss Kennel Club. Some years later, The English Springers joined with the Retrievers to form a joint Club. The President is Frau L. Bernhauser of Rapperswill who has given much time and effort towards building up a good Springer blood lines in the country.

Emphasis is being laid on the working side of the breed and in 1960 an experienced breeder and trainer was appointed to develop the practical side of the club's activities, while Herr Hans

Demuth, the club's first president, published an article in the Swiss dog journal *Hundesport*, on the English Springer as a working dog.

The classification for all breeds, with dogs and bitches judged separately, is as follows: Open Class, for all dogs over fifteen months old; National Class, for all dogs over fifteen months bred in Switzerland; Young Class, for dogs between ten and fifteen months; and Working Class, for dogs which hold certificates as working dogs, either at field trials or as police dogs, etc.

No placings as first, second or third are made, but a judge may give 'Excellent', 'Very Good', and 'Good'. No dog in the Young Class may be awarded more than 'Very Good'.

A judge may give the Schonheits Ziegertitel, literally the Beauty Victor title, equivalent to our Challenge Certificate, to one dog and one bitch from the National Class and the Open Class together, once a year. A dog can win the Beauty Title several times, just as dogs here can win many Challenge Certificates, but, as with us, it does not give a further title; it is merely recognized as a greater honour.

With no quarantine regulations to restrict movement from one country to another dogs may be shown at international championship shows, under the Brussels International Federation, and then the title of International Champion is given. To obtain this title a Springer would have to win two International Beauty Titles and pass a full official field trial examination. So far no English Springer from Switzerland has qualified for this title.

ITALY

I am indebted to Signor Marco Valcarenghi, who is known to so many of us from our meeting him at shows and field trials here in England, for information about Springers in his country. He is, in fact, responsible for starting interest in English Springers in Italy, as he first imported Ch. Stokeley Gay Boy from Mr D. C. Hannah's kennel and then purchased Higham Turvey from Miss C. M. Francis. Before that, Springers were practically unknown. There are some extremely good pointing breeds in Italy, and, although Signor Valcarenghi hopes that Springers will soon become well known, he doubts if they will ever attain the popularity that they have here or in the U.S.A. or Canada. Still, they are getting to be known and are attracting the interest of a number of shooting people.

A Spaniel Club was formed in 1958, again largely through the enthusiasm of Signor Valcarenghi; this caters for both Cockers and Springers, these being the only varieties of Spaniels in Italy. The club organises a championship show every year, which is judged by a specialist. Three or four field trials are held each season, at which both varieties run. They are carried on on similar lines to our own Spaniel trials and the dogs work entirely on pheasants.

Challenge Certificates are awarded for both trials and shows. To become a Show Champion a Springer needs three Challenge Certificates from three different judges and is required to qualify at work. To become a Field Trial Champion a Springer needs two field trial Challenge Certificates from different judges and has to qualify at a show.

Of the foundation stock imported from England, Ch. Stokeley Gay Boy died before he could make much contribution to the breed in Italy, but Italian F.T.Ch. Higham Turvey won three Open Stakes at trials and a Challenge Certificate on the bench. Stokeley Marco won seven Challenge Certificates at shows and one Challenge Certificate at field trials and was placed in five other trials. Stokeley Rogue has won one Open Stake and Challenge Certificate. Of the Italian bred Springers, Dolly of Valmarco (F.T.Ch. Silver Star of Chrishall ex Italian F.T.Ch. Higham Turvey) has already won one Open Stake with Challenge Certificate and Gilda of Valmarco (Ch. Stokeley Marco ex Dolly of Valmarco) has won a Junior Stake.

Two other enthusiastic Springer owners have started kennels, and working on the lines indicated above the breed should have a successful future in Italy.

SPAIN

There are very few English Springers in Spain; only two were registered in 1960, and both were bred by Miss J. Robinson and registered here as Solstar of Stubham and Hawkhill Narcissus. They are owned by the Earl of Valle de San Juan.

Two international championship shows are held each year, one in Madrid and one in Barcelona. A dog must win three Challenge Certificates to become a Spanish champion, but if it competes for an International Beauty Championship under the International Kennel Federation, four certificates are required.

BELGIUM

There are very few owners of English Springers in Belgium, and little or no breeding. A few dogs have been imported from England, but at shows only two, three or four Springers are entered, compared with from ninety to one hundred Cockers. At field trials there are never more than one or two entered, and they run in competition with the Cockers as their number does not warrant a separate stake.

HOLLAND

In Holland the registrations of English Springers have been increasing and in the 1960's the imported dog, Winch Crocidolite, became a Champion. In the past two years the imported bitch, Dutch Champion Larkstoke Sarcelle, has taken top honours in breed classes and has been Best in Show All Breeds, including Utrecht 1972 when 1,500 dogs of all breeds were exhibited.

To become a Champion a Springer has to win four championship prizes at four shows, or three when one of the championship prizes has been won at the Winner Show in Amsterdam.

For the title of Field Trial Champion two Field Trial Championship prizes are necessary and the qualification 'Good', 'Very Good' or 'Excellent' at a championship show, which ensures that not merely working ability but good Springer type is maintained in all the leading dogs.

SWEDEN

At shows Springers are given the same classes as other gundogs.

Field Trials for Spaniels, both Springer and Cocker, are held each autumn.

Springers in Sweden are descended from both American and English dogs, and a number of Springers have been imported from England carrying Whaddon Chase, Higham and Woodbay blood lines.

To be full Champions, dogs must qualify on the Bench and in the Field.

DENMARK

English Springers are steadily increasing in numbers in Denmark, as shown by the registrations for the following five years: 1956, 37; 1957, 39; 1958, 56; 1959, 73; and 1960, 114. These numbers, however, have not justified the formation of a specialist club for the breed, and owners of Springers belong to the Spanielklubben, the secretary for which is Mr A. F. Norland, Ordrupvej 6, Carlottenlund, Denmark.

The Danish Kennel Club arranges four championship shows. Two of these are under international auspices, and specialist clubs can hold two championship shows for their members, so enabling Springers to complete at six shows in Denmark each year. They can also compete at shows in Norway, Sweden and Finland, so that a Springer is able to enter for thirty shows a year in the three Scandinavian countries and Finland. Only two classes are scheduled for each breed, one for 'Youngsters', for dogs from ten to fifteen months old and an Open Class for dogs above fifteen months. In the Open Class four prizes are awarded and all first prize-winners enter a Winners Class, from which the judge selects his four best dogs as prize-winners, a process somewhat similar to our Best in Show judging, except that four dogs are placed instead of only Best in Show and Reserve Best in Show.

Between 1937 and 1942 there were three English Springer Champions, but since the war only two have attained championship status, a litter brother and sister, born in November 1954 and bred and owned by Mr Axel Peterson, Ch. Solveigs Bob and Ch. Solveigs Leila.

U.S.A AND CANADA

The United States of America and Canada are the two countries in which the English Springer has become most popular and the most numerous. In the U.S.A. they were first registered as a separate variety of Spaniel in 1910. In 1958, 1959 and 1960 the registrations numbered 4,578, 4,305 and 4,027 respectively. In considering these numbers one must, of course, remember the difference in size between that country and Great Britain and Northern Ireland and so realise that in proportion to population and area our registrations of 1,477, 1,535 and 1,613 for the same three years are greater.

Mr Charles S. Goodall, in his book *The Complete English Springer*, published by The Howell Book House Inc. of New York, quotes G. Mourt's *Journal of the Beginning of the English Plantation at Plymouth*, written in 1623, as recording that one of the Pilgrims had a 'Spanell' which chased deer. He also says that another early reference to Spaniels in America is to be found in the *Sportsman's Companion*, published about 1780, which describes several varieties as most effective shooting dogs when carefully trained. His book has a most attractive illustration, reproduced from a portrait painted in 1712 by Justus Kuhn, of a little girl named Eleanor Darnall, who lived in Baltimore, Maryland, standing with her hand on the head of an undoubted Springer, with ears long enough for a present-day show specimen, but with a muzzle of field trial type. This picture is now owned by the Baltimore Historical Society.

Spaniels of all varieties increased in number during the nineteenth and early twentieth centuries, but were almost entirely used as gundogs.

The first English Springer registered by the American Kennel Club was Denne Lucy, in 1910. In 1924 the English Springer Spaniel Field Trial Association was formed and became the parent body of all springer Societies, issuing a standard of points for Springers and rules for the conduct of field trials. The first show at which English Springers were specially classified was in 1923, at the Madison Square Garden in New York, and the first Show Champion was Horsford Highness. The first field trial held in the United States of America was at Fishers Island, in 1924, the winners being English dogs: first, Aughrim Flashing and second: Horsford Hale.

As in Great Britain the owners of English Springers in America have developed separate types for show and for work and trials, and even the most enthusiastic, as are Colonel and Mrs J. C. Quirk, keep their breeding lines in their famous Greenfair Kennels for show and work quite distinct. I must admit, though, judging from the many photographs I have seen of U.S.A.-bred trial Springers, that many of the dogs are very definitely Springers of a good type, more so than many of our English trial dogs. Three English Springers that had a great influence on the breed as workers in America were Triple F.T.Ch. Wake Wager of Greenfair, bred by Mr F. M. Prime of Farnham, Bishop's Stortford, and the only English Springer to become a Field Trial Champion in three continents—Europe (in England), Asia (in India), and America (U.S.A.)—and F.T.Ch. Dalshangan Dandy Boy and his

L

son, F.T.Ch. Tedwyns Trex. I saw Wager running as quite a young dog and was struck by his speed and style, and I well remember the day on which Dandy Boy won the stake which made him a Field Trial Champion. This was at Grindleford, Derbyshire, when the Northern and Midland Society was one of the greatest field trial societies in the country. The weather was appalling, with sleet and rain driving across the high moors, but I think we were all so pleased to see Dandy Boy win his third Open Stake that we forgot how cold we were. Until very much later, a dog had to win three Open Stakes with at least eight dogs running before obtaining the title. F.T.Ch. Tedwyn's Tres and his brother F.T.Ch. Tedwyns Trump were brilliant young dogs, and I feel that I was lucky to be able to breed a litter by Trex before they went to America. Dandy Boy and Trex each sired eight Field Trial Champions in the States, besides leaving a large number of field trial winners in their homeland, showing very clearly what a wonderful working strain Mr Trotter and his son-in-law Mr Byrnes had established.

In the years between the two World Wars many of the best of our English Springers of both show and working strains travelled to the United States and Canada, from such kennels as the Rivington, O'Vara, Banchory, Denne, Avendale, Inveresk, Ware, Cairnies, L'ile and Rufton. A number of Mr Lewis D. Wigan's dogs descended from his famous Cornwallis Cavalier (Port), and particularly F.T.Ch. Jed of the Cairnies did a lot for the working strains in America, as did Mr H. S. Lloyd's Ch. Springbok and Ch. Jambok of Ware. One of the Springers I always regarded as one of the most beautiful we had here in the 1920s was Mr D. MacDonald's Ch. Nuthill Dignity, and looking at a picture of him taken in the States years afterwards he completely satisfies me as a typical and beautiful Springer, which yet looks capable of a good job of work, as I know he was. I wish we had more like him now.

Since World War II English Springers have advanced steadily in popularity, both as show dogs and as workers. I must say how much I admire the enthusiasm and energy of the owners of Springers in America when I think of the tremendous distances that have to be covered, both in the United States of America and in Canada, to reach the great inter-State shows and the field trials of the Eastern Seaboard, the Mid-West and the Western Coast.

By the kindness of Mr and Mrs Greeno and Mrs Gasow I have

been given many details of recent trials, and of particular interest is the book of the National Championship Field Trial, the equivalent in the States of our Kennel Club Spaniel Championship. It is a beautiful production, and gives a picture of every Springer winning the National Championship since 1947. Among them it is most pleasing to recognise many of our English Springers: F.T.Ch. Whittlemoor George, 1950; F.T.Ch. Micklewood Scud, 1953 and 1955; F.T.Ch. Ludlovian Bruce (now of Greenfair), 1954 and 1956; F.T.Ch. Staindrop Breckonhill Chip, 1957 and 1958; F.T.Ch. Brackenbank Tangle, 1959; and F.T.Ch. Carswell Contessa, 1960. Contessa's win provides several points of special interest. She is a bitch, bred by a woman, Mrs P. M. Badenach-Nicolson, and run for the first time ever at the National Championship by a woman handler, an *amateur* handler, Mrs Julia Armour. That nine of the fourteen National Championships since 1947 should have been won by Springers from this side of the 'pond' is gratifying, and we should be proud to think that they have upheld the honour of their homeland in the country of their adoption.

There are about thirty field trials held each year and these are of two types: Sanction and championship or licensed trials. The sanction trials are less formal than championship or licensed trials, and the conditions are less strict. Pigeons are used for retrieving and so these trials can be held at any time in the year.

Licensed and championship trials must use pheasants for retrieving, or else rabbits, but the latter are not popular, as most American dogs are trained on pheasants and are not used to rabbits. Pheasants, however, have to be purchased and the cost is high, making the trials expensive, as five or six are used for each dog. The stakes at a licensed or championship trial are Puppy, Shooting Dog, and All Aged, Amateur All Aged and Novice.

A Springer qualifies as a Field Trial Champion if it wins two All Aged Stakes in which there are ten or more dogs actually running, and no dog can become a Field Trial Champion if it has not passed a water test. At the National Field Trial Championship five land tests and two water tests are given each dog, and none that fails to complete all seven satisfactorily is given an award of any sort.

As in Great Britain there are two judges; one takes the dogs for the odd numbers, the other the evens, but there is no change-over as here, where all the dogs are seen by both judges. In America, when all the dogs have been seen by one or the other judge, they call for the dogs they want again and these are run under the judge who has not seen them previously. These dogs may be called in a third or even a fourth time. First, second, third and fourth prizes and Certificates of Merit are given, but no dog can receive an award unless he has worked under both judges.

There are about 650 championship shows held each year, and practically all give classes for English Springers, and there are from ten to fifteen specialist shows for the breed. Classification is somewhat different from ours and is given in great detail in the American Kennel Club rules for registration and shows and field trials. The Puppy Class is, like ours, for those between six and twelve months old. The Novice Class is for dogs six months or over who have never won a first prize except in Puppy Class. The Bred-by-Exhibitor Class brings in very different conditions from ours of the same name, for a dog in this class can be handled in the ring only by the actual breeder or a member of his immediate family, i.e. husband, wife, father, mother, son, daughter, brother or sister. The American Bred Class is for all dogs except Champions, six months of age or over, whelped in the United States and the result of a mating in the United States. The Open Class is for all dogs over six months old, unless it is at a Speciality Club show held only for American-bred dogs. The Winners Class is for unbeaten dogs and bitches only or, if this is divided by sex, the best in each, after which, as here, the two meet for Best of Breed. The group system is used, and from that the Best in Show is selected.

The winning of a championship title does not depend, as in England, on the award of three Challenge Certificates, but on the number of points gained, five being the maximum that can be awarded at any one show, and the points are estimated on the number of exhibits of the same sex entered and actually competing in the five classes above. If the breed is a very popular one thirty-five entries may be required to score the five points; in less popular breeds (sixty of the 112 registered breeds) six entries of the same sex give the five points, but with fewer competitors the points are reduced. No dog can become a Champion in less than three shows, and it may take more shows if the entry is small. This method, although it sounds rather complicated to us, with our three-certificate system, seems to work well and is in use in a

(*W. Baron*)

Ch. (S.A.) and Ch. (Rhodesia) Studley Hussar of Renfrew

(*W. Baron*)

Ch. (S.A.) and Ch. (Rhodesia) Kim of Renfrew

Indian Ch. Winch Kainite

N.Z.Ch. Sandhurst Sherman, Q.C.

number of other countries. It does at least prevent the possibility
of 'cheap certificates' if the entry should be small.

It is a somewhat rare occurrence for an English Springer to be
the Best in Show at one of our English championship shows, and
when it happens we Springerites are all very gratified. In the
States one very wonderful dog, Frejax Royal Salute, owned and
bred in 1945 by Mr Fred Jackson, and sired by Mrs F. Gasow's
Ch. Sir Lancelot of Salilyn ex Ch. Frejax Lilac Time, won this
award thirty-eight times, thirty-one times in the U.S.A. and
seven times in Canada. He won the sporting group fifty-five times
in the U.S.A. and eleven times in Canada and was Best of Breed
eighty-three times in the U.S.A. and twelve times in Canada,
surely the most wonderful record any Springer has ever put up.
In addition he sired forty-four champions in the U.S.A. and ten
in Canada. And all this in a comparatively short lifetime, for he
died while at an age considered to be a Springer's prime.

A gay note at both trials and shows is added to the competition
by the presentation of rosettes—always called 'ribbons': first,
blue; second, red; third, green; and fourth, white. Best of Sex
(winners), purple; and Best of Breed, purple and gold.

Springers are as popular in Canada as in the United States,
and during the 1920s Mr R. Chevrier was largely responsible for
the importation of many dogs from England and Scotland. He
wrote to all of us who had achieved any measure of success either
on the bench or in the field and was keen to purchase the best we
had to offer—these included Dual Ch. Flint of Avendale and Ch.
Springbok of Ware—while Mr H. J. Placey imported two of Mr
McNab Chassel's breeding, Ch. Inveresk Chancellor and Ch.
Inveresk Cocksure.

A Springer called Longbranch Teal, owned by Mr C. E.
Thomas of Victoria, B.C., was registered in the *Canadian Kennel
Club Stud Book* in 1914, bred from a Clumber and of stock im-
ported from Mr F. Winton-Smith. Mr G. T. Wolfe of Toronto
imported Beechgrove Fly and Beechgrove Bounce from Mr
Winton-Smith, and the mating of these two produced the dog
Niagara Prince, all three being registered with the Canadian
Kennel Club in 1915. Other Beechgrove dogs imported by Mr
Hoyes Lloyd between 1910 and 1920 were Nutty, Florette and
Roddy, but the dog which had perhaps the greatest influence in
popularising Springers in Canada was Ch. Don Juan of Gerwyn.
imported from Wales by Mr W. H. Gardiner of Winnipeg in 1914,

This dog, although black and white, was bred from the famous Corrin of Gerwyn, a red-and-white dog and a famous worker, as well as a prize-winner at championship shows, and whose name is found in all the old Welsh Springer pedigrees. Mr Chevrier saw Don Juan at work when he was eleven years old and was so impressed by him that he started his kennel of Avendale Springers which afterwards became so famous.

In the United States there are at least sixteen English Springer Spaniel clubs or societies in addition to a number of Any Variety Spaniel clubs. There is also a periodical entirely devoted to Springer news and interests, known as *Springer Barks*.

With such vast territories as those of the U.S.A. and Canada there are naturally very many owners of English Springers interested in both shows and work, and it is impossible to give a complete list—it would occupy many pages. A few of the leading owners whose names come to mind, however, are Col and Mrs J. C. Quirk, Mr and Mrs P. D. Armour, Mr E. W. Wunderlich, Mr Chevrier, Mrs J. Hutcheson, Mr Dean Bedford, Mr and Mrs H. Gilman Smith (whose kennels house thirty Show Champions), Mr C. M. Kline, Mrs F. H. Gasow, Mr and Mrs J. Greeno, Mr F. Jackson, Mr and Mrs G. Dodson, Mr W. T. Gibson, Dr Sabin and Mr E. A. Klokke.

The Canadian Kennel Club is completely separate from the American Kennel Club but the Breed Standards are identical for English Springers. However, Show and Field Trial Championships and Working Tests have completely different requirements.

I.B.H.

AUSTRALIA

There are separate authorities for kennel interests in each of the six Australian states, but I understand that there are few Springers in either South or Western Australia. I am indebted to the secretaries of the R.A.S. Kennel Club, Sydney, and the Kennel Control Council, Melbourne, Miss L. Hood of Mortlake, Victoria, Dr M. M. Wilson of Dilby, Ferntree Gully, Victoria, and Mr and Mrs L. B. Matthews of Fawkner, Victoria, for a great deal of interesting information about Springers in Australia.

Owing to the restrictions imposed by the Game Laws in New South Wales, interest in working Springers has fallen during the last few years. Certain gundog clubs hold non-slip retrieving trials and water tests, but no Springer has competed for the past two years. Classes are scheduled for Springers at all championship and other shows and the points system for the title of Champion is in use. Springers can also obtain the title of Field Trial Champion, competing in classes for 'Spaniels and Retrievers'.

In Victoria, although only twenty-five Springers have been registered in the last three years (1960–1963), there are a number of the breed in the state and considerable interest is maintained in them both as show and shooting dogs. About ninety-five shows are held each year and in addition there is the nine-day Royal Melbourne Show held each September. (English exhibitors need not shudder; no breed has to be present for more than one day!) Clubs affiliated to the Kennel Control Council hold open parades for all breedes and for specialist clubs.

As in New South Wales, and indeed throughout Australia, the points system is in use. For the title of Champion, 100 points and four Challenge Certificates, won under four different judges, are needed before a dog can take the title of Champion.

Early in the 1930s Mr C. Little of Tasmania imported Beauchief Bocara and Beauchief Belle, Dr A. B. Corkhill Research of Ranscombe (Noll of Harting ex Regalia of Ranscombe), and Dr J. Silberberg Joy of the Cairnies (F.T.Ch. Jed of the Cairnies ex Molly's Beanie of Landermere). The last two went to Melbourne, and combined two strains which went back to the old Aqualate Springers and from these four Springers and another, Cavalier of Gilderbrook (grandson of Ch. Marmion of Marmion), brought out by Mr F. Fildes, developed the principal strains in Victoria and several other parts of Australia. Another newcomer to the breed, Mrs Coyle, purchased from Mr Little a bitch, bred from his Bocora and Belle, called Bocora Radiant, and this bitch she mated, in turn, to Research and Cavalier. Four of the pups resulting from these matings, registered as Regal, Goldilocks Cavalier and Artist's Model of Wialla, she sent to New Zealand, where they became the foundation stock of three or four kennels.

In 1947 Dr Wilson took Whittlemoor Flicker (Whittleford Spitfire ex Whittlemoor Flick) back from Mr A. E. Curtis's kennels. Her breeding went back to the famous F.T.Ch. Don O'Vara and F.T.Ch. Bee of Blair and she was mated to Rasil of Romford, a son of Research and Joy. Flicker bred a number of very good-looking winning and working Springers, among them Aust. Dual

Ch. Curtsey George. Mated to Aust. Ch. Ranger of Rathlar, Flicker produced the first Aust. Dual Ch. Curtsey Chicquita, owned jointly by Mr L. F. Matthews and Dr Wilson, but trained and handled in field trials and shows by Mr Matthews.

Miss L. Hood, of Mortlake, Victoria, visited England in 1950 and purchased Winch Pyrites from Mrs G. G. Crawford. This bitch soon became a Champion, and in spite of dying quite young was the dam of two Champions and claims at least eight Champions among her descendants, while nearly every Springer winning at present carries her blood. Her early death was a great loss to the breed in Australia. Miss Hood has recently imported a Springer puppy from Mrs Cooper of New Zealand to combine with her own strain.

The principal Springer kennel in Queensland is owned by Mrs Sapio who had lived for many years in New Zealand, where she had started her kennel with a brace from Mrs C. Cooper's Sandhurst Kennel, Penelope of Sandhurst and Regal of Wialla, afterwards importing Strathblane Renown and Strathblane Warspite, Sir Echo of Chastleton and Higham Tobit from England. Her most notable winners in Australia have been Ch. Puni Maiden of Cruchfield, a field trial winner, and her daughter Ch. Cruchfield Punihuia and Cruchfield Kiwa, who won Best of Breed at the Sydney Royal Show.

Field trials are very popular in Victoria and some other parts of Australia, but they can be run only on rabbits and quail, as there are no pheasants in Australia, their importation being forbidden for fear of their bringing disease to other Australian birds. There are pheasants on King Island, but permits to shoot them have to be obtained and the number shot is strictly limited.

As in New Zealand, Springers do well in Tasmania, where the climate, much more like the temperature of our own, suits them.

Springers in Australia have two major troubles to contend with: particularly sharp, hard grass-seeds which, during two months of the year, penetrate into their ears and between their toes and are much worse than our English grass-seeds, and snakes, which I am told Springers are very keen on hunting and become adepts at killing, though their owners would prefer, probably, that the task should be left to themselves, rather than see their dogs take what must be grave risks.

NEW ZEALAND

For a great deal of the information on English Springers in New Zealand I am indebted to Mrs C. Cooper of Ashburton, for she is one of the earliest owners of the breed, and for more than thirty years has bred and shown her dogs as well as being the first woman to train and handle Springers at field trials.

Springers are more numerous, in proportion to the size of the country, than in Australia. The climate is ideal for them. There are more in the South Island than in the North, in fact the large majority are in the South.

Mrs Cooper tells me that it is the versatility of the breed which so greatly appeals to the average New Zealand sportsman, who shoots rabbits in the summer and duck and quail in the winter, for the Springer does all his work most efficiently, and works as well on land as in water. In fact, as in England, the Springer is the handyman of the gundog breeds.

Four Springers were imported in 1930, but only two, Dickens of Bourne, bred by Mr Eversham, and Horsford Hummingbird (a grand-daughter of Dual Ch. Horsford Hetman), bred by Dr A. J. Little, survived to breed any stock in their new homes. Early in the 1930s Mr H. Ayers brought out to the South Island F.T.Ch. Welford Trump, a son of F.T.Ch. Don O'Vara, bred by Captain Holford, and Anthony of Somersby, bred by the late Mr Richard Sharp. From these two dogs have come very many of New Zealand's show and field trial Springers. Major Hunter-Blair returned from England with Rajah of Broomhouse, a son of F.T.Ch. Tedwyns Trex, bred by Miss Ogilvie, and Mrs Cooper had one of his daughters, Ranee of Sandhurst, who won both at shows and field trials, and from matings to Trump and Anthony established a line of Springers which has come right down to the present. Of the four Australian-bred puppies, Regal, Goldilocks, Cavalier and Artist's Model, who came from Mrs Coyle's Wialla Kennels, Regal and Artist's Model also went to Mrs Cooper's kennel.

Mr P. Hennessey and Mr Broad at this time owned outstanding workers in F.T.Ch. Three Star and F.T.Ch. Chum respectively; the dog with whom they were in keenest competition was Ch. Sandhurst Solitaire, and perhaps pride of place should go to this dog, for not only was he a Bench Champion but he also won the land section of the All Breeds Championship and the Provincial All Breeds Championship, with fifteen placings in Open

Trials. The coming of World War II stopped all trials and so prevented him getting just that one point more that would have given him the title of Field Trial Champion.

Later in the 1930s Mr F. A. Elliot started his kennel of Springers with the prefix 'Brackenfield' and won well at trials with Ch. Brackenfield Sherry. When, later, he imported Slice O'Vara his strain was successful at trials all over New Zealand.

Another new Springer enthusiast at this time was Mr N. Leathem, who has two Field Trial Champions in Patsy's Pride (a daughter of Welford Trump) and her son Patchet of Pridevilla.

Mr J. Stanton has the Dalkey Kennel. This strain started with two bitches, Sandhurst Souvenir and Cruchfield Copper Coin, and the imported Strike O'Vara. As might be expected Strike made a great name as a field trial winner, and his daughter F.T.Ch. Dalkey Dabble is the only Springer to have won the New Zealand All Breeds Championship. Mated to Ch. Sandhurst Royal Salute, Dabble bred F.T.Ch. Dalkey Sharon and Dalkey Shamus, also field trial winners.

Among the Springers which have attained high honours on the bench are Ch. Sandhurst Royal Salute, Q.C., who won thirty-six Challenge Certificates, two Best of all Breeds and fifteen field trial awards. Ch. Sandhurst Sherman, Q.C., also a Best of all Breeds winner and holder of fourteen field trial awards, Ch. Patricia of Worthy Down, Ch. Brackenfield Broom, and many others well on their way to championship status.

The control of all shows is in the hands of the New Zealand Kennel Club, while the Dominion Gundog Club is responsible for field trials. There are field trial clubs all over both islands, and to begin with any gundogs were allowed to compete at trials. Now all such clubs have to be affiliated with the Kennel Club, rules and regulations are standard for all trials, and all dogs running at them have to be registered. Q.C. after a dog's name indicates that it has obtained the equivalent of our Qualifying Certificate.

Obedience training and tests are becoming popular in New Zealand and Springers take part in them.

With all the activity on both the show and trial sides there is no doubt that the future of the English Springer in New Zealand is a bright one.

INDIA

The great days of the English Springer in India were in the 1920s, when both the Maharajah of Patiala and the Maharajah of Jind imported some of our best dogs both for shows and for work.

Springer classes were very well supported and competition was very keen, for many of the British resident in India then showed their dogs and competed at trials.

Among the best-known winners of those days were Int.Ch. L'ile Buccaneer, Ch. Standard, Ashborne Stroller, Int.Ch. Crusader of Malwa (Buccaneer's son) who came to England and became a Champion here, and Ch. Mischief of Malwa. These dogs will be remembered by those of us who were exhibiting in those far-off days, and I would be happy if I could take any one of them into the ring today, for they were all beautiful and typical Springers and should win against any being shown now.

Many of our best trial dogs also ran at Indian trials and gained the title of Field Trial Champion there; among them was that famous dog Triple Int.F.T.Ch. Wakes Wager.

Since India has become an independent state many fewer Springers have been bred there and very few imported. Only thirteen have been registered during the last three years, but renewed interest is being taken in all varieties of Spaniels lately and the Spaniel Club of India has held its first championship show, when Miss M. C. P. Wadia's English Springer Indian Ch. Winch Kainite was Best Exhibit in Show.

There are a number of English Springers in Ceylon, and the English Show Champion Hazel of Stubham, a most attractive liver, white and tan, owned by Mr K. Arnolda and now a champion in her new home, is certainly outstanding.

RHODESIA

The Rhodesian Federation Kennel Club is affiliated to the South Africa Kennel Union, but owing to the great distances to be covered—from Cape Town to Bankcroft in Northern Rhodesia is 2,500 miles—the Rhodesias are allowed to possess their own title: Ch.(Rho.). To obtain this title a Springer must win four Challenge Certificates under four different judges in two different provinces. (Northern Rhodesia has one province and Southern Rhodesia has two provinces.) These Challenge Certificates can count towards the South African title of Champion, for which a dog must win four Challenge Certificates under three different judges in three

different provinces under the jurisdiction of the South African
Kennel Union. From this it will be seen that while certificates
won in the South African Republic *and* the Rhodesias qualify a
dog for the South African title, only certificates won in the
Rhodesias qualify a dog for the title Ch.(Rho.). Distance is the
great problem in showing in Rhodesia; for example, Janey of
Stubham attained the titles of Ch. and Ch.(Rho.) in seven shows,
but to do this she had to travel 5,000 miles. A Springer living in
Bancroft would have to travel a minimum of 2,000 miles to obtain
the title of Rhodesian Champion, and a distance of 3,000 miles
for the South African title, even if it were lucky enough to win its
Challenge Certificates at four successive shows. The Rhodesians,
like the Australians and the people of the U.S.A. and Canada,
have enthusiasm and energy, and, I might add, courage, that puts
us to shame, since some of us complain at having to travel 200
miles. Think of the following programme carried out by Mr and
Mrs Foden of Salisbury, S. Rhodesia. Leave home at 1 a.m. to
drive 280 miles to arrive at Bulawayo for the 8.30 a.m. start (note
the time of the start) and arrive home next morning after another
280 miles of night driving, and on roads not as good as ours. And
this journey was followed the next week by a 600-mile flight from
Salisbury up to Kilwe, starting at 4.30 a.m. and returning the
same day. And these are only moderate distances to some of the
journeys they must take!

The South African Kennel Union, after long negotiations, has
been persuaded by the Rhodesias to accept the Kennel Club
Field Trial rules, and when the show season was over in October
1961 a Gun Dog Association was formed in the Federation and
field trials organised. The owners of Springers tell me that they are
anxious to avoid any cleavage between show and working dogs,
as has arisen in some other countries. They hope that the present
rules will be altered so that only Springers possessing a working
qualification may be called Champions. This should be a definite
help towards maintaining both a good type and working ability.

I expect many of the pre-war exhibitors of Springers will remember meeting Princess Radziwill at our principal shows; she
took a number of our Springers back to her home in Poland, but
when the Russians and the Germans both overran that country
she got away to England, where she stayed until the war was
over. While here she had at least two of Lady Lambe's Whaddon
Chase Springers; she took a great interest in our war-time

Corrin (registered as a Welsh Springer in 1902)

(*D. J. Adams*)

Ch. Rushbrooke Runner

Ch. Rockhill Rhiwderin at 12 years old

Stokecourt Susan
(*F. W. Simms*)

shows and, I remember, judged at one of them. After the war she went to Africa and started a kennel with the prefix 'Ira', importing Whaddon Chase Harmony and Roundwood Laddie. She bred and showed for a number of years, and her strain had a great influence on the breed, but though she still retains her interest in the breed she has given up showing.

Mrs L. R. Penny, of the 'Renfrew' prefix, imported Hope Mountain Stronghold, which became a South African Champion in 1948. She added Studley Huzzar and Diamond of Stubham to her kennel, and when she left South Africa to live in Rhodesia they both became Ch. and Ch.(Rho.). Mrs Penny is still an active breeder and exhibitor, and so many more Renfrews are likely to uphold the Springer interests.

Mr and Mrs Raesides, of Salisbury, who purchased their first Springer in 1941, while in Nairobi, and later came to Rhodesia, acquired first Ch. and Ch.(Rho.) Bob of Ira, afterwards importing Totonian Charmer from Mrs Travers in 1955. They still take a great interest in Springers, although no longer showing.

In Bulawayo Mr C. H. Jordan imported a bitch, Candyfloss of Crosslane (Ch. Clintonhouse George ex Candida of Crosslane), from Mr Anderson. This bitch has won five Challenge Certificates and two Reserve Challenge Certificates and in her three litters, registered under the prefix 'Ramleh', has produced young stock which is proving of great value to the breed, in particular one bitch owned by Mr N. Goode.

Mr and Mrs H. Foden of Salisbury are two more of the most enthusiastic Springer breeders and exhibitors, and both look forward to taking an active part in the formation of the Gundog Association. Their home-bred Ch. and Ch.(Rho.) Kim of Renfrew, winner of thirteen certificates, is a son of Ch. and Ch.(Rho.) Studley Huzzar of Renfrew and Ch. and Ch.(Rho.) Diamond of Stubham of Renfrew. As Kim is still quite young he should have a rosy future as well as also being of great value to the breed. Ch. and Ch.(Rho.) Janey of Stubham, imported as a four-months puppy from Mrs Till, has made Springer history by not only winning eight Challenge Certificates but by being the first Springer bitch to win an Open Challenge (all breeds) and by being the first Springer of either sex to be Best Opposite Sex in Show, which she has done twice.

Until his death, the late Lord Llewellyn, the first Governor General of the Rhodesias, was a great supporter of Springers, particularly of working dogs, and in this he was helped by Mr Bruford of Beatrice, Southern Rhodesia, who owns dogs of the O'Vara strain.

Another keen owner and admirer of English Springers in the Federation is Sir Hugh Beadle, the Chief Justice, and there are, to my knowledge, a considerable number of regular exhibitors and breeders, in addition to the very many other Springer admirers, who show occasionally and who work their dogs. Lack of space prevents my naming them all.

Again, in Rhodesia, as in New Zealand, there is a growing interest in Springers due to their kind and charming temperaments, their intelligence and their ability and keenness for work.

I wish I could give as happy a report on Springers in the South African Republic, but from what one learns from judges coming from there, there is now an almost complete dearth of the breed. This is thought to be caused by the uncertainty of the political situation, and I hope that as this grows more settled Springers will regain the position they once held.

KENYA

The political unrest in Kenya had its effect on the dog world there and Miss N. McDowell, one of the keenest supporters of the English Springer, who has bred and shown them for many years, told me that breeding practically ceased because of uncertainty as to future conditions.

The East African Kennel Club is the controlling authority, and two championship shows are held annually. Classes for Springers are scheduled but are not being supported too well at the moment. Breed club shows are held and, recently, a Spaniel Breed Club was formed, but its members are mainly drawn from the ranks of Cocker owners.

Mrs Spencer Tryon, for very many years the great supporter of English Springers, who imported some of the best dogs from England, had to give up breeding owing to ill-health, and this has been a great loss to the breed.

During the years 1958 to 1960 eighteen English Springers were registered, but none has been recorded for 1961.

As in England, a dog needs to win three Challenge Certificates in order to become a Champion, and at the moment the only two are Miss McDowell's Ch. Sandylands Sweet Sue, which she imported, and Ch. Glengarry Rona, bred in Kenya. Another dog, Chastleton Whistlers Boy, was imported in 1959.

Springers, with their heavy coats, feel the heat of East Africa severely, and it is rare for them to live beyond ten years of age. Their long ears also are found to be a handicap in working in the type of thick cover common in Kenya.

Mr Robin Wylie, who returned from Kenya in the early 60's, told me that there have been no official Spaniel trials promoted by the Kennel Club since the war. The late Mr G. Cooke ran Springer trials in pre-war days, since then the only Springer that has been run is Mr G. Littlewood's dog, Copes Jistrine, which was awarded a Certificate of Merit in competition with Labradors at the Labrador Retriever Club of East Africa trials.

The administration of the dog fancy involves many processes which the novice owner/breeder and outsider find quite complicated and at times even frustrating. It is now 'big business' and change is inevitable involving policy and administration.

Many Continental Show and Field Trial Regulations are different from those laid down by our own Kennel Club. Like our own, they are revised from time to time and there are variations from the author's original text. I can only attempt to revise this chapter on a very broad basis.

A visit to a continental show is very interesting. Every dog in the class is given an assessment by the Judge before being placed. Here it is usual for the Judge to select his first four dogs and then place them in order of merit. At a large show, such as Cruft's, the Judge will most likely place up to six dogs in a class.

A great talking point at the 1970 European Spaniel Congress held at Oxford was Trial Regulations. For example, in Germany and Switzerland a dog running in a Trial is required to give tongue. Under our rules this would be a disqualification. The problem arising from exporting trained dogs is obvious. There is need for some form of standardisation in rules if only all can agree.

It might be advisable to mention here the problem of paper work involved in exporting stock. Always be sure that you are in possession of the latest information regarding the entry of your export into a foreign country. A wrong form, or a missing one, can cause much delay and possible expense. Remember that your dog is being held in restricted conditions while the muddle is being sorted out. A telephone call to the Embassy or Consulate of the country concerned is well worth while if you are not sure.

I.B.H.

Chapter XIV

THE WELSH SPRINGER SPANIEL

THE Welsh Springer Spaniel, that attractive red-and-white Spaniel, which in size is between the English Springer and the Cocker, and from 35 lb. to 45 lb. in weight, is absolutely distinct in type and character in every way. No other Spaniel has its colour, and it never breeds away from that colour. Its muzzle is not so deep as that of the English Springer, and its ears, hanging close to the head, are of vine-leaf shape, and besides being shorter and set lower are not so profusely covered or fringed with hair. Although, now, most Welsh Springers have black noses and dark eyes, it must not be forgotten that flesh-coloured noses and hazel eyes were the original colours, and are still seen at times and given as correct in the breed standard. Another distinction is the slight arching of the loin, instead of the straight line of the bodies of the other Spaniel breeds.

I had their character described to me by a great supporter of the breed, who has loved and lived with them, shown and worked them for many years: proud dogs, quick-witted and clever; forceful and competent at work, though perhaps a little impulsive; tough both mentally and physically; most courageous, willing to go through the thickest of brambles; wonderful swimmers. They are very faithful and give all their love and devotion to their owners and are very happy and anxious to please them.

It is doubtful whether the Welsh Springer Spaniel is of more ancient lineage than the other Spaniel varieties, but there is certainly the very old law of Wales of A.D. 300 which speaks of Spaniels, and Dr Caius in his *Historie of Englishe Dogges*, written in 1570, describes the 'Spaniell whose skynnes are white and if marked with any spottes they are commonly red'. As he also writes of 'brown-and-black pied Spaniells', we may take it that he saw these distinctive red-and-white Spaniels running on the Welsh hills, as they have done through the centuries down to the present time.

We know that on the Welsh hills, and in the valleys, numbers of these dogs can be seen and that they breed true to type in size, colour and character. During the nineteenth and early part of this century these dogs were known as 'starters', from the fact that they were largely used to 'start' the game for the gun, Retrievers being used for gathering what was shot.

Coming nearer to our own times, the first owners who appeared with their dogs at trials and shows were Mr A. T. Williams of Ynis-y-gerwn, Glamorgan, whose family had kept its distinct strain for 100 years, Sir John Talbot Llewelyn of Pentlargaer, Colonel Lewis of Greenmeadow and Colonel K. J. Blandy Jenkins of Llanharon, where there had been red-and-white Spaniels as long as living memory went back. Even now Welsh Springers are referred to as belonging to the Llanharon strain. All these strains were kept for shooting and were noted as gundogs. They first ran at trials in 1899, at the Sporting Spaniel Society trials held at Ynis-y-gerwn, Mr A. T. Williams's estate, and his team beat all other varieties of Spaniels. They repeated this success the following year on Mr W. Arkwright's ground at Sutton Scarsdale in Derbyshire, thus disposing of the suggestion that they had won previously on ground with which they were familiar.

The dog to whom practically all present-day Welsh Springers go back was one called 'Corrin' (known at home as 'Flirt'). He was first registered as a Cocker, but when, in 1902, Welsh Springers were given separate registration at the Kennel Club he was re-registered as a Welsh Springer. The picture of him here is one taken when he was about ten years old, and a life-size copy of this picture, owned now by Mr H. Leopard, had the following inscription on the back:

'Corrin (Kennel name Flirt). This Spaniel was, prior to the present date, bred and kept at Llanharon House and was given to me by Colonel K. J. Blandy Jenkins, J.P. (Chairman of the Glamorganshire County Council), as a great personal kindness and on condition that I would never part with him. He is full of intelligence, a magnificent worker, a devoted companion, with the best of tempers. He will face the thickest and worst of coverts, is full of courage and yet perfectly gentle. He will push through any covert that the smallest Cocker can get through. Flirt has been the best-looking sporting Spaniel in England, certainly for the last four years. He was exhibited at the following shows: 1899, Birmingham, First; 1900, Manchester, First; Crystal Palace (under Mr Arkwright), First and Challenge Cup; 1901, Brecon, First and

Special; I only showed him at Brecon after 1900 and after Brecon withdrew him altogether from competition. Flirt is a true representative of the Llanharon family of Spaniels. I have never owned a better-looking Spaniel and have never seen a better worker.

A. T. Williams. 4th August, 1901. Ynis-y-gerwn.'

KENNEL CLUB STANDARD OF THE BREED

Points of the Welsh Springer

Characteristics.—The 'Welsh Spaniel' or 'Springer' is also known and referred to in Wales as a 'Starter'. He is of very ancient and pure origin, and is a distinct variety which has been bred and preserved purely for working purposes.

General Appearance.—A symmetrical, compact, strong, merry, very active dog; not stilty; obviously built for endurance and hard work. A quick and active mover displaying plenty of push and drive.

Head and Skull.—Skull proportionate, of moderate length, slightly domed, with clearly defined stop and well-chiselled below the eyes. Muzzle of medium length, straight, fairly square; the nostrils well developed and flesh-coloured or dark. A short chubby head is objectionable.

Eyes.—Hazel or dark, medium size, not prominent, nor sunken, nor showing haw.

Ears.—Set moderately low and hanging close to the cheeks, comparatively small and gradually narrowing towards the tip and shaped somewhat like a vine leaf, covered with setter-like feathering.

Mouth.—Jaw strong, neither under nor overshot.

Neck.—Long and muscular, clean in throat, neatly set into long sloping shoulders.

Forequarters.—Forelegs of meduim length, straight, well boned, moderately feathered.

Body.—Not long; strong and muscular with deep brisket, well-sprung ribs; length of body should be proportionate to length of leg, and very well balanced; muscular loin slightly arched and well coupled up.

Hindquarters.—Strong and muscular, wide and fully developed with deep second thighs. Hind legs, hocks well let down; stifles moderately bent (neither twisted in nor out); moderately feathered.

Feet.—Round, with thick pads. Firm and cat-like, not too large or spreading.

Tail.—Well set on and low, never carried above the level of the back; lightly feathered and lively in action.

Coat.—Straight or flat, and thick, of a nice silky texture, never wiry nor wavy. A curly coat is most objectionable.

Colour.—Dark rich red and white only.

Weight and Size.—Weight 35 lb. to 45 lb.

Faults.—Coarse skull, light bone, long or curly coat, bad shoulders, poor movement.

The Welsh Spaniel Club was formed early after 1902, with Mrs H. D. Greene as its honorary secretary, and continued until World War I, when it ceased to function. During these years keen supporters of the club were Sir John Llewelyn of Pentlargaer, Colonel Lewis, The Rev. H. Thomas of Pentyrch and Mrs H. D. Greene of Craven Arms, all of whom developed excellent strains of Welsh Springers. Mrs Greene was particularly notable as a breeder and exhibitor and at one time, shortly before 1914, she owned six or seven Champions. Tragically, when the war came she felt so sure that there would be no food available for feeding dogs that she had every dog in her kennel put down, a very great loss to the breed, as she owned some of the most typical Welsh Springers in the country.

Big winners before 1914 were Tawney Patch, Bacchus, Ch. Col Fash and Ch. Cinela Dash.

After World War I breeding and shows started again and, following a meeting in 1922, the present Welsh Springer Spaniel Club was established in 1923, with Colonel J. H. R. Downes-Powell as the honorary secretary and treasurer. In the 1948 *Year Book* of the club he gives a very interesting account of its formation and progress.

For twenty-five years 'The Colonel', as he was always so affectionately referred to, guided the affairs of the club, as secretary, until in 1948 he became chairman of committee, Mr Hal Leopard taking over the duties of secretary and treasurer. In 1957 'The Colonel' became president, on the death of Commander A. T. Wison, but he held this position for far too short a time, for he died early in 1958. Since then the club has not elected a new president, it being felt that at present no one could fill his place.

The first field trials of the present club were held at Ruperra Park, and since then, except for the war years, and on one or two occasions when myxomatosis rendered the ground chosen impossible, trials have been held each year. For very many years they took place at Marglam, on the ground of the president, Captain A. Talbot Fletcher, and afterwards several times at Powis Castle, Lydney Park and Garth, with single visits to venues in other parts of both England and Wales.

Challenge Certificates were granted at ten shows last year and it is encouraging to note that entries are increasing steadily. The cult of the breed is certainly spreading far beyond the confines of Wales. In the first few years after the club was formed members lived principally in Wales and its adjacent counties, but the *Year Book* for 1961 shows that the majority of the members now live outside the Principality, with addresses as far apart as Scotland, Ireland and the Channel Islands.

Perhaps the dogs which had the most influence on the breed in the years between the two wars were Ch. Barglam Bang and his son, Ch. Marglam Bang. The latter was mated many times to a bitch called Goitre Lass and although she was alleged to have some English Springer blood their puppies were always the correct Welsh colour. Instead of their all having the flesh-coloured nose and hazel eyes, however, they frequently had black noses and dark eyes, which was very attractive with the bright red of the coat, but away from the original type.

The very best dog of the Ch. Marglam Bang—Goitre Lass matings was unquestionably Colonel Downes-Powell's Ch Marksman O'Mathern, a winner at trials as well as on the bench; a dog that stood out in the inter-war period and is still considered to be the best Welsh Springer ever bred. He was the rich red and white so typical of the breed, and had the flesh-coloured nose and hazel eye so rarely seen now. He was the particular favourite of his master, who refused an offer of £2,500 for him from the United States of America.

Other well-known winners during this period were Ch. Musketeer O'Mathern, Ch. Felcourt Flapper, Serenade O'Silian, Dere M'laen, Lass and Lad of Tolworth, Master Gun, Lady of Moile, Gunner of Tolworth, Cwn d u Maid, Lady of Usk, Judy of Knaphill and Judy of Blaina, Gun Major, Madrigal O'Mathern, Marglam Marquis, Tawney Patch, Topsy and Tess of Shill, Tawney Pippin, Marionette O'Mathern, Rockhill Rock, Shot of Canonmoor and Llanwern Advent, all Challenge Certificate winners and/or field trial winners. A dog specially to be remembered on the working side of the breed was Legacy Lex, by Tawney Pippin ex Tawney Pansy, and owned by Mr R. H. Sprake of Earsham, Norfolk. Lex won the Puppy Stake and the cup for the Best Welsh Springer at the Welsh Springer Club meeting at Marglam in 1931, and later the Eastern Counties Spaniel Society's Open Stake for Any Variety Spaniel, the first Welsh Springer to achieve this against all the English Springer competitors. I saw him at this trial and admired his work and style immensely. This great little dog worked gaily until he was over sixteen years old, and died with a rabbit in his mouth as he was retrieving it to his master.

To think of Welsh Springers is to think of Colonel Downes-Powell, who, right from his earliest days to the time of his death at the age of eighty-four, worked devotedly for his favourite breed, both on the show and working sides. He guided the affairs of the Welsh Springer Spaniel Club in one capacity or another for over thirty-five years, and although he had owned and worked most breeds of Spaniels, and was an authority and judge of many breeds of dogs, of them all he loved the Welsh Springer the best. I remember he sat at the ringside at a show when I was judging Welsh Springers. I put up a young bitch and gave her the certificate over a number of well-known winners, I think to the surprise of some of the newer exhibitors. Afterwards I was told that the Colonel had said that I had done exactly as he would have done, and, hearing that, I felt that I had had my 'degree' in judging Welsh Springers awarded me by the greatest authority in the breed. He will remain a memory and an inspiration to all those who have the breed at heart. I cannot refrain from concluding with what Mr Hal Leopard told me of what occurred at the Colonel's funeral. As he reached the lych-gate to go into the church for the service, a very fine Welsh Springer came up the road and waited at the gate and so was there to pay a last tribute and farewell from the breed the Colonel had loved so much. A coincidence, perhaps, but a very touching one.

Another great supporter of Welsh Springers, and one much loved by all who knew her, was Mrs M. Mayall, who for thirty-three years on both the working and the show sides bred and owned many of the outstanding specimens of the breed. Ch. Rockhill Rhiwderin, a very beautiful dog and winner of twelve Challenge Certificates, was perhaps the best known. Others, to mention but a few, were Rock, Rona, Regina, Regalia and Ruffle, all typical and all good workers. Her death in 1956 left a gap which it is impossible to fill.

To the post-war exhibitor the Rev. D. Stewart was not known well as he was to many of us in the 1920s and 1930s. He then lived in Suffolk, and his O'Silians could win against many of the other Spaniel varieties. For thirty years a member of the club, and one who worked as well as showed his Welsh Springers, his death was another great loss to the breed.

During the war breeding practically ceased, but Mr H. Newman continued his kennel, although on a reduced scale. He acquired a dog called Dewi Sant from Miss M. O. Evans which he showed at some of the war-time shows and at championship shows directly they were resumed, when he won three Challenge Certificates in succession at the first three of them. This most attractive dog has sired a number of winners and he has had a considerable influence on the post-war breeding of Welsh Springers. Ch. Branksone Beauty, and the Show Champions Stokecourt Jonathan, Jester of Downland, Cofios Bon, Taliesin Ye Ail, Denethorp Dido and Welsh Lady all own him as sire.

Mr H. Leopard, secretary of the Welsh Springer Spaniel Club for many years, has established his prefix 'Rushbrooke' as one to be reckoned with at both trials and shows. He has bred a large number of winners: Ch. Runner, Sh.Ch. Rustle, Racer, Runelle, Race-along, Rustic and many others, all bearing the Rushbrooke hall-mark.

Mr H. C. Payne is also one of the most enthusiastic supporters of the breed, which he has shown and run at trials for many years past. He is usually to be seen at the big championship shows and very frequently in the big ring with the Welsh Springer Best of Breed. His latest Champion is Statesman of Tregwillym. Others he owns are the Show Champions Token, Trigger and Top Score.

The 'Denethorp' prefix of Mr F. A Hart is well known for its winners. Ch. Denethorp Danny holds pride of place as, in addition to being a Bench Champion, he is a prize-winner at field trials. Rockhill Rona was bred in these kennels, and since Mrs Mayall's death her favourite, Ch. Rockhill Rhiwderin, has come to live with the Denethorps.

Mr L. Hughes owns the two Champions Snowdonian Lad and Lassie of Menai, and to Mrs M. F. Morgan goes the honour of breeding and owning the first post-war Champion, Branksome Beauty. Later, owned jointly by Mr and Mrs T. H. Morgan, Brancourt Bang became a Champion.

Miss D. Ellis has owned Welsh Springers for many years. Sh.Ch. Jester of Downland and Philosopher of Downland are two of her best-known winners. Some years ago she flew to the United States with a team of five Welsh Springers and exhibited them successfully at the big shows there.

In 1946 Mrs D. Morriss showed a young dog named Stokecourt Beau, whom she had bought for rough shooting—a most attractive dog and an excellent worker. He won a Challenge Certificate, and his daughter, Stokecourt Susan, has been one of the outstanding Welsh Springers at trials, winning the Spaniel Club Stake for Any Variety except English Springers and Cockers in 1953, 1957 and 1961, and again being first at the Welsh Springer Spaniel Club Stake in 1960 at the age of nine and a half years. She has two Awards of Honour and numerous Certificates of Merit in Open Any Variety Stakes and, in addition, has won well on the bench, including a First and Reserve Challenge Certificate. Mrs Morriss has bred a number of other winners, including Sh.Ch. Stokecourt Jonathan and Sh.Ch. Stokecourt Gillian and trial prize-winners Simon, Saki and Satan, as well as other show winners.

Of recent years a number of new owners have fallen for the charm of the Welsh Springer and shown successfully. Dr E. Rickards has three Show Champions in her kennel: Tarbay Florian of Broomleaf, Mikado of Broomleaf, both bred by Mrs K. Doxford, and Stokecourt Judith, bred by Mrs Morriss. Other supporters of the breed are Miss A. West, owner of Ch. Belinda of Linkton and Sh.Ch. Arabella of Linkhill, Mr A. Hubert Arthur, Mr E. Painter and Brig. C. P. G. Wills who was the chairman of committee for several years. Dr Rickards now holds office. Well to the fore with winning stock at the present time are Mr and Mrs

Burgess, Mr and Mrs Mullins, Mr and Mrs Hunton-Morgan, Mr Perkins and Mr Pattinson.

The Welsh Springer has not attained the popularity of the English Springer and the Cocker in the U.S.A. and other countries, but, although not seen in large numbers at shows abroad, a considerable number have been exported. In Holland, for instance, during the last three years four Welsh Springers have become Dutch Champions—Rushbrooke Rhoda, Rusty of Riverland, Welsh Gala of Riverland and Red Rust of Downland— while in the same period only one English Springer has attained the Dutch title—Winch Crocidolite.

Recently a Welsh Springer Spaniel Club was formed in the United States, with Mr Randolph as president and Mr James Parker, of Fort Glover, Marblehead, Mass., as secretary and treasurer.

The Welsh Springer Spaniel Club used to hold a Field Trial with Stakes for Any Variety Spaniel and also Stakes restricted to Welsh Springer Spaniels only. The Club then decided to provide Stakes for Welsh Springers only until 1965 when it sponsored the formation of the Welsh and English Counties Spaniel Club and this body now holds the Field Trials.

Miss W. J. Painter took over as Secretary of the Welsh Springer Spaniel Club and its former Secretary, Mr Hal Leopard, became Secretary of the new Welsh and English Counties Spaniel Club.

Miss W. J. Painter resigned on becoming Mrs Hitchcock and is now concerned with raising a younger generation of Welsh enthusiasts. She handed over the office in 1971 to Mrs J. Walton.

I.B.H.

APPENDIX A
BREED STATISTICS

POST-WAR REGISTRATIONS OF ENGLISH SPRINGER SPANIELS

Year			Year			Year		
1946	..	.. 3,250	1955	..	.. 1,341	1964	..	.. 1,832
1947	..	.. 3,172	1956	..	.. 1,328	1965	..	.. 2,004
1948	..	.. 2,740	1957	..	.. 1,305	1966	..	.. 1,796
1949	..	.. 2,327	1958	..	.. 1,477	1967	..	.. 2,054
1950	..	.. 2,316	1959	..	.. 1,535	1968	..	.. 2,147
1951	..	.. 1,699	1960	..	.. 1,613	1969	..	.. 2,529
1952	..	.. 1,458	1961	..	.. 1,616	1970	..	.. 2,894
1953	..	.. 1,398	1962	..	.. 1,941	1971	..	.. 2,683
1954	..	.. 1,376	1963	..	.. 1,944			

POST-WAR REGISTRATIONS OF WELSH SPRINGER SPANIELS

Year			Year			Year		
1946	..	.. 160	1955	..	.. 82	1964	..	.. 195
1947	..	.. 168	1956	..	.. 101	1965	..	.. 208
1948	..	.. 126	1957	..	.. 143	1966	..	.. 157
1949	..	.. 116	1958	..	.. 105	1967	..	.. 253
1950	..	.. 136	1959	..	.. 139	1968	..	.. 229
1951	..	.. 102	1960	..	.. 128	1969	..	.. 385
1952	..	.. 109	1961	..	.. 153	1970	..	.. 335
1953	..	.. 99	1962	..	.. 210	1971	..	.. 409
1954	..	.. 122	1963	..	.. 124			

APPENDIX B

SPECIALIST CLUBS HOLDING SHOWS FOR ENGLISH SPRINGER SPANIELS ONLY

Championship Shows	*Secretary*
The English Springer Spaniel Club	Mrs I. B. Hampton, Larkstoke Cottage, Bourton-on-the-Hill, Moreton-in-Marsh, Glos
The Midland English Springer Spaniel Society	Mrs J. Backhouse, 121 Silcoates Lane, Wrenthorpe, Wakefield, Yorks

The English Springer Spaniel   Mr. J. Sharpe,
    Club of Scotland   21D Fulton's Lane, Kilmarnock, Ayrshire
The English Springer Spaniel   Mr. P. A. Davies,
    Club of Wales   Springfields, Blackton Lane, Penmark,
                               Barry, Glam

Open Shows	*Secretary*
The London and Home Counties English Springer Spaniel Society	Mr A. E. Spearing, 'Kilrennan', 3 Raps Close, Creech Barrow Laxton Road, Taunton, Somerset
The Welsh Springer Spaniel Club	Mrs. J. Walton, The Lodge, Wrotham, Sevenoaks, Kent

APPENDIX C

SOCIETIES RUNNING FIELD TRIALS
FOR SPANIELS

Society or Club	*Secretary*	*Stakes*
1. *Societies for English Springer Spaniels only*		
The English Springer Spaniel Club	Mrs I. B. Hampton, Larkstoke Cottage, Bourton-on-the-Hill, Moreton-on-Marsh, Glos	Novice Open
	Field Trial Sec. Lt Col. L. T. Spittle, Cinders Wood, Tenbury Wells, Worcs	
The English Springer Spaniel Club of Scotland	Mrs E. K. Thomson, Over Linkins, Castle Douglas, N.B.	Novice Open
The Midland English Springer Spaniel Society	Mrs J. Backhouse, 121, Silcoates Lane, Wrenthorpe, Wakefield, Yorks	Novice Open
	Field Trial Sec. Mrs W. Oakey, Takoradi, Eydon, Daventry, Northants NN11 6QE	
The English Springer Spaniel Club of Northern Ireland	Mr J. Blaikie, 58, Springhill Road, Bangor, N.I.	Novice Open
The Antrim and Down Springer Spaniel Club	Mr J. S. Burrow, 92, Locksley Park, Finaghy, Belfast BT10 0AT	Open
2. *Societies for Any Variety Spaniel*		
Eastern Counties Spaniel Society	Miss A. Busuttil, The Old Rectory, Swardeston, Norwich ,Norfolk	A.V. Open A.V. Members Open A.V. Novice Dog A.V. Novice Handlers
The Spaniel Club	Mr T. J. Greatorex, 212, Andover Rd, Newbury, Berkshire	A.V. Open
Western Counties, and South Wales Spaniel Club	Mr A. M. Pearce, 23, Durleigh Rd, Bridgwater, Somerset	A.V. Open A.V. Novice

Society or Club	*Secretary*	*Stakes*

3. *General Field Trial Societies holding Field Trials for Spaniels*

Ulster Gundog League	Mr S. B. Cunningham, The Northern Whig, Bridge Street, Belfast	A.V. Open
North Western Counties Field Trial Association	Mr A. Mason, 21, King St, Carnforth, Lancs	A.V. Open
Cambridge Field Trial Society	Mrs M. J. Curtis, The Moors, Whittlesford, Cambs	A.V. Open A.V. Novice
Gamekeepers' National Association	Mr J. Aldridge, Kerrysdale Gundog Kennels, Windyridge, Warrenhill, Collin, Dumfries, Scotland	A.V. Open A.V. Novice
Scottish Gundog Association	Mr A. H. Syme, The Moss, Dunblane, Perthshire	A.V. Open A.V. Novice
Scottish Field Trials Association	Mr A. H. Syme, The Moss, Dunblane, Perthshire	A.V. Open A.V. Novice
Yorkshire Gundog Club	Mrs E. H. Bailey, Longclose, Bessacarr, Doncaster	A.V. Open
Essex Field Trial Society	Mr L. G. Kinsella, The Mount, Fingringhoe, Colchester, Essex	A.V. Open A.V. Novice
West Midland Field Trial Society	Mr C. Sutcliffe, Gravel Pit Cottage, The Green, Barton-under-Needwood, Burton-on-Trent, Staffs	A.V. Open A.V. Novice
North of Scotland Gundog Association	Mr D. M. Douglas, Frogfield, Laurencekirk, Kincardineshire, Scotland	A.V. Open A.V. Novice
Cheshire, North Wales and Shropshire Retriever and Spaniel Society	Mr Hobley Eaves, Keren, St Hilary's Drive, Deganwy, Caerns	A.V. Open A.V. Novice
Midland Counties Field Trial Society	Mr J. A. Taylor, 420 London Road, Leicester LE2 2PT	A.V. Open A.V. Novice
Southern and Western Counties Field Trial Society	Mrs D. Purbrick, Dores Hill, North Sydmonton, Newbury, Berkshire	A.V. Open A.V. Novice
Welsh and English Counties Spaniel Club	Mr H. J. H. Leopard, The Boynes, Upton-on-Severn, Worcestershire	A.V. Open

APPENDIX D

POST-WAR ENGLISH SPRINGER SPANIEL CHAMPIONS 1947–71

Name	Sex	Sire	Dam	Owner	Breeder	Born
1947 Ch. Whaddon Chase Bonny Tom	D	Ch. Higham Tom Tit	Butter	Lady Lambe	Mr T. M. P. Hill	15·5·44
Ch. Whaddon Chase Snipe	B	Ch. Higham Tom Tit	Butter	Lady Lambe	Mr T. M. P. Hill	15·5·44
1948 Ch. Invader of Ide	D	Templecorran Spotback	Glenmount Lass	Mr J. H. G. Braddon	Mr T. Richie	5·8·45
Ch. Sandylands Shrubley	D	Starshine of Ide	Solo of Shotton	Mrs G. Broadley	Mr M. D. Withers	30·5·44
Ch. Sandylands Soubranie	D	Peter of Shotton	Sandylands Sherry	Mr E. Lumb Taylor	Mrs G. Broadley	14·5·45
Ch. Solitaire of Happeedaze	D	Peter of Shotton	Drumcree Joan	Mr W. R. Hepplewhite	Mr S. P. Phipp	4·9·45
Ch. Stokeley Bonny Boy	D	Ch. Whaddon Chase Bonny Tom	Clintonhouse Elizabeth	Mr D. C. Hannah	Mr D. C. Hannah	23·3·47
Ch. Painted Lady	B	Hercules of Rafehill	Sunnemede Lass	Mr E. J. Burton	Mr J. Mineely	1·9·44
Ch. Sprightley of Happeedaze	B	Templecorran Spotback	Miss Clodagh	Mr W. R. Hepplewhite	Mr E. N. Power	1·4·45
Ch. Staitley May Queen	B	Velikie Luke	Raceview Beauty	Mr G. G. M. Harwell	Mr F. D. Taggart	17·5·45

Name	Sex	Sire	Dam	Owner	Breeder	Born
1949						
Ch. Carnfield Chick	B	Carnfield Commodore	Carnfield Florrie	Mr G. A. Taylor	Mr G. A. Taylor	14.8.47
Ch. Carnfield Florrie	B	Mountain Crest	Clintonhouse Elizabeth	Mr G. A. Taylor	Mr D. C. Hannah	20.12.45
Ch. Higham Topsy	B	Higham Tristram	Ch. Whaddon Chase Snipe	Miss C. M. Francis	Lady Lambe	15.3.47
1950						
Ch. Carnfield Albvic Legioner	D	Albvic Scholar	Sparton	Mr G. A. Taylor	Mr A. V. Blake	28.6.47
Ch. Castlecary Cameronian	D	Staitley Solo	Morneborough Dot	Mrs G. Broadley	Mr F. T. Chalmers	15.4.47
Ch. Whaddon Chase Prince	D	Higham Tristram	Ch. Whaddon Chase Snipe	Lady Lambe	Lady Lambe	15.3.47
Ch. Sandylands Shandy	D	Ch. Sandylands Shrubley	Sandylands Sherry	Mrs G. Broadley	Mrs G. Broadley	8.2.48
Ch. Strathblane Bonnie	D	Ch. Whaddon Chase Bonny Tom	Strathblane Cartridge	Mr S. O'Flynn	Major A. M. Horsbrugh	24.6.47
Ch. Jess of Montcrief	B	Chastleton Waxwing	Sally of Montcrief	Mr E. W. Dugeon	Mr E. W. Dugeon	6.10.48
Ch. Light of Ashleigh	B	Boxer of Bramhope	Alwinton Faithful Maid	Mr A. B. Nicholson	Mr F. L. Davey	29.6.48
1951						
Ch. Banner of Beechfield	D	Sh.Ch. Grand Lodge	Soubrette of Happeedaze	Miss J. Wilkins	Mrs F. Thompson	20.5.49
Ch. Leymor Recorder	D	Leymor Cracksman	Leymor Perfect Harmony	Mr R. A. Morgan	Mr R. A. Morgan	21.2.45

Name	Sex	Sire	Dam	Owner	Breeder	Born
1951—*cont.*						
Ch. Stokeley Gay Boy	D	Ch. Whaddon Chase Bonny Tom	Clintonhouse Elizabeth	Mr D. C. Hannah	Mr D. C. Hannah	24.4.48
Ch. Stokeley Lucky	D	Ambergris Sportsman	Clintonhouse Elizabeth	Mr D. C. Hannah	Mr D. C. Hannah	22.2.50
Ch. Birkdale Beggermaid	B	Joe of Highbarn	Northdown Style	Mrs N. Ireland	Mr W. Manin	25.5.49
1952						
Ch. Clintonhouse George	D	Boxer of Bramhope	Clintonhouse Hazeltong Judith	Mr I. Davies	Mrs G. Thomson	3.7.50
Ch. Alexander of Stubham	D	Boxer of Bramhope	Susan of Stubham	Mrs F. O. Till	Mrs F. O. Till	20.2.50
Ch. Peter of Lorton Fell	D	Boxer of Bramhope	Alwinton Faithful Maid	Mr J. C. Hanning	Mr F. L. Davey	29.6.48
Ch. Whaddon Chase Bonny Lass	B	Ch. Whaddon Chase Bonny Tom	Whaddon Chase Melody	Lady Lambe	Lady Lambe	6.8.48
Ch. Whaddon Chase Bracken	B	Higham Tristram	Ch. Whaddon Chase Snipe	Lady Lambe	Lady Lambe	15.3.47
Ch. Bramhope Recorder	D	Ideal Stamp	Bramhope Suzette	Mr E. Froggott	Mr and Mrs J. Scott	20.4.48
1953						
Ch. Colmaris Contessa	B	Colmaris Toreador	Clintonhouse Hazeltong Judith	Mr T. Davies	Mr T. Davies	8.12.51
Ch. Dinah of Stubham	B	Boxer of Bramhope	Susan of Stubham	Mr R. Grant	Mrs F. O. Till	26.2.57
Ch. Tillan Toddy	B	Ch. Solitaire of Happeedaze	Staghorn Pinkfoot	Mr J. M. Bolton	Lady Belhaven	30.5.48

Name	Sex	Sire	Dam	Owner	Breeder	Born
1954 Ch. Studley Major	D	Boxer of Bramhope	Bountiful of Beechfield	Mrs S. G. Smithson	Mrs. S. G. Smithson	13.1.52
Ch. Belarosa of Bramhope	B	Boxer of Bramhope	Reurut Rose	Mr and Mrs J. Scott	Mr A. Laing	23.3.52
1955 Ch. Camdin Chief	D	Boxer of Bramhope	Camdin Mistress	Mrs V. Hare-Dinsley	Mrs V. Hare-Dinsley	26.6.50
Ch. Beanmore Camdin Greta	B	Gay Lord of Beanmore	Camdin Mistress Lucy	Mrs H. P. Frankish	Mrs V. Hare-Dinsley	8.6.52
1956 Ch. Inverruel Raider	D	Aristocrat of Stubham	Barnes Mill Cherry	Mr D. Campbell	Mr T. Robb	3.10.57
Ch. Whaddon Chase Grouse	B	Higham Tar	Ch. Whaddon Chase Bracken	Lady Lambe	Lady Lambe	12.8.50
Ch. Print of Ardrick	D	Ch. Clintonhouse George	Patsey of Ardrick	Mr F. G. Burton	Mr F. G. Burton	2.8.54
Ch. Bonnie Wee Teal	B	Crescent Starlight	Balnathany Bonnie Lass	Mr J. S. Webster	Mr A. R. Webster	8.6.52
1957 Ch. Mowgrain Mr. Chips	D	Ch. Sandylands Soubranie	Bambino of Bramhope	Mrs J. Midgley	Mrs J. Midgley	15.10.53
Ch. Royal Salue of Stubham	D	Ch. Alexander of Stubham	Empress of Stubham	Mrs F. O. Till	Mrs F. O. Till	20.5.55
Ch. Bathsheba of Bramhope	B	Boxer of Bramhope	Clintonhouse Hazeltong Judith	Mrs M. Scott	Mr and Mrs J. Scott	2.8.53

Name	Sex	Sire	Dam	Owner	Breeder	Born
1957—cont. Ch. Duchess of Stubham	B	Boxer of Bramhope	Susan of Stubham	Mrs J. Spence	Mrs F. O. Till	26.2.51
Ch. Northdown Donna	B	Ch. Clintonhouse George	Sh.Ch. Northdown Fancy	Mrs F. Sherwood and Mr W. Manin	Mr W. Manin	25.12.54
1958 Ch. Colmaris Chancellor	D	Sh.Ch. Stokeley Sea Sprite	Colmaris Clover	Mrs H. P. Frankish	Mr I. Davies	22.4.56
Ch. Studley Diadem	B	Banker of Bramhope	Bountiful of Beechfield	Mrs F. O. Till	Mrs S. G. Smithson	13.12.54
1959 Ch. Hawkhill Brave	D	Ch. Studley Major	Starlet of Stubham	Miss J. Robinson	Miss J. Robinson	9.7.55
Ch. Floravon Silverstar	B	Ch. Studley Major	Starlet of Stubham	Miss J. Robinson	Mr H. Sweeney	24.4.54
1960 Ch. Winch Starturn	D	Winch Crocidolite	Winch Olivine	Mrs G. G. Crawford	Mrs G. G. Crawford	30.7.57
Ch. Tyneview Margaret	B	Sh.Ch. Studley Brave Buccaneer	Tyneview Sarina	Mrs E. Dobson	Mr G. Scott	21.11.55
1961 Ch. Hyperion of Stubham	D	Ch. Alexander of Stubham	Ch. Floravon Silverstar	Mrs F. O. Till	Miss J. Robinson	7.11.58
Ch. Sir Knight	D	Int.Ch. Print of Ardrick	Hart of Oak	Mr J. Cranston	Mr J. Cranston	30.7.57
Ch. Brandyhole Diadem	B	Brandyhole Commodore	Brandyhole Bellflower	Mrs J. Spence	Mrs J. Spence	25.4.57
1962 Ch. Beanmore George	D	Ch. Colmaris Chancellor	Beanmore Jennifer	Mrs H. P. Frankish	Mrs H. P. Frankish	17.5.58

Name	Sex	Sire	Dam	Owner	Breeder	Born
1962—cont. Ch. Glenford Gamester	D	Redbank Ranger	Doleful Damsel	Mr H. F. Lock	Mr H. F. Lock	17.10.56
Ch. Maydown Ripple	B	Peter of Pinecrest	Black Cygnet	Mrs L. Bunting	Mr H. Bunting	16.7.55
1964 Ch. Pencloe Driftwood	D	Douglas of Freetwood	Dalhanna Dew	Miss M. H. Bolton	Miss M. H. Bolton	30.6.61.
1965 Ch. Conneil Casket	B	Ch. Alexander of Stubham	Conneil	Mr D. Storie	Mrs C. Crawford	28.8.60
Ch. Stokeley Teesview Telstar	B	(Amer.Ch.) Stokeley Toreador	Ch. Tyneview Margaret	Mr. D. C. Hannah	Mrs E. Bobson	22.6.62
Ch. Pats Boy of Stodhart	D	Hawkhill Nebuchadnezzar	Hawkhill Margaret	Mr and Mrs T. P. and Mr N. P. Campbell	Mrs A. Campbell	15.3.61
1966 Ch. Moorcliff Dougal of Truelindale	D	Sh.Ch. Douglas of Freetwood	Sh.Ch. Lessudden Linnet	Mr E. Froggatt	Miss M. Alder	10.1.64
Ch. Blossomtime of Bramhope	B	(Amer.Ch.) Melilotus Shooting Star	Ch. Bathsheba of Bramhope	Mr and Mrs J. Backhouse	Mrs M. C. Scott	29.4.61
Ch. Chipmunk of Stubham	D	Ch. Hyperion of Stubham	Whaddon Chase Honeysuckle of Stubham	Mr F. J. Robinson	Mrs F. O. Till	2.12.62
1967 Ch. Ranjoa Roberta	B	Redport Major	Jessica of Chatsmith	Mr A. Lupton	Mr A. Lupton	22.10.62
Ch. Woodbay Gay Charmer	B	Northdown Diplomat	Sh.Ch.Vanity Fair of Stubham	Mr N. H. Jenkins	Mrs F. Sherwood	28.6.60

Name	Sex	Sire	Dam	Owner	Breeder	Born
1967—cont. Ch. Teesview Titus	D	(Amer.Ch.) Stokeley Toreador	Ch. Tyneview Margaret	Mrs E. Dobson	Mrs E. Dobson	22.6.62
Ch. Larkstoke Ptarmigan	B	Larkstoke Black Grouse	Larkstoke Higham Tidy	Mrs I. B. Hampton	Mrs I. B. Hampton	10.1.64
1968 Ch. Inverruel Pacemaker	D	Pemberton Prince	Inverruel Jasmine	Mr D. P. B. Camp-bell	Mr D. P. B. Camp-bell	7.7.65
Ch. Teesview Tarmac	D	Ch. Teesview Titmus	Cleavehill Cilla	Mrs E. Dobson	Mrs E. Dobson	30.8.65
Ch. Weaversvale Moorcliff Farewell	B	Sh.Ch. Moorcliff Freetwood Game-cock	Sh.Ch. Moorcliff Bye-Bye of Bramhope	Mr A. G. Nicholls	Mr E. Froggatt	15.5.66
1970 Ch. Swallowtail of Shipden	D	Sh. Ch. Persimmon of Shipden	Sombre Beauty	Mr and Mrs C. J. Muirhead	Mr P. Snowley	5.5.67

APPENDIX E

POST-WAR ENGLISH SPRINGER SPANIEL FIELD TRIAL CHAMPIONS 1947–71

Name	Sex	Sire	Dam	Owner	Breeder	Born
1947 F.T.Ch. Pinehawk Roger	D	Staindrop Spitfire	Pinehawk	Mr A. Wylie	Mr A. Wylie	1.3.44
F.T.Ch. Silverstar of Chrishall	D	Whittlesford Beesting	Teggie of Chrishall	Mr J. Kent	Mr J. Kent	30.11.44
F.T.Ch. Spark O'Vara	D	Sprint O'Vara	Sprigg O'Vara	Mr Selwyn C. Jones	Mr Selwyn C. Jones	15.4.45
1948 F.T.Ch. Caerleon Comet	D	Searle O'Vara	Garreg Busy	Mr H. Thornel Brown	Mr T. Evans	2.6.46
F.T.Ch. Sarkie O'Vara	D	Sprint O'Vara	Starlette O'Vara	Mr Selwyn C. Jones	Mr Selwyn C. Jones	26.6.42
1949 F.T.Ch. Racedale Rover	D	F.T.Ch. Beson of Blair	Pinehawk	Mrs A. Beale	Mr A. Wylie	20.6.43
F.T.Ch. Spurt O'Vara	D	F.T.Ch. Pinehawk Roger	Skip O'Vara	Mr Selwyn C. Jones	Mr Selwyn C. Jones	18.7.47
F.T.Ch. Whittlemoor George	D	Whittlesford Spitfire	Whittlemoor Betty	Col C. McNeill	Mr A. E. Curtis	30.9.46
F.T.Ch. Breckonhill Bee	B	F.T.Ch. Sarkie O'Vara	Breckonhill Bustle	Mr G. Curle	Mr T. H. Graham	18.4.46
1950 F.T.Ch. Kinmount Pat	D	Kinmount Punch	Kinmount Trixie	Mr J. Buie	Capt. E. W. Brook	26.7.42

Name	Sex	Sire	Dam	Owner	Breeder	Born
1950—cont.						
F.T.Ch. Rivington Glensaugh Glean	D	F.T.Ch. Silverstar of Chrishall	Kingsham Keepsake	Messrs E. and M. Ainsworth	Mr D. Munro	16.5.48
F.T.Ch. Whittlesford Record	D	Whittlesford Spitfire	Jean Laird	Col C. McNeill	Col C. McNeill	24.6.47
F.T.Ch. Acheron Pat	B	Spy Hawk	Dochfour Trixie	Mr R. N. Burton	Capt A. McNeill Farquhar	11.5.47
1951						
F.T.Ch. Dauntless Monty	D	F.T.Ch. Pinehawk Roger	Victory Vee	Mr W. G. Sheldon	Mr W. G. Sheldon	1.5.48
F.T.Ch. Sleet O'Vara	D	Sprint O'Vara	Stress O'Vara	Mr Selwyn C. Jones	Mr Selwyn C. Jones	17.4.49
F.T.Ch. Acheron Trick	B	Spy Hawk	Dochfour Trixie	Dr E. B. Sunderland	Capt. A. McNeill Farquhar	11.5.47
1952						
F.T.Ch. Greatford Kim	D	Harpersbrook Apethorpe Teazle	Bobble of Rothwell	Major H. Peacock	Mr A. Sergeant	3.7.49
F.T.Ch. Stranwood Superior	D	Searle O'Vara	Curley Caroline	Mr J. McHarrie	Mr J. McHarrie	16.5.49
F.T.Ch. Griffel Daisy Bell	B	Glennewton Prince	Barlochan Patsy	Mr T. B. Laird	Mr T. B. Laird	23.4.48
F.T.Ch. Griffel Pamela	B	Glennewton Prince	Barlochan Patsy	Mr T. B. Laird	Mr T. B. Laird	23.4.48
F.T.Ch. Ludlow Gyp	B	F.T.Ch. Pinehawk Roger	Victory Vee	Mr W. G. Sheldon	Mr W. G. Sheldon	1.5.49
1953						
F.T.Ch. Carlo of Chrishall	D	F.T.Ch. Silverstar of Chrishall	Bekesbourne Rozzi	Mr J. Kent	Mr P. R. A. Moxon	23.5.51

Name	Sex	Sire	Dam	Owner	Breeder	Born
1953—cont.						
F.T.Ch. Ludlovian Darkie	D	F.T.Ch. Spark O'Vara	F.T.Ch. Ludlow Gyp	Mr W. G. Sheldon	Mr W. G. Sheldon	12.6.51
F.T.Ch. Stranwood Speed	D	Sarkie O'Vara	Westwood Sally	Mr J. McHarrie	Mr J. McHarrie	24.3.50
F.T.Ch. Scramble O'Vara	B	Searle O'Vara	Skid O'Vara	Mr Selwyn C. Jones	Mr Selwyn C. Jones	9.11.51
F.T.Ch. Staxegoe Sensation	B	Panda of Culnaightry	Prudence of Mull	Mr W. Emsleigh	Mr J. Lindsay	24.2.51
F.T.Ch. Streonshalh Comet	B	Harpersbrook Apethorpe Teazle	Streonshalh Tempest	Mr F. George	Mr R. Baker	8.6.51
1954						
F.T.Ch. Criffel Prince	D	Glennewton Prince	Barlochan Patsy	Mr T. B. Laird	Mr T. B. Laird	7.1.52
F.T.Ch. Ludlovian Bruce	D	F.T.Ch. Rivington Glensaugh Glean	F.T.Ch. Ludlow Gyp	Mr W. G. Sheldon	Mr W. G. Sheldon	14.5.52
F.T.Ch. Saighton's Sentry	D	Saighton's Sam	Saighton's Scent	Mr Talbot Radcliffe	Mr Talbot Radcliffe	22.1.53
F.T.Ch. Cammas Tiny	B	Bramble of Chrishall	Bang of Landwade	Mr J. M. Lukies	Mr G. Gibson	1.4.51
F.T.Ch. Carswell Cornelia	B	Carswell Sprightley	Carswell Conquest	Mrs P. M. Badenach-Nicolson	Mrs P. M. Badenach-Nicolson	5.1.51
F.T.Ch. Criffel Nellie	B	F.T.Ch. Rivington Clensaugh Glean	F.T.Ch. Criffel Pamela	Mr T. B. Laird	Mr T. B. Laird	9.5.53
F.T.Ch. Ludlovian Ruby	B	Micklewood Scud	Ludlovian Beauty	Mr W. G. Sheldon	Mr W. G. Sheldon	5.6.51

Name	Sex	Sire	Dam	Owner	Breeder	Born
1954—cont. F.T.Ch. Rivington Michele	B	F.T.Ch. Rivington Glensaugh Glean	F.T.Ch. Ludlow Gyp	Mrs C. A. Thomson	Mr W. G. Sheldon	14-5-52
F.T.Ch. Saighton's Scent	B	F.T.Ch. Spark O'Vara	Saighton's Slice	Mr T. Radcliffe	Mr T. Radcliffe	27.6.49
1955 F.T.Ch. Criffel Danny	D	Whittlemoor Renrut Brightstar	F.T.Ch. Creffel Pamela	Mr T. B. Laird	Mr T. B. Laird	2.7.54
F.T.Ch. Harpersbrook Sammy	D	Harpersbrook Apethorpe Teazle	Peggie of the Manor	Dr J. Hurndall Gann	Col R. H. Palmer	31-5-52
F.T.Ch. Ludlovian Socks	D	Micklewood Scud	F.T.Ch. Ludlovian Gyp	Mrs F. E. Waller	Mr W. G. Sheldon	25.2.53
F.T.Ch. Rivington Landmark	D	Dungarry	Lockelrig Ruth	Mr C. A. Thomson	Mr J. Windle	22.5.54
F.T.Ch. Bryanston Bess	B	Harpersbrook Apethorpe Teazle	Oldshire Empress	Mr D. A. S. Bowlby	Mr S. Folwell	9.5.52
F.T.Ch. Gwen of Barnacre	B	Searle O'Vara	Saighton's Slice	Mr H. Jackson	Mr T. Radcliffe	19.5.53
1956 F.T.Ch. Breckonhill Brave	D	Breckonhill Buddy	Breckonhill Bee	Mr R. Garvin	Mr G. Curle	10.8.54
F.T.Ch. Rossend Prince	D	Handy of Glenmorag	Tirelands Janet	Lt Com. E. A. J. Collard	Mr J. P. Winterbourne	16.8.53
F.T.Ch. Carswell Contessa	B	F.T.Ch. Stranwood Speed	F.T.Ch. Carswell Cornelia	Mrs P. M. Bradenach-Nicolson	Mrs P. M. Bradenach-Nicolson	30.12.54
F.T.Ch. Posterngate Jet	B	Brockenhill Pim	Cinders of Lincliff	Dr D. A. White	Mr C. Weighton	2-3-53

Name	Sex	Sire	Dam	Owner	Breeder	Born
1956—cont.						
F.T.Ch. Staxigoe Seawaif	B	F.T.Ch. Rivington Glensaugh Glean	Staxigoe Seashell	Mr W. J. McCoubray	Mr D. McKenzie	29.4.52
1957						
F.T.Ch. Breckonhill Bridegroom	D	Breckonhill Buddie	Breckonhill Bee	Mr G. Curle	Mr G. Curle	16.4.55
F.T.Ch. Pinehawk Sark	D	F.T.Ch. Ludlovian Socks	Garwgarreg Jet	Mr A. Wylie	Mr T. Evans	27.3.56
F.T.Ch. Richard of Elan	D	F.T.Ch. Rossend Prince	Ludlovian Shelly	Lt-Com. E. A. J. Collard	Mr A. Winterbourne	15.2.55
F.T.Ch. Saighton's Spree	D	F.T.Ch. Saighton's Sentry	Linwhinny Jess	Mr H. Blackburn	Mr H. Blackburn	14.4.55
F.T.Ch. Rivington Raechele	B	Whittlemoor Renrut Brightstar	F.T.Ch. Rivington Michele	Mrs C. A. Thomson	Mrs C. A. Thomson	20.3.55
1958						
F.T.Ch. Breckonhill Borderance Bounce	D	Breckonhill Buddie	Breckonhill Brag	Mr G. Curle	Mr D. S. Nicholson	27.10.53
F.T.Ch. Criffel Snipe	D	Rivington Dale	F.T.Ch. Criffel Pamela	Mr T. B. Laird	Mr T. B. Laird	16.7.55
F.T.Ch. Harpersbrook Boots	D	F.T.Ch. Ludlovian Socks	Meadowcourt Martha	Mrs F. George	Mr R. B. Weston-Webb	26.4.56
F.T.Ch. Jordieland Glean	D	F.T.Ch. Rivington Glensaugh Glean	Lockside Flo	Mr J. A. Windle	Mr J. A. Windle	4.6.55
F.T.Ch. Shineradee	D	Scamp O'Vara	Ninadee	Mr F. George	Mr F. Bell	20.5.56
F.T.Ch. Entonlee Cherry	B	F.T.Ch. Ludlovian Socks	Entonlee Blackberry	Mr F. George	Mrs J. C. Lee	12.5.56

Name	Sex	Sire	Dam	Owner	Breeder	Born
1959						
F.T.Ch. Blatherwycke Meadowcourt Hector	D	Great Meadowcourt Stephen	Meadowcourt Mistress	Mrs F. George	Mr R. B. Weston-Webb	26.5.57
F.T.Ch. Pinehawk Spur	D	F.T.Ch. Ludlovian Socks	Garwgarreg Jet	Mr H. A. J. Silley	Mr T. Evans	27.3.56
F.T.Ch. Wakefares Sprigg	D	F.T.Ch. Harpersbrook Sammy	Wakefares Sugar	Mr F. M. Prime	Mr F. M. Prime	1.6.57
F.T.Ch. Willy of Barnacre	D	Conygree Simon	F.T.Ch. Gwen of Barnacre	Mr H. Jackson	Mr H. Jackson	7.6.56
F.T.Ch. Jontis Jezebel	B	Breckonhill Brien	Ballygawly Flash	Mr R. J. Fettis	Mr K. Patterson	12.6.56
1960						
F.T.Ch. Harpersbrook Reed	D	Greatforl Meadowcourt Stephen	Thurwood Sally	Mr F. George	Mr H. Woodfield	25.6.57
F.T.Ch. Jonkit Jasper	D	F.T.Ch. Pinehawk Sark	Jonkit Julia	Dr T. K. Davidson	Dr T. K. Davidson	7.6.58
F.T.Ch. Markdown Muffin	D	F.T.Ch. Rivington Glensaugh Glean	Ludlovian Diana	Mr F. Thomas	Mr F. Thomas	16.12.57
F.T.Ch. Saighton's Swing	D	Saighton's Sputnik	Saighton's Sickle	Mr T. Radcliffe	Mr T. Radcliffe	9.4.58
F.T.Ch. Criffel Melody	B	F.T.Ch. Pinehawk Sark	F.T.Ch. Criffel Pamela	Mr T. B. Laird	Mr T. B. Laird	9.8.58
F.T.Ch. Micklewood Slip	B	F.T.Ch. Rivington Glensaugh Glean	Ludlovian Diana	Capt. R. W. Corbett	Mr F. Thomas	16.12.57
F.T.Ch. Red Siren	B	Straight Shot	Shooting Pal	Mr H. Thompson	Mr W. Plunkett	22.10.57
F.T.Ch. Speckle of Chrishall	B	Tim of Chrishall	Higham Tell	Mr J. Kent	Miss C. M. Francis	8.4.57

Name	Sex	Sire	Dam	Owner	Breeder	Born
1961						
F.T.Ch. Breckonhill Bilko	D	Brackenbank Solo	Houghton Lady	Mr G. Curle	Mr W. C. Kyle	25.6.58
F.T.Ch. Harpersbrook Reed	D	Greatford Meadowcourt Stephen	Thurwood Sally	Mr F. George	Mr H. A. Woodfield	25.6.57
F.T.Ch. Dinas Dewi Sele	B	Rivington Sailor	Dinas Dewi Scottie	Major L. T. Spittle	Mr W. Llewellyn	15.7.59
F.T.Ch. Kate of Barnacre	B	Conygree Simon	F.T.Ch. Gwen of Barnacre	Mr H. Jackson	Mr H. Jackson	7.5.58
F.T.Ch. Meadowcourt Judy	B	F.T.Ch. Pinehawk Spur	Meadowcourt Mistress	Mr R. B. Weston-Webb	Mr R. B. Weston-Webb	6.6.59
F.T.Ch. Rivington Judy	B	F.T.Ch. Rivington Glensaugh Glean	Ludlovian Perle	Mr R. D. Methven	Mr C. A. Thomson	14.8.57
1962						
F.T.Ch. Halebrook Saighton's Shingle	B	Saighton's Squire	Saighton's Speed	Mrs R. Hadcock	Mr T. Radcliffe	1.5.59
F.T.Ch. Markdown Mag	D	Conygree Simon	Jordieland Jane	Mrs C. M. Thomas	Mr J. B. Taylor	12.7.59
F.T.Ch. Templegrafton Hardy	D	Tim of Chrishall	Warrenmere Frisky	Captain T. L. M. Lonsdale	Mrs W. H. Whitbread	5.1.59
F.T.Ch. Ballyvoy Dandy	D	Cadet Jeff	F.T.Ch. Red Siren	Mr H. Thompson	Mr H. Thompson	8.3.60
F.T.Ch. Jonkit Jandy	B	F.T.Ch. Pinehawk Sark	Jonkit Julia	Mr B. B. Dutton	Dr T. K. Davidson	9.6.58
F.T.Ch. Gwibernant Abereithy Skip	D	F.T.Ch. Pinehawk Sark	Dinas Dewi Scottie	Mr K. Erlandson	Mr W. Llewellyn	13.3.61
F.T.Ch. Ruffin Tuff	D	F.T.Ch. Saighton's Swing	Dainty Lady of Ards	Mr J. M. Kelvey	Mr H. Johnston	2.4.61

Name	Sex	Sire	Dam	Owner	Breeder	Born
1963 F.T.Ch. Gwibernant Gynan	D	Conygree Simon	Breckenhill Brando	R. J. Fettis	K. A. Erlandson	14.7.60
F.T.Ch. Saighton's Stinger	D	Saighton's Salmon	Creevanmore Brownie	T. Radcliffe	T. Radcliffe	24.7.62
F.T.Ch. Wilby Trigger	D	F.T.Ch. Jonkit Jasper	Jonkit Juno	F. George	Dr T. K. Davidson	7.4.60
F.T.Ch. Berrystead Freckle	B	F.T.Ch. Jonkit Jasper	Jonkit Juno	W. C. Williams	Dr T. K. Davidson	7.4.60
F.T.Ch. Criffel Patsy	B	F.T.Ch. Markdown Muffin	F.T.Ch. Criffel Melody	T. B. Laird	T. B. Laird	16.5.61
F.T.Ch. Gardez	B	F.T.Ch. Saighton's Swing	Dainty Lady of Ards	R. Garvan	H. Johnston	2.4.61
1964 F.T.Ch. Bradenham Socks	D	Pannier of Chrishall	Kenswick Tango	Mrs K. Luttmer and Dr D. A. White	Mrs K. Luttmer	20.6.60
F.T.Ch. Denhead Walnut	D	F.T.Ch. Markdown Muffin	Denhead Scamper	G. S. Drummond	D. M. Douglas	21.5.61
F.T.Ch. Willie Snaffles	D	Gwibernant Gadwaladr	Micklewood Slip	Mrs J. W. Sloan	Capt. W. Corbett	24.8.61
F.T.Ch. Lytchmore Hamers Jean	B	Meadowcourt Wise Boy	Wilby Bess	M. H. Hopper	R. Dutton	26.6.60
F.T.Ch. Meadowcourt Polly	B	F.T.Ch. Markdown Muffin	F.T.Ch. Meadow-court Judy	Mrs S. Weston Webb	R. B. Weston Webb	15.7.61
F.T.Ch. Wivenwood Fofo	B	F.T.Ch. Wakefares Sprigg	Mizzen	J. W. Davey	J. W. Davey	3.7.61

Name	Sex	Sire	Dam	Owner	Breeder	Born
1965						
F.T.Ch. Blatherwycke Teal	D	F.T.Ch. Harpersbrook Reed	Meadowcourt Record	Mrs F. George	M. Jackson	5.3.62
F.T.Ch. Denhead Warrior	D	F.T.Ch. Markdown Muffin	Denhead Scamper	D. M. Douglas	D. M. Douglas	21.5.61
F.T.Ch. Hiwood Rosso	D	Hiwood Andy	Shani of Snowdell	The Hon. Lady Hill Wood	R. Haddow	31.3.63
F.T.Ch. Saighton's Saulson	D	(Amer.F.T.Ch.) Saighton's Saul	F.T.Ch. Halebrook Saighton's Shingle	T. Radcliffe	T. Radcliffe	17.6.63
F.T.Ch. Sliguy of Ardoon	D	Hales Smut	Gwibernant Gwenellian	J. Magee	W. Sloan	1.6.63
F.T.Ch. Harwes Mitten	B	F.T.Ch. Markdown Muffin	Nestfell Kestrel	Dr D. Bovill	E. E. Dougill	8.6.62
F.T.Ch. Meadowcourt Della	B	F.T.Ch. Markdown Mag	F.T.Ch. Meadowcourt Judy	R. B. Weston Webb	R. B. Weston Webb	18.4.63
1966						
F.T.Ch. Hamers Hansel	D	F.T.Ch. Markdown Muffin	F.T.Ch. Jonkit Jandy	B. B. Dutton	B. B. Dutton	17.6.62
F.T.Ch. Jonkit Joel	D	Hales Smut	Jonkit Janet	Dr T. K. Davidson	Dr T. K. Davidson	21.2.64
F.T.Ch. Lytchmore Logan	D	F.T.Ch. Wakefares Sprigg	Jordieland Lily	F. George	M. Hopper	27.2.63
F.T.Ch. Micklewood Story	B	Hales Smut	F.T.Ch. Micklewood Slip	Capt R. W. Corbett	Capt R. W. Corbett	27.10.63
F.T.Ch. Wakefares Scamp	D	F.T.Ch. Wakefares Sprigg	Wilby Flare	F. M. Prime	H. Martineau	24.1.63

Name	Sex	Sire	Dam	Owner	Breeder	Born
F.T.Ch. Carswell Blanche	B	Rivington Starturn	Carswell Berengaria	Mrs P. Badenoch Nicolson	Mrs P. Badenoch Nicolson	17.5.62
F.T.Ch. Sallie of Barnacre	B	F.T.Ch. Markdown Muffin	Markdown Mischief	P. Jackson	R. Greenbank	26.11.61
1968						
F.T.Ch. Goldeneye Jock	D	Hales Smut	Bricksclose Rika	M. Greenwood	J. W. Gillett	4.10.64
F.T.Ch. Joss of Barnacre	D	F.T.Ch. Markdown Muffin	Tuft of Barnacre	H. Jackson	Mrs B. Jackson	19.6.64
F.T.Ch. Markdown Marcus	D	F.T.Ch. Markdown Mag	Shelcot Sheena	F. Thomas	J. Sherlock	18.3.65
F.T.Ch. Rivington Santa Claus	D	Griffel Ranger	Rivington Shellagh	Mrs E. K. Thomson	Mrs E. K. Thomson	8.8.64
F.T.Ch. Bricksclose Scilla	B	Hales Smut	Bricksclose Cherry	Mrs M. Pratt	Mrs M. Pratt	14.4.64
F.T.Ch. Drumbro Daisy	B	F.T.Ch. Denhead Walnut	Reece of Elan	Major G. Yool	G. Easton	4.5.65
F.T.Ch. Gwibernant Garran	B	Hales Smut	Gwibernant Gwaed	Lt-Col L. Spittle	Lt-Col L. Spittle	27.5.65
F.T.Ch. Lady of Ardoon	B	Hales Smut	Gwibernant Gwaed	W. Slaon	C. Spittle	27.5.65
1969						
F.T.Ch. Layerbrook Michelle	B	Hales Smut	Layerbrook Dusty Susan	M. Scales	M. Scales	12.4.67
F.T.Ch. Lancshot Laser	D	Gwibernant G.I. Bach	Gwibernant Garw-graig	C. C. Lamb	K. Erlandson	31.3.67
F.T.Ch. Braiswood Pimm	B	Hales Smut	F.T.Ch. Wivenwood Fofo	Mrs E. M. Hartt	J. W. Davey	4.6.65

Name	Sex	Sire	Dam	Owner	Breeder	Born
1970 F.T.Ch. Harwes Silas	D	Saighton's Stinger	Harwes Mitten	Dr D. Bovill	Dr D. Bovill	20.2.67
F.T.Ch. Staxigoe Swank	D	F.T.Ch. Rivington Santa Claus	Staxigoe Skim	Hon Mrs F. Hopkinson	Mr D. Mackenzie	8.6.67
1971 F.T.Ch. Homerton Rock	B	Wivenwood Bonzo	Rivington Hetherette	Mr A. F. Ebbs	Mr A. F. Ebbs	7.2.68
F.T.Ch. Berrystead Finch	D	F.T.Ch. Berrystead Factor	Wivenwood Trudie	Mr. W. C. Williams	Mr. J. W. Davey	1.3.66
F.T.Ch. Stanleyregis Premier	D	Pinewarren Punch	Bekesbourne Fizz	Mr P. Wilkins	Mr P. Wilkins	4.9.68
F.T.Ch. Gwibernant Ashley Robb	D	Hales Smut	Nell of Ardoon	Mr P. A. Huet	Mr W. C. Sloan	6.8.68
F.T.Ch. Robbie of Barnacre	D	F.T.Ch. Markdown Mag	F.T.Ch. Sallie of Barnacre	Mr H. Jackson	Mr H. Jackson	14.7.67
F.T.Ch. Ballyrobert Bess	B	F.T.Ch. Sliguy of Ardoon	Ballyrobert Hamers Helen	Mr R. E. Clemitson	Mr R. E. Clemitson	5.8.67
F.T.Ch. Philray Tern	D	F.T.Ch. Berrystead Factor	F.T.Ch. Braiswood Pimm	Mr P. R. Elsey	Mrs E. M. Hartt	24.3.67
F.T.Ch. Criffel Ruth	B	Birkwood Sailor	Criffel Suzanne	Mr T. B. Laird	Mr T. B. Laird	29.5.66
F.T.Ch. Coppicewood Carla	B	Wivenwood Bonzo	Wivenwood Susan	Mr T. Lawton Evans	Capt. C. E. Owen	28.5.67

APPENDIX F

POST-WAR ENGLISH SPRINGER SPANIEL SHOW CHAMPIONS 1947–71

Name	Sex	Sire	Dam	Owner	Breeder	Born
Sh.Ch. Sandylands Show Girl	B	Peter of Shotton	Ch. Jess of Shelcot	Mr G. Broadley	Mr M. D. Withers	10.5.43
Sh.Ch. Starshine of Ide	D	Peter of Shotton	Ch. Jess of Shelcot	Mr J. A. Braddon	Mr M. D. Withers	11.6.41
Sh.Ch. Sandylands Sherry	B	Steady of Shotton	Sandylands Salvage	Mrs G. Broadley	Mrs G. Broadley	17.5.43
Sh.Ch. Carnfield Christabelle	B	Belchamp Casson	Clintonhouse Janet	Mrs R. Perridge	Mr H. Jarvis	13.9.45
Sh.Ch. Sandylands Shot	D	Peter of Shotton	Sandylands Sherry	Mrs G. Broadley	Mrs G. Broadley	14.5.45
Sh.Ch. Grand Lodge	D	Boxer of Bramhope	Jordanstown Lass	Mr R. Cleland	Miss E. Gault	14.4.47
Sh.Ch. Skipper of Happeedaze	D	Peter's Benefactor	Belchamp Cedilla	Mr R. G. Thomas	Mr W. R. Hepplewhite	14.3.46
Sh.Ch. Cavehill Maid	B	Rambler of Chastleton	Elaine	Mr W. R. Gardiner	Mr W. R. Gardiner	26.7.47
Sh.Ch. Wintonhill Tessa	B	Northern Command	Beautility Brocade	Messrs W. R. and J. Johnston	Mr W. R. Johnston	26.4.56
Sh.Ch.Ambergris Alert	B	Replica of Ranscombe	Sue of Amberside	Miss D. Cupit	Miss D. Cupit	1.4.43
Sh.Ch. Roundwood Haynford Lady	B	Replica of Ranscombe	Springdale Primrose	Mr and Mrs S. H. Till	Mr I. T. Whitaker	10.4.45

Name	Sex	Sire	Dam	Owner	Breeder	Born
Sh.Ch. Bauker of Bramhope	D	Boxer of Bramhope	Bramhope Brown Betty	Miss B. Cripps	Miss E. McShane	7.4.49
Sh.Ch. My Love of Bourneview	B	Rambler of Chastleton	Lassie of Wood Vale	Mr H. Hunt	Mr H. Hunt	23.10.47
Sh.Ch. Deana of Glenbervie	B	Ch. Sandylands Shrubley	Sweet Memory	Mr A. B. Nicolson	Miss A. Steele	8.2.49
Sh.Ch. Sandylands Secret	B	Ch. Sandylands Shrubley	Sandylands Sherry	Mrs G. Broadley	Mrs G. Broadley	11.4.49
Sh.Ch. Northdown Fancy	B	Boxer of Bramhope	Northdown Style	Mr W. E. Manin	Mr W. E. Manin	25.1.51
Sh.Ch. Whaddon Chase Romance	B	Sh.Ch. Whaddon Chase Robin	Ch. Whaddon Chase Snipe	Lady Lambe	Lady Lambe	12.1.49
Sh.Ch. Wollburn Wallflower	B	Boxer of Bramhope	Wollburn Wattle	Mrs H. M. S. Bell	Mrs H. M. S. Bell	1.6.51
Sh.Ch. Bonaventure of Bramhope	D	Boxer of Bramhope	Bramhope Stonebrig Seraph	Mr E. E. A. Stevenson	Mrs E. A. T. Sawter	22.4.51
Sh.Ch. Studley Brave Buccaneer	D	Boxer of Bramhope	Bountiful of Beechfield	Mrs S. G. Smithson	Mrs S. G. Smithson	25.2.53
Sh.Ch. Hazel of Stubham	B	Ch. Alexander of Stubham	Empress of Stubham	Mrs F. O. Till	Mrs F. O. Till	1.9.52
Sh.Ch. Pride of Abbotscross	B	Green Boy	Lassie of Orzona	Mr T. Gordon	Mr J. Orr	19.6.52
Sh.Ch. Mallard of Glenbervie	D	Boxer of Bramhope	Whintonhill Tessa	Mr A. B. Nicolson	Mr A. B. Nicolson	7.8.53
Sh.Ch. Stokeley Sea Sprite	D	Ch. Clintonhouse George	Stokeley Flight	Mr D. C. Hannah	Mr D. C. Hannah	22.9.54

Name	Sex	Sire	Dam	Owner	Breeder	Born
Sh.Ch. Brandyhole Brown Berry	B	Ch. Clintonhouse George	Ch. Duchess of Stubham	Mrs I. C. Durie	Mrs J. Spence	7.7.53
Sh.Ch. Jessica of Stubham	B	Ch. Alexander of Stubham	Empress of Stubham	Mr J. Glyn Lewis	Mrs F. O. Till	10.2.53
Sh.Ch. Mably Sharon	B	Skipper of Happeedaze	Dainty Girl	Mr J. Williams	Mr F. L. Martin	20.10.54
Sh.Ch. Whaddon Chase Salote	B	Whaddon Chase Duke	Ch. Whaddon Chase Swift	Lady Lambe	Lady Lambe	10.2.54
Sh.Ch. Brown Bess of Bramhope	B	Bentinto of Bramhope	Studley Bernadette	Mrs M. Scott	Mrs S. G. Smithson	26.7.54
Sh.Ch. Onyx of Stubham	B	Ch. Alexander of Stubham	Empress of Stubham	Mr A. Wright	Mrs F. O. Till	13.8.54
Sh.Ch. Stokeley Sea Princess	B	Ch. Clintonhouse George	Stokeley Flight	Mr D. C. Hannah	Mr D. C. Hannah	22.9.54
Sh.Ch. Studley Debutante	B	Banker of Bramhope	Bountiful of Beechfield	Mrs S. G. Smithson	Mrs S. G. Smithson	13.12.54
Sh.Ch. Beauvallet of Cross Lane	D	Ch. Clintonhouse George	Candida of Cross Lane	Mr E. A. Anderson	Mr. E. A. Anderson	8.2.55
Sh.Ch. Colmaris Nice Fella	D	Sh. Ch. Stokeley Sea Sprite	Colmaris Clover	Mr I. Davies	Mr I. Davies	22.4.56
Sh.Ch. Vanity Fair of Stubham	B	Ch. Alexander of Stubham	Bronte of Bramhope	Mrs F. Sherwood	Mrs F. O. Till	29.2.56
Sh.Ch. Sheilah of Stubham	B	Ch. Aleaxnder of Stubham	Winter Cloud	Mrs F. O. Till	Miss A. Redlich	9.1.57
Sh.Ch. Colmaris Ranger	D	Sh.Ch. Stokeley Sea Sprite	Colmaris Clover	Mr I Davies	Mr I. Davies	28.11.58

Name	Sex	Sire	Dam	Owner	Breeder	Born
Sh.Ch. Glenford Gamester	D	Redbank Ranger	Doleful Damsel	Mr H. F. Locke	Mr H. F. Locke	17.10.56
Sh.Ch. Glencora Country Maid	B	Ch. Alexander of Stubham	Glencora Tonga	Mr J. Auld	Mr J. Auld	13.9.58
Sh.Ch. Judith of Cloudbrook	B	Ch. Studley Major	Nanette of Stubham	Mr K. Jones	Mr K. Jones	15.6.57
Sh.Ch. Sandylands Susanna	B	Sandylands Scotsman	Sandylands Susie	Mrs G. Broadley and Miss A. Woolgar	Mrs G. Broadley	16.6.57
Sh.Ch. Colmaris Bonny Lad	D	Sh.Ch. Stokeley Sea Sprite	Colmaris Clover	Mr D. C. Hannah	Mr I. Davies	28.10.58
Sh.Ch. Stokeley Carmen	B	Colmaris Son of George	Sh.Ch. Stokeley Sea Princess	Mr I. Davies	Mr D. C. Hannah	23.8.59
Sh.Ch. Dovehouse Wonder Boy	D	Dovehouse Godley Boy	Rose of Bramhope	Miss J. Manifold	Mrs B. Lancashire	10.5.55
Sh.Ch. Moorcliffe Keeper	D	Moorcliffe Masterpiece	Moorcliffe Suzette	Mr A. Froggatt	Mr A. Froggatt	5.8.57
Sh.Ch. Studley Oscar	D	Ch. Studley Major	Sh.Ch. Studley Debutante	Mrs M. Smithson	Mrs M. Smithson	4.12.59
Sh.Ch. Colmaris Bonny Lad	D	Sh.Ch. Stokeley Sea Sprite	Colmaris Clover	Mr D. C. Hannah	Mr I. Davies	28.11.58
Sh.Ch. Scarlet Ribbons of Stubham	B	Ch. Alexander of Stubham	Glencora Tonga	Mrs F. O. Till	Mr A. Stevenson	4.6.60
Sh.Ch. Wollburn Water Music	B	(Amer.Ch.) Melilotus Shooting Star	Wollburn Wren	Mrs H. M. S. Bell	Mrs H. M. S. Bell	1.6.59
Sh.Ch. Benefactor of Roundfield	D	Ch. Colmaris Chancellor	Sh.Ch. Jessica of Stubham	Mr J. G. Lewis	Mr J. G. Lewis	9.6.59

Name	Sex	Sire	Dam	Owner	Breeder	Born
Sh.Ch. O'Malley's Tango of Glenbervie	B	Hemlington Record	Dhu Varren Lass	A. B. Nicolson	W. J. McCall	3.3.58
Sh.Ch. Pencloe Driftwood	D	Sh.Ch. Douglas of Freetwood	Dalhanna Dew	Miss M. H. Bolton	Miss M. H. Bolton	30.6.61
Sh.Ch. Pencloe Dynamo	D	Sh.Ch. Douglas of Freetwood	Dalhanna Dew	Miss M. H. Bolton	Miss M. H. Bolton	30.6.61
Sh.Ch. Conneil Covergirl	B	Ch. Alexander of Stubham	Conneil	Mr and Mrs A. Bower	Mrs C. Crawford	23.8.60
Sh.Ch. Lessudden Linnet	B	Conneil Cavalier	Conneil Countrygirl of Lessudden	Miss M. Alder	Mrs R. Clark	21.7.59
Sh.Ch. Weavervales Luckystar	B	Wendover Fearless	Weavervales Gay Lady	A. G. Nicholls	A. G. Nicholls	27.7.60
Sh.Ch. Woodbay Prima Donna	B	Ch. Alexander of Stubham	Northdown Donna	Mrs F. Sherwood	Mrs F. Sherwood and W. Manin	31.5.58
Sh.Ch. Douglas of Freetwood	D	Ch. Alexander of Stubham	Glencora Tonga	A. Stevenson	J. Auld	13.9.58
Sh.Ch. Paidmyre Mallard	D	Glencora Great Guns	Duskie Princess	A. Stevenson	J. Lynch	29.7.61
Sh.Ch. Rollencourt Danny Boy	D	Kirkvale Venture	Lady of Twentywell	Mrs D. M. Senior	F. Newsham	30.6.55
Sh.Ch. Whaddon Chase Drake	D	Ch. Alexander of Stubham	Whaddon Chase Destiny	Lady Lambe	Lady Lambe	28.4.60
Sh.Ch. Elmerglade Early Dawn	B	Ch. Alexander of Stubham	Brandyhole Delight of Elmerglade	Mrs R. Campion	Mrs R. Campion	19.3.60
Sh.Ch. Moorcliff Wigeon	B	Sh.Ch. Moorcliff Keeper	Moorcliff Trudy	E. Froggatt	E. Froggatt	24.11.62

Name	Sex	Sire	Dam	Owner	Breeder	Born
Sh.Ch. Witching Eye of Freetwood	B	Ch. Alexander of Stubham	Glencora Tonga	J. Lindsay	A. Stevenson	4.6.60
Sh.Ch. Kennersleigh Drummer Boy	D	Sh.Ch. Studley Oscar	Belize of Bramhope	Mrs M. Keighley	Mrs M. Keighley	25.9.62
Sh.Ch. Lochardils Ghillie of Bramhope	D	Sh.Ch. Douglas of Freetwood	Brandy Sour of Bramhope	A. Wylie	A. Wylie	27.6.63
Sh.Ch. Moorcliff Freetwood Gamecock	D	Sh.Ch. Douglas of Freetwood	Game Bird of Freetwood	E. Froggatt	A. Stevenson	29.6.64
Sh.Ch. Dulcie of Kennersleigh	B	Sh.Ch. Studley Oscar	Belize of Bramhope	Mrs J. M. Taylor	Mrs M. Keighley	25.9.62
Sh.Ch. Linzy Maid	B	Ch. Studley Major	Sh.Ch. Witching Eye of Freetwood	A. Lindsay	A. Lindsay	4.5.62
Sh.Ch. Moorcliff Bye Bye of Bramhope	B	(Amer. Ch.) Melilotus Shooting-star	Barnardine of Bramhope	E. Froggatt	Mrs Scott	10.12.61
Sh.Ch. Slayleigh Paulina	B	Sh.Ch. Whaddon Chase Drake	Quaker Girl of Stubham	Mrs J. A. Hancock	Maj. A. W. G. Scott	19.12.63
Sh.Ch. Water Gypsy of Stubham	B	Douglas of Freetwood	Hawkhill Harmony of Stubham	Mr and Mrs R. Townley	Mrs K. Till	2.1.62
Sh.Ch. Bella Bee of Kennersleigh	B	Ch. Studley Major	Belize of Bramhope	Mrs J. M. Taylor	Mrs M. Keighley	20.8.61
Sh.Ch. Lisdalgin Babbling Brook	B	Ch. Sir Knight	Zilla of Lisdalgin	W. McClenaghan	W. McClenaghan	4.5.63
Sh.Ch. Cavalier of Loweview	D	Sh.Ch. Douglas of Freetwood	Judy of Loweview	C. P. Jackson	C. P. Jackson	8.3.65
Sh.Ch. Persimmon of Shipden	D	Kublai Kahn of Shipden	High Circle of Shipden	Mr and Mrs C. Muirhead	Mr and Mrs C. Muirhead	20.5.63

Name	Sex	Sire	Dam	Owner	Breeder	Born
Sh.Ch. Miss Chataway	B	Sh.Ch. Douglas of Freetwood	Mischievous Maid	Miss M. Bolton	Miss M. Bolton	25.4.65
Sh.Ch. Cleavehill Dandini	D	Glencora Shootingstar	Dulcie of Kennersleigh	Mrs J. M. Taylor	Mrs J. M. Taylor	17.8.64
Sh.Ch. Majeba Mac	D	Sh.Ch. Douglas of Freetwood	Brandy Sour of Bramhope	Mr and Mrs J. Backhouse	A. A. Wylie	15.7.65
Sh.Ch. Hawkhill Derby Daydream	B	Ch. Moorcliffe Dougal of Truelindale	Sh. Ch. Shayleigh Paulina	Miss F. Bagshawe	Mrs Hancock and Mr Cudworth	7.6.67
Sh.Ch. Moorcliff Camilla	B	Ch. Moorcliff Dougal of Truelindale	Moorcliff Hi There	E. Froggatt	E. Froggatt	22.4.66
Sh.Ch. Sapphire of Shipden	B	Studley Indian Prince	Francesca of Poppyland	A. C. Fowle	Mr and Mrs C. J. Muirhead	30.8.59
Sh.Ch. Hawkhill Royal Palace	D	Ch. Moorcliff Dougal of Truelindale	Sh.Ch. Slayleigh Paulina	Mrs J. A. Hancock and Mr J. P. Cudworth	Mrs J. A. Hancock and Mr J. P. Cudworth	7.6.67
Sh.Ch. Hawkhill Hello Dolly	B	Ch. Moorcliff Dougla of Truelindale	Hawkhill Starshine	Mrs J. A. Hancock	Mrs Buchan	14.9.66
Sh.Ch. Teesview Tarama	B	Ch. Teesview Tarmac	Teesview Topaz	Mrs E. Dobson	Mrs E. Dobson	30.4.67
Sh.Ch. Hawkhill St. Pauli Girl of Moorcliff	B	Ch. Moorcliff Dougal of Truelindale	Sh.Ch. Slayleigh Paulina	Mr E. Froggatt	Mrs J. A. Hancock and Mr J. P. Cudworth	7.6.67
Sh.Ch. Stokeley Son of Laddie	D	Sh.Ch. Colmaris Bonny Ladd	Ch. Stokeley Teesview Telstar	Mrs K. Hannah	Mr D. C. Hannah	1.4.65
Sh.Ch. Wollburn Wild Drake	D	Sh.Ch. Paidmyre Mallard	Wollburn Western Honey	Mr R. L. Davis	Mr C. Campbell	6.10.68

Name	Sex	Sire	Dam	Owner	Breeder	Born
Sh.Ch. Whadhill Alicia	B	Ch. Teesview Titus	Mable of Annetlea	Miss V. Phillips	Mrs E. Stephenson	9.4.66
Sh.Ch. Cleavehill Corn Dolly	B	Andrew of Etton	Cleavehill Bumble Bee	Mrs J. M. Taylor	Mrs J. M. Taylor	25.8.67
Sh.Ch. Woodbay Don Derry	D	Sh.Ch. Benefactor of Roundfield	Sh.Ch. Woodbay Prima Donna	Mrs F. Sherwood	Mr V. Thomas	13.12.63
Sh.Ch. Lady Caroline of Hortonbank	B	Sh.Ch. Lochardils Ghillie of Bramhope	Lady Jane of Hortonbank	Mrs L. W. Carstairs	Mr L. Charlesworth	18.5.67
Sh.Ch. Elizabeth of Hortonbank	B	Sh.Ch. Lochardils Ghillie of Bramhope	Lady Jane of Hortonbank	Mrs. J. Boyce	Mr L. Charlesworth	15.10.68
Sh.Ch. Hawkhill Connaught	D	Ch. Moorcliff Dougal of Truelindale	Sh.Ch. Slayleigh Paulina	Mrs Hancock and Mr Cudworth	Mrs Hancock and Mr Cudworth	11.7.69
Sh.Ch. Gewdore Apollo of Moorcliffe	D	Conneil Cock O' the North	Scotch Lassie	Mrs J. Froggatt	Mr R. K. Robertson	17.11.69
Sh.Ch. Hawkhill Harmonious	B	Sh.Ch. Cavalier of Loweview	Sh.Ch. Hawkhill Hello Dolly	Mrs H. Jackson	Mrs J. A. Hancock	30.3.68
Sh.Ch. Fairleigh Chocolate Bar	B	Game Lad of Fairleigh	Lovely Bride of Fairleigh	Mrs J. Boyce	Mrs J. Boyce	15.2.69
Sh.Ch. Fairleigh Trentside	D	Game Lad of Fairleigh	Lovely Bride of Fairleigh	Mrs J. Boyce	Mrs J. Boyce	24.10.70
Sh.Ch. Teesview Pandora of Truelindale	B	Ch. Teesview Titus	Morag of Truelindale	Mrs E. Dobson	Miss M. Alder	2.1.70

POST-WAR WELSH SPRINGER SPANIEL CHAMPIONS 1947–71

Name	Sex	Sire	Dam	Owner	Breeder	Born
1949 Ch. Branksome Beauty	B	Dewi Sant	Castlewood Counetss	Mrs M. L. Morgan	Mrs M. L. Morgan	17.5.48
1950 Ch. Rushbrooke Runner	B	Rushbrooke Rufus	Rushbrooke Ruff	Mr H. J. H. Leopard	Mr H. J. H. Leopard	16.4.47
1952 Ch. Denethorp Danny	D	Rushbrooke Rufus	Jenny of Denethorp	Mr F. A. M. Hart	Mr F. A. M. Hart	3.5.49
Ch. Snowdonian Lad	D	Gay Rebel	Freckled Fanny	Mr L. Hughes	Miss D. H. Ellis	7.1.148
1953 Ch. Rockhill Rhiwderin	D	Myrydd Marksman of Tregwillym	Rockhill Rona	Mr Hart, previously Mrs Mayall	Mrs M. Mayall	26.9.51
1954 Ch. Broadweir Bracken	B	Rushbrooke Rust	Rushbrooke R Rum	Mrs J. A. Foster	Mrs J. A. Foster	13.4.51
Ch. Lassie of Menai	B	Ch. Snowdonian Lad	Ceri Menai	Mr L. Hughes	Mr D. F. Hughes	1.3.52
1955 Ch. Belinda of Linkton	B	Downland Diplomat	Elizabeth Judy	Miss A. West	Mr D. Lawrie	12.7.53
1956 Ch. Brancourt Bang	D	Lucky Laddie	Ashfield Aristocrat	Mr and Mrs T. H. Morgan	Mrs D. Thomas	30.11.51
1959 Ch. Tulita of Tregwillym	B	Tehran of Tregwillym	Gilly of Beameads	Mr H. C. Payne	Mr L. Bourne	11.9.56

Name	Sex	Sire	Dam	Owner	Breeder	Born
1960 Ch. Kim of Cwm	D	Sh.Ch. Top-Score of Tregwillym	Tudor Lass of Tregwillym	Mr B. G. Thorpe	Mr H. C. Payne	21.9.57
1962 Ch. Mandy of Tregwillym	B	Sh.Ch. Trigger of Tregwillym	Lady Blanche of Broomleaf	Mr H. C. Payne	Lt Col. J. C. Lewis	26.8.59
1962 Ch. Statesman of Tregwillym	D	Sh.Ch. Token of Tregwillym	Trinket of Tregwillym	Mr H. C. Payne	Mr H. C. Payne	20.9.58
1965 Ch. Talysarn Calon Dewr	D	Tehran of Tregwillym	Shot Silk of Tregwillym	Mr D. Dobson	Miss C. Potter	1.1.62
1969 Ch. Tidemarsh Rip	D	Stokecourt Sam	Lingholm Rhoda	Mr G. H. Pattinson	Mr G. H. Pattinson	11.5.67
1970 Ch. Krackton Surprise Packet	B	Nobleman of Tregwillym	Prue of Gliffaes	Mr G. W. R. Couzens	Mr S. G. Brabner	18.8.67
1971 Ch. Tidemarsh Tidemark	D	Ch. Tidemarsh Rip	Titian Beauty	Mr G. H. Pattinson	Mrs Russen	24.9.69

APPENDIX H

POST-WAR WELSH SPRINGER SPANIEL SHOW CHAMPIONS 1947–71

Name	Sex	Sire	Dam	Owner	Breeder	Born
Sh.Ch. Dewi Sant	D	Deri Di	Tresco Thornycroft	Mr H. Newman	Mrs M. C. Evans	10.6.43
Sh.Ch. Rushbrooke Rustle	B	Goblin Goch	Rushbrooke Rose	Mr H. J. H. Leopard	Mr H. J. H. Leopard	30.3.46
Sh.Ch. Jester of Downland	D	Dewi Sant	Merry Madcap of Downland	Miss D. Ellis	Miss D. Ellis	12.6.45
Sh.Ch. Cofois Bon	B	Dewi Sant	Doweli Meweh Nol	Mr H. Newman	Mr H. Newman	6.9.45
Sh.Ch. Rushbrooke Ruadh	D	Dere Nol	Rushbrooke Ruff	Mr H. J. H. Leopard	Mr H. J. H. Leopard	7.2.46
Sh.Ch. Stokecourt Jonathan	D	Dewi Sant	Camrose Lass	Mrs D. Morriss	Mr G. Hooper	17.2.46
Sh.Ch. Denethorp Dido	B	Dewi Sant	Treorchy Megan	Mr H. Newman	Mr F. A. M. Hart	26.7.49
Sh.Ch. Taliesin Ye Ail	D	Dewi Sant	Gillian of Tregwillym	Mr G. Taylor	Mr J. Kemp	10.5.47
Sh.Ch. Moelwyn Melody	B	Melwyn Marksman	Tebay	Mr E. W. Painter	Mr T. Jones	27.6.46
Sh.Ch. Kestrel of Kenswick	B	Glenross of Tregwillym	Fidget of Fosseway	Mrs M. G. King	Mrs M. G. King	4.5.50
Sh.Ch. Rushbrooke Rustic	B	Rushbrooke Rust	Rushbrooke Rum	Mr H. J. H. Leopard	Mrs J. A. Foster	13.4.57
Sh.Ch. Kim of Kenswick	D	Glenross of Tregwillym	Fidget of Fosseway	Mrs M. G. King	Mrs M. G. King	4.5.50

Name	Sex	Sire	Dam	Owner	Breeder	Born
Sh.Ch. Welsh Lady	B	Dewi Sant	Merch Dewi	Mr H. Newman	Mr H. Newman	28.9.49
Sh.Ch. Brancourt Bushranger	D	Ch. Brancourt Bang	Ch. Branksome Beauty	Mr and Mrs T. H. Morgan	Mrs M. L. Morgan	23.12.53
Sh.Ch. Token of Tregwillym	D	Taliesin Ye Ail	Titian of Tregwillym	Mr H. C. Payne	Mr H. C. Payne	22.6.54
Sh.Ch. Gwyneth	B	Beggar Me Boy	Gwenlilian Goch	Mr G. E. Bounds	Mr G. E. Bounds	19.6.52
Sh.Ch. Mikado of Broomleaf	D	Sh.Ch. Stokecourt Jonathan	Broomleaf Dimple of Empshott	Dr E. Rickards	Mrs K. Doxford	2.10.54
Sh.Ch. Stokecourt Gillian	B	Sh.Ch. Stokecourt Jonathan	Gwyneth Allt Bedw	Mrs D. Morriss	Col C. R. Smith	30.4.53
Sh.Ch. Top Score of Tregwillym	D	Tehran of Tregwillym	Rockhill Rosewell	Mr H. C. Payne	Mr H. C. Payne	11.1.57
Sh.Ch. Brancourt Belinda	B	Ch. Brancourt Bang	Ch. Branksome Beauty	Mr and Mrs T. H. Morgan	Mrs M. L. Morgan	22.5.57
Sh.Ch. Coombelane Fidelia	B	Ch. Brancourt Bang	Sh.Ch. Gwyneth	Miss D. M. Norman	Mr G. E. Bounds	4.5.55
Sh.Ch. Trigger of Tregwillym	D	Tehran of Tregwillym	Terlesa of Tregwillym	Mr H. C. Payne	Mr H. C. Payne	13.8.56
Sh.Ch. Arabella of Linkhill	B	Ch. Brancourt Bang	Ch. Belinda of Linkton	Miss A. West	Miss A. West	4.10.56
Sh.Ch. Tarbay Florian of Broomleaf	D	Hilarion of Broomleaf	Broomleaf Little Buttercup	Dr E. Rickards	Mrs K. Doxford	17.3.58
Sh.Ch. Statesman of Tregwillym	D	Sh.Ch. Token of Tregwillym	Trinket of Tregwillym	Mr H. C. Payne	Mr H. C. Payne	20.9.58

Name	Sex	Sire	Dam	Owner	Breeder	Born
Sh.Ch. Stokecourt Judith	B	Stokecourt Simon	Sh.Ch. Stokecourt Gillian	Dr E. Rickards	Mrs D. Morriss	27.5.55
Sh.Ch. Jenny of Tarbay	B	Sh.Ch. Mikado of Broomleaf	Sh.Ch. Stokecourt Judith	Dr E. Rickards	Dr E. Rickards	25.8.58
Sh.Ch. Deri Darrell of Linkhill	D	Sh.Ch. Statesman of Tregwillym	Sh.Ch. Arabella of Linkhill	Miss A. West	Miss A. West	3.9.60
Sh.Ch. Denethorp Dihewyd	D	Ch. Rockhill Rhiwderin	Denethorp Danella	Mr F. A. M. Hart	Mr F. A. M. Hart	2.8.58
Sh.Ch. Rambler of Miellette	D	Hackpen Redwyn Lad	Thora of Empshott	Mr A. H. Corbett and Miss C. Potter	Mrs E. A. Rowe	24.7.57
Sh.Ch. Amber Rose of Tregwillym	B	Ch. Statesman of Tregwillym	Tete-a-Tete of Tregwillym	Mr H. C. Payne	Mr H. C. Payne	1.11.59
Sh.Ch. Liza of Linkhill	B	Ch. Statesman of Tregwillym	Sh.Ch. Arabella of Linkhill	Miss A. West	Miss A. West	26.10.61
Sh.Ch. Gamefeather of Siani	B	Sh.Ch. Mikado of Broomleaf	Blodyn Gwanwyn	Major and Mrs K. Stevens	Mr H. Newman	14.7.60
Sh.Ch. Fashion Plate of Hearts	B	Ch. Statesman of Tregwillym	Sh.Ch. Brancourt Belinda	Mr T. H. Arthur	Mr T. H. Arthur	7.8.62
Sh.Ch. Mountararat of Broomleaf	D	Sh.Ch. Deri Darrell of Linkhill	Iolanthe of Broomleaf	Mr C. J. Kitchener	Mrs K. Doxford	12.6.62
Sh.Ch. Diplomat of Hearts	D	Ch. Statesman of Tregwillym	Sh.Ch. Brancourt Belinda	Mr T. H. Arthur	Mr T. H. Arthur	7.8.62
Sh.Ch. Easter Parade	D	Sh.Ch. Topscore of Tregwillym	Blodyn Gwanwyn	Mr H. Newman	Mr H. Newman	1.4.61
Sh.Ch. Lady of Llangarna	B	Ch. Statesman of Tregwillym	Tete-a-Tete of Tregwillym	Mr H. Pocock	Mr H. C. Payne	7.12.61

Name	Sex	Sire	Dam	Owner	Breeder	Born
Sh.Ch. Golden Tint of Tregwillym	B	Sportsman of Tregwillym	Sh.Ch. Lady of Llangarna	Mr H. C. Payne	Mr H. Pocock	18.6.64
Sh.Ch. Plattburn Paramount	D	Sh.Ch. Denethorp Dihewyd	Patmyn Pie Powder	Mr and Mrs J. K. Burgess	Mr and Mrs J. K. Burgess	7.2.65
Sh.Ch. Golden Guinea	B	Mynyddislwyn Lad	Talysarn Blodeuyn	Mr D. Dobson	Mr D. Dobson	26.5.65
Sh.Ch. Plattburn Penny	B	Ch. Rockhill Rhiwderin	Patmyn Pie Powder	Mr and Mrs J. K. Burgess	Mr and Mrs J. K. Burgess	27.11.63
Sh.Ch. Bruce of Brent	D	Benefactor of Brent	Bronwyn Trixie	Mrs D. M. Perkins	Mrs N. Hall	28.8.66
Sh.Ch. Dewi of Hearts	D	Ch. Talysarn Calon Dewr	Fashion Model of Hearts	Mr T. H. Arthur	Mr and Mrs N. P. Campbell	30.3.66
Sh.Ch. Plattburn Progressor	D	Plattburn Proclamation	Plattburn Penelope	Mr and Mrs J. K. Burgess	Mr and Mrs J. K. Burgess	16.9.68
Sh.Ch. Maria of Pencelli	B	Priory Major	Bony Legend	Mr H. Newman	Mr H. Newman	14.3.67
Sh.Ch. Dalati Anwylyd	B	Sh.Ch. Diplomat of Hearts	Freesia of Hearts	Mr and Mrs N. Hunton-Morgan	Mr and Mrs N. Hunton-Morgan	3.5.67
Sh.Ch. Athelwood Daiperoxide	D	Nobleman of Tregwillym	Atalanta of Athelstone	Mr and Mr B. J. Mullins	Mr and Mrs B. J. Mullins	26.3.68
Sh.Ch. Dalati Swynwyr	D	Sh.Ch. Bruce of Brent	Freesia of Hearts	Mr and Mrs N. Hunton-Morgan	Mr and Mrs N. Hunton-Morgan	17.7.68
Sh.Ch. Golden Sunset	B	Talysarn Golden Finch	Sh.Ch. Talysarn Golden Guinea	Mr N. H. Bazeley	Mr D. Dobson	6.11.68
Sh.Ch. Plattburn Perchance	D	Plattburn Poacher	Emma of Glenary	Mr and Mrs J. K. Burgess	Mrs Short	4.1.69

Name	Sex	Sire	Dam	Owner	Breeder	Born
Sh.Ch. Plattburn Pegasus	B	Sh.Ch. Plattburn Pen Rip	Sh.Ch. Plattburn Penny	Mr and Mrs J. K. Burgess	Mr and Mrs J. K. Burgess	24.4.69
Sh.Ch. Athelwood Lily the Pink	B	Stokecourt Sam	Atalanta of Athelstone	Mr and Mrs B. J. Mullins	Mr and Mrs B. J. Mullins	12.9.69
Sh.Ch. Dalati Del	B	Sh.Ch. Athelwood Daiperoxide	Delati Sidan	Mr and Mrs N. Hunton-Morgan	Mr and Mrs N. Hunton-Morgan	12.8.70

INDEX